American Lives

Volume Two:
Since 1877

American Lives

Volume Two: Since 1877

Willard Sterne Randall

John Cabot University, Rome

Nancy Nahra

John Cabot University, Rome

 LONGMAN

An imprint of Addison Wesley Longman, Inc.

New York • Reading, Massachusetts • Menlo Park, California • Harlow, England
Don Mills, Ontario • Sydney • Mexico City • Madrid • Amsterdam

Executive Editor: Bruce Borland
Developmental Editor: James Strandberg
Text Design and Project Coordination: Ruttle Graphics, Inc.
Cover Designer: Paul Lacy
Cover Illustration: City Activities with Dance Hall from America Today, 1930. Thomas Hart
             Benton Collection, The Equitable Life Assurance Society of the U.S.
Photo Researcher: Carol Parden
Electronic Production Manager: Angel Gonzalez Jr.
Manufacturing Manager: Willie Lane
Electronic Page Makeup: Ruttle Graphics, Inc.
Printer and Binder: R R Donnelley & Sons Company
Cover Printer: The Lehigh Press, Inc.

Library of Congress Cataloging-in-Publication Data
Randall, Willard Sterne.
     American lives/ Willard Sterne Randall, Nancy Nahra.
          p.   cm.
     Includes bibliographical references and index.
     Contents: v. 2. Since 1877
     ISBN 0–673–46987–5
     1. United States—Biography. I. Nahra, Nancy Ann. II. Title.
CT214.R36   1996   96–11929
920.073—dc20   CIP

ISBN 0673-46987-5

345678910-DOC-9998

To Lucy
so full of
American life

Contents

Preface

History is about people.

It is impossible to write or to study history without considering the lives of people. Perhaps nowhere is this more true than in studying the history of America, where diversity has encouraged individualism. Even great social, economic, intellectual, and political forces took shape in the minds of individual Americans. The record of their lives documents their personal actions.

All of these forces and the great ideas of these individuals are bound up in the fortress of memory called history. But how is the interested student to approach this great mass of ideas, actions, and struggles? Too often, the historical record has been rendered impenetrable. There must be some accessible way, some pathway or bridge to approach the study of history. Biographies, especially short biographies, provide one such approach.

The idea of using biography—the study of human lives—to teach is certainly not new. Plutarch's forty-six *Parallel Lives*, written in the second century, long remained the model for others who sought to teach by showing a system of ethics, by recording the exploits, the virtues, and the maxims of kings and generals. As late as the mid-nineteenth century, biography was considered an all-male business for author and subject alike. The English historian Thomas Carlyle pronounced it "the story of the great men." It was only in the past century that a significant number of biographies written by and about women began to appear.

Writing about great men and great women prompts discussions of leadership, of charisma, and of relationships between leadership and power, between leaders and the people. But the lives of the not-so-great more and more are attracting biographers who use them to show how people in everyday life react to the same events and problems. Short biographies of the great and not-so-great also serve as case studies of the periods in which people live, using individuals to study ideas.

Each of these lives puts us in another time and place. Each one shows what we can and cannot comprehend about the past. And each life invites us to remember these remarkable people and the problems they faced, and to see, in their memories, links to history, their past and ours.

Acknowledgments

The authors think that the collective subject of this book helped inspire a constructive spirit of cooperation that left many people encouraged and hopeful. In a project like this, different kinds of assistance made a crucial difference at moments when we needed help. Here are some of the people who have our gratitude. At Addison Wesley Longman, we owe thanks to Bruce Borland, Executive Editor, who listened to the idea for the book and boldly signed it up. James Strandberg, Developmental Editor, did many jobs meticulously and cheerfully to transform the idea into bound pages. Ray Lincoln, agent and friend, gave exactly the suggestions and opinions that we would have asked for. Ruth Gminski helped a great deal with the early library searches. Dr. Vincent Naramore, emeritus professor of mathematics at St. Michael's College, helped us with many useful observations. Diann Varricchione helped us, as usual, in her competent and unflappable way as she prepared the many drafts of the manuscripts. And our thanks, too, to Kimberly Thompson at Ruttle Graphics for her thoroughgoing copyediting.

The manuscript got better as it passed through the hands of a team of careful historians whose expertise sharpened points and refined factual distinctions at different stages. These include: Anne B. Harris, Old Dominion University; Philip H. Vaughan, Rose State College; Theresa Kaminski, University of Wisconsin-Stevens Point; Hilliard J. Goldman, Meramec Community College; Jerry Thompson, Texas A&M International University; Timothy Koerner, Oakland Community College-Royal Oak Campus; B. B. McCool, Arkansas Tech University; David Dixon, Slippery Rock University; Michael Weiss, Linn-Benton Community College; Mark C. Herman, Edison Community College; David A. Walker, University of Northern Iowa; Deborah M. Jones, Bristol Community College; Tommy Stringer, Navarro College; Kenneth H. Williams, Alcorn State University; Ellen Shockrow, Pasadena City College; Valeen T. Avery, Northern Arizona University; and David Godshalk, Shippensburg University. Errors that may remain, of course, can be attributed not to them but to us. For the photos that illustrate our book, we thank Carol Parden, who saw to that aspect of the research.

Willard Sterne Randall
Nancy Nahra

1

Mark Twain

*P*eople who came to America, more than people already living there in the early to mid-nineteenth century, had to believe in starting over. Before the Civil War, partisans of the Confederacy trusted their dream of transforming a rich agricultural region to a new country. After the fighting ended, the entire nation needed to believe in a new beginning. That credo motivated the South where rebuilding had to pull recovery along, and the North where women wanted a voice in remaking the entire society. The man who would become famous worldwide as a professional Southerner left an intact Dixie before he could see it violated. For a long time he seemed to go everywhere except back home, and as he traveled he wrote about it. When America needed to stay home and mend, he went out of his way to feel uprooted and to write about being a stranger. The writing itself meant a deliberate starting over, and he conveyed that condition with no self-pity. To the relief of all Americans, he made it hilarious.

Mark Twain so deeply loved his boyhood version of the South as viewed from the Mississippi, that he refused to admit that the place he knew had been lost to the world. He needed years away before he could confront his memory and make his South immortal. Success allowed, and perhaps required, that he live in exile from his origins. While he waited, he had to become Mark Twain and start over—more than once.

THE DEVASTATION OF the South following the Civil War required courage and capital for recovery, while in the North personal losses made it difficult for Union families to feel exultant. Not until 1877, twelve years after the Civil War, did General Grant meet cheering veterans for a triumphant entrance to Chicago—some compared him to Napoleon—and then a progression on to other Northern cities. In this time of remembered suffering, an unusual literary mind and sensibility let one American original appreciate a new axis and a different pattern for seeing America that looked past the nearly fatal split of North and South. Samuel Clemens, better known as Mark Twain, recognized that the two emerging cultures in America were the East and the West. His experience, especially in the varied and apparently unrelated jobs he had held as a young man, let him understand that in many ways the relation of East to West corresponded to an older difference known to many Americans, that of the Old World from the New.

Because he had been born in 1835 in Missouri, a slave state, Mark Twain found himself, at age twenty-six, in a Confederate unit (that is, he did not seek regular military duty) in the Civil War. Perhaps no other account of military life makes armed conflict seem so pointless and, consequently, so poignant as Twain's rendition of it in "The Private History of a Campaign That Failed" which appeared in *Century magazine* in 1885. The group of just over a dozen old friends who organized themselves into the "Marion Rangers" camped near a farm and mostly discussed reports that came to them about "the enemy." When a lone man arrived on horseback, the story reports, the imperfect moonlight made Mark Twain, and maybe others, believe that more of the enemy followed. Just as the word "Fire!" broke the silence, Twain shot the man. Only later did he find out that five shots were fired in response to that same command. When he saw the man fall, and later when the Rangers discovered that the man was unarmed and not even wearing a uniform, the horror of the incident taught the young Twain as much as he needed to know about battle:

> I was down by him in a moment, helplessly stroking his forehead; and I would have given anything then—my own life freely—to make him what he had been five minutes before. All the boys seemed to be feeling the same way; they hung over him, full of pitying interest . . . . In a little while the man was dead. It seemed an epitome of war; that all war must be just that—the killing of strangers against whom you feel no personal animosity; strangers whom, in other circumstances, you would help if you found them in trouble, and who would help you if you needed it.

After spending all of two weeks in the service, more or less of the Confederacy, Mark Twain and his entire unit deserted. He moved West to Nevada where his older, less talented brother Orion (the family pronounced the name with the accent on the first syllable) had a position as secretary to Governor James W. Nye of the Nevada Territory. Sam Clemens's working experience up to that time had been first as a steamboat pilot (an occupation which the war ended for him when the blockade of the Mississippi by Union warships made river traffic impossible) and then as a printer, working for Orion in Hannibal, Missouri. In Nevada the younger Clemens had to find work, an effort in which his older brother's help proved characteristically ineffectual. Not long after his arrival, he found a position as a reporter for the *Virginia City Territorial Enterprise*. He would have preferred a different line of work because of the lack of respect attached to journalism of any kind in those times. As part of the circulation wars that raged among frontier newspapers, winning readers was far more important than details such as truthfulness. Worse, the young Clemens behaved in a way which did not enhance community approval. His tendency to stand around and have long talks with people gave the impression that his drawl in speaking corresponded to general laziness. In other journalism jobs which he later held, employers noticed his habit of waiting a long time before beginning an assignment. According to one newspaper owner, he was intolerably slow in getting started on his news beat and even slower in writing up what he had found.

While working in Virginia City, Clemens followed a practice not unusual among young journalists: he took a pseudonym. As a steamboat pilot, he had read letters in the New Orleans *Picayune* from a cranky pilot who styled himself "Mark Twain," steamboat parlance for two fathoms (or twelve feet) of water, the shallowest depth in which a steamboat pilot dared pass without serious risk to his vessel. Clemens, knowing that the old pilot had died and no longer needed the name, took it for himself.

As a newspaper writer in Nevada, his horizon did not reach far enough to satisfy his curiosity or his ambition. In the rough life of frontier mining towns, stabbing and murders occurred so frequently that they could not be counted as worthy of news stories. Stirred by something he later called "spring fever," Mark Twain headed farther west to California. *Roughing It* (1872) is his own account of his time in Nevada and California. In fact, he had to get out of Nevada. The "spring fever" that prompted the move might have been the bad hangover he suffered when he wrote a piece mocking the Confederate ladies of Carson City, Nevada, and their war relief efforts. Stunts in print appeared almost daily in the Nevada press, but Mark Twain's must have seemed too plausible. He left town optimistically, sure that his shares of stock in Hale and Norcross silver mines would save him by going up in value at about the time he reached California. In fact, flirting with fortune would more than once let him down by reversing the direction of his career.

In the spring of 1864 when Mark Twain left Nevada and arrived in California, he found a state full of "building, building, building." This expansion had begun when the discovery of gold in 1849 transformed that territory and, at least in some way, all those who pursued gold. San Francisco in 1864 could not have been more suited to the blank sheet facing a young writer. Twenty newspapers in the community of 150,000 people wanted stories about the city and its rich cultural life, the by-product of its six theaters and more than one opera house. The style of journalism he had practiced in Nevada suited the taste of San Francisco's readers. According to Mark Twain himself, he and the other young writers scraped together "such material as we might, wherewith to fill our required columns—and if there were no fires to report we started some."

During his stay in San Francisco the value of his Nevada stock sank to nothing. In his own words, Twain says that "for two months my sole occupation was avoiding acquaintances . . . I became very adept at 'slinking.'" Not long afterwards he tried recovering from his risky circumstances by doing more newspaper work by contributing to the *Golden Era,* the *Californian,* the Sacramento *Union,* the *Daily Dramatic Chronicle* (which became the *San Francisco Chronicle*), and sending letters about San Francisco to the *Territorial Enterprise.* In these letters he covered many sides of San Francisco life, including its airs and pretensions as a cultural center. He used the style of a music critic, for example, to describe what sounded like an opera performance, when he was evaluating the skill of a furniture mover: "I was particularly impressed by the able manner in which Signor Bellindo Alphonso Cellini, the accomplished bass-relievo furniture scout and sofa shifter, performed his part." Writing in that spirit may not have always pleased his employers, but it shows his skill with a form that has nearly disappeared from American life, the hoax. He did not restrict his wit to the printed page. A friend who asked him for a photograph, for example, received different photographs of Mark Twain every day for over a month.

That same taste for the outrageous let him turn into a famous short story a yarn he had heard from a miner when he briefly left San Francisco for mining country in the northern part of California. In its most boiled-down form, the story tells of a miner who claims to have a frog that can outjump any other. A stranger arrives who challenges the miner and accepts bets. But the stranger also feeds the miner's frog a bellyful of quail shot (tiny shotgun pellets) and, predictably, wins. That simple tale became the hilarious story "The Celebrated Jumping Frog of Calaveras County." While Mark Twain did not get rich from the story, he did earn a reputation, even in the East where it was reprinted.

The reason Twain happened to be away from San Francisco to hear the story was due to his rocky relations with the San Francisco police. He wrote such unflattering stories about their role in the unjust treatment of citizens, especially the city's growing Chinese population—stories that were not easy to get published—that the police considered him trouble. And trouble knew to leave town for a while.

In March 1866 Mark Twain arrived on the steamer *Ajax* in Honolulu Harbor, on assignment for the Sacramento *Union*. The paper had engaged him to travel to the Sandwich Islands, as Hawaii was then called, and report on his adventures for readers. Twain filed twenty-five dispatches for which he was paid twenty dollars each. So successful was Twain in reporting his travels that when he returned to California, where the public associated his name with the islands, he was able to give public lectures. These lectures kept some of the flavor of frontier journalism. To help cope with the stage fright he experienced at first as a lecturer, Twain came up with ways of engaging his audience as participants in the talks. He promised, for example, to demonstrate cannibalism as it is practiced in the Sandwich Islands, if any mother in the audience would simply volunteer a child, and then he would wait. While Twain stood there stony faced, as if he really expected a volunteer, the belly laughs began.

Soon his lecturing, which started as an experimental or even a stopgap measure, turned into what he would eventually call his "other career." Lecturing remained an important activity for his reputation and his financial solvency. Later in his life he was able to recover repeatedly, even from bankruptcy, by lecturing. He could eventually demand and receive as much as ten thousand dollars for a lecture engagement. His lavish way of life and a long pattern of bitter relations with publishers he did not feel he could trust made Twain rely more and more on public talks to help reduce his debts.

Having made his name known by writing for newspapers, Mark Twain imagined that his lecture audiences would increase if he could enhance their expectations. Not bound by any concept of truth in advertising, he promised whatever he thought would draw a crowd, even if that included freshly captured wild animals. As one tantalizing announcement said, "The trouble begins at eight."

On stage Twain understood first by instinct and then by experience the importance of "having" the audience. He studied the performances of other successful

Emily Driscoll, Shepherdstown, West Virginia

Mark Twain spent two and a half years as a steamboat pilot before the Civil War stopped river traffic and started his career as an observer of America.

speakers throughout his life, including the famous humorist Artemus Ward and the riveting preacher Henry Ward Beecher, brother of Harriet Beecher Stowe. Twain mastered the use of silence on the stage. By saying absolutely nothing and looking expectantly at a large audience before beginning, or at strategic moments, he could make hundreds and later thousands of people double over with laughter.

Sometimes he would be on stage playing the piano when the curtain opened, or pretend to be a bumbling introducer before letting on that he was really the entertainment. In leaving the stage he would stumble or try the wrong exit. The performances attracted huge crowds and earned him a reputation as lecturer and Western humorist, when he decided at the age of thirty-one to head East.

An arrangement with the *Alta California* let Mark Twain believe that he could continue to sell travel reports on any trip he might make. He had earlier thought of leaving from San Francisco for China and then traveling around the world, stopping off in Europe for the Paris Exposition, a great worldwide attraction, but he had not seen his mother in six years. Long before, he had vowed not to lay eyes on his mother, Jane Clemens, nor on his sister Pamela "until I am a rich man." By now, not really settled in a career and still unmarried, Twain was not rich but had made a reputation of sorts, or rather, a story of his had. "The Celebrated Jumping Frog" had been widely published all over the country, but not always for the material benefit of its author.

To reach New York from San Francisco in 1866 required time and good luck. When the railroad linked the country in 1869 the journey would require only ten days. But before the railroad was complete and before the Panama Canal, ships had to leave California and sail down the coast of Mexico to the west coast of Nicaragua where passengers disembarked before crossing the jungle by mule and wagon. On the eastern side of Nicaragua, they had to board another steamer and sail up the coast to New York. If all went well, this could be accomplished in twenty-eight days. On Mark Twain's trip cholera claimed at least eight lives before they arrived in New York. Only after he recovered from this journey did he begin the eleven hours of rail travel to see his mother and sister in Missouri.

While in New York Mark Twain heard about a trip that he was sure would provide a wealth of reportable material. The *Quaker City* was accepting passengers for travel not only to Europe but to continue all the way to the Holy Land. Its passengers would come from the well-heeled Brooklyn congregation of Henry Ward Beecher, pastor of Plymouth Church. Mark Twain's instinct as a journalist and travel writer told him that readers of the *Alta California* would want to learn about the cruise, but also about the socially important New York passengers.

This forerunner of the modern luxury cruise would be the first such expedition from New York. The necessary suspension of travel between North America and Europe during the Civil War gave the project great appeal. A well-off group of serious "pilgrims," as they would be called, signed up full of fervid expectations. The same unsatisfied desire for travel, the editor of the *Alta* had no doubt imagined, would make his readers want to know about such an adventure. In writing his reports, Twain sounded like a lecturer addressing an audience waiting to be entertained.

Mark Twain agreed to write letters describing the voyage of the *Quaker City* because he needed a job and saw in it a chance to build on his reputation as the travel reporter known in the West for his Sandwich Island lectures. But that temporary job would change his life, his career, and profoundly redefine his future possibilities. Among the passengers, most of whom he found easy to caricature for their sanctimonious habits, Twain also met Charles Langdon, close to his own age and descendant of a wealthy New York family whose fortune had been made in coal.

More importantly, Langdon showed Mark Twain a picture, an ivory miniature, of his beautiful sister, Olivia Langdon. Ten years younger than Mark Twain, Olivia would meet him two years later. She became his wife, and for years, his first reader, critic, and confidant. By marrying Olivia, or Livy as Twain called her, Mark Twain let go his identity with the American West, to which he very rarely returned, and became part of his wife's world, a society of a different order. The beautiful, refined, and sickly Miss Langdon had already spent two years suffering from a paralysis (which left her mysteriously) which had started for poorly understood reasons after she fell on the ice at age sixteen. As Mark Twain's wife she would have four children, but continue to be subject to periods of collapse from nervous prostration.

Mark Twain's widowed mother Susan, who saw New York society as a world too different from her respectable and familiar milieu in Missouri, made no attempt to project herself into her son's new social circumstances. She did not even come East for the wedding, which took place two years after the young couple had first met. Her son, who had not yet written one word about the world of his boyhood, had gone to live in the North among abolitionists.

Jervis Langdon, father of Olivia and Charles, overcame his initial misgivings about the prospective marriage and helped assure his frail daughter's comfort by helping his son-in-law buy a share of a newspaper in Buffalo. By the time of his marriage in February 1870, Mark Twain had become well known as the author of *The Innocents Abroad*, his hilarious account of the passengers on the *Quaker City* and their visits to Old World sites, with which they refused to be excessively impressed. The soap of Marseilles, then as now, ranked as a famous French product, but Mark Twain reported only that in that city he found no soap at all in his hotel room, a shortcoming that he did not even notice until he had started, or tried to start, his bath. When shown works by such artists as Michelangelo, the American tourist who served as narrator of the book had only one question: Is he still alive? Twain tried to claim that no book had ever sold as well as *Innocents Abroad*, knowing that it came nowhere near *Uncle Tom's Cabin*.

His father-in-law, Jervis Langdon, showed some of the same love of hoax for which his daughter's new husband was already known. For their honeymoon, the couple looked forward to a trip to Buffalo where they would stay at a boarding house. Mark Twain intended to live in that city where he now had the position of associate editor of the *Buffalo Express*. What confused Twain was the fancy neighborhood in which their car kept driving. He had seen enough of the world to know that boarding houses ordinarily could not be found in such grand surroundings. The cab stopped before a splendid house at 472 Delaware Avenue. The bridegroom did not know that the house, its furnishings, and its staff of servants were all the wedding present from his magnanimous father-in-law.

After an early and difficult time in Buffalo where their first child was born in November 1870, where Livy had typhoid the following winter, and where at age two their son died, the young couple moved to Connecticut. In Hartford the flamboyant Mr. Twain planned to build a house which would become for many years a passion and a burden, almost a character in the story of his life. He entertained Bret Harte, William Dean Howells, Rudyard Kipling, and other important literary figures in that house, and happily made sacrifices to keep on furnishing it. During trips to Europe, for example, Mr. and Mrs. Twain observed frugal habits about car-fare and hotel bills in order to bring back for the house such luxuries as a four-hun-dred-dollar music box, thousands of dollars in furniture and European trimmings, and a massive bed decorated with wood carvings including cherubs.

The book which put Mark Twain on the literary scene, *The Innocents Abroad*, succeeded in part because it matched so well the mood of the country. Compared to Europeans, Americans were younger in many ways, and their nation lacked cen-turies of political experience. Having just survived the Civil War, the great crisis in its coming of age, America could now look toward the rest of the world with great curiosity, but also with energy and hope at a time of growth and especially in the multiplication of fortunes. (That book earned enough money to let Twain move his mother, his widowed sister, and her children to New York.) What Mark Twain called the few decades after the Civil War, "The Gilded Age," became the title of a book on which he collaborated and also the name historians have since used to refer to the period. Not a golden age, nor a lost pastime of perfection, the Gilded Age was an age of conspicuous opulence, gilded maybe to conceal a marred sur-face, recently scarred. Innocent, but with some knowledge of pain, the young republic found a representative in the irreverent humorist, lecturer, reporter, and travel writer who said what so many of his countrymen thought.

In England, the public reception of Mark Twain showed no sign of the reserve and the hesitation about acceptance that Boston, the literary center of America, had made him feel. He had gone to England to reduce living expenses, but found reasons for prolonging his stay quite unrelated to money. The English loved the cigar-smoking, whiskey-drinking, bushy-browed commentator, a man of letters without the conventional air of serious dignity. They saw him as the essence of America—so original, so bright, and so free from the restraints of a system based on social rank and privilege. Twain, for his part, experienced a period of Anglophil-ia. That trip in 1872 would be only his first. Taken altogether, over the rest of his life Twain spent what amounted to eleven years in England. In 1872 he thought that if he were able to, he would like to live in England. But America pulled at him as the strong ties of his wife's family back in Connecticut made England too far from "home." Olivia's uncertain health always made it hard for her to travel. At sev-eral different times over the years she suffered nervous collapse, usually related to the stress of her husband's demanding work plans. To remain in England was out of the question. They sailed home.

An odd Southerner, Mark Twain left his Missouri home when he was young. Although he was just twelve years old when his father, John Marshall Clemens, died, he could not remain steadily in school. His father, a respected lawyer, came from a good family and distinguished himself in community service, however he never succeeded as a businessman nor as a speculator and left the family with very little that was of value. He did leave them 70,000 acres of land in Fentress County, Tennessee, a patrimony that turned into more of a burden than an asset. The fam-ily land inspired dreams of a fortune from the discovery of minerals while in reali-ty the family lacked ready money and the sons had to do what work they could to "help out." The young Mark Twain did find work, but did not consider it the kind he wanted because he could not see exactly how it was enriching him. The kinds of work he did find gave him a wealth of experience, the raw material he would use to enrich American literature and set a powerful model for future writers: the literature of American writers has always been rooted in experience.

Not by intention, it happened that the work Mark Twain found repeatedly brought him near writing in various forms. Working first as a printer on a newspaper in Hannibal where his brother was editor, he learned about setting type before he had done much reading and even before he learned about stories and their power first hand. That knowledge came from the river. The arrival of steamboats along the Mississippi brought excitement and transient glamour to towns like Hannibal where the Clemens family lived. Bigger than any building in town, a steamboat, so enormous and at night so bright, exposed the town to proof of a kind of life somewhere else that had little to do with "drowsing" Hannibal, as Mark Twain called it. The heroes of these transient events, of course, were the wonders of courage and masters of technology who drove the boats, the highly respected and highly paid pilots. As a young boy, Mark Twain knew that more than anything he wanted to be part of the flamboyant, white-suited aristocracy of the river.

After serving a year and a half as apprentice, he had worked as a licensed steamboat pilot for two and a half years. His strong emotional ties to the job that transformed his life made the blow hit hard when he had to give it up, since all the river traffic had come to a stop because of the war. Silence gives proof of how he suffered. He was well-established as a travel writer before he started writing about the South of his boyhood, and it was not until 1882 when he was forty-seven that he experienced a strong desire to see "the river" again. When he revisited the waterway that he had not just known but memorized, as a steamboat pilot had to do, he found it completely transformed. Worse still, electric light along its bank had taken away the look and the atmosphere he remembered, as he reports in *Life on the Mississippi* (1883).

The question of slavery, Mark Twain understood, could not be dismissed as easily as his Connecticut neighbors would have believed. His family in Missouri, always far from being rich, had owned some slaves, and as a boy Mark Twain had not seen the arrangement as necessarily cruel. But many years later, looking back, he remembered a particular child, a memory which brought with it his mother's words:

> We had a little slave boy whom we had hired from some one, there in Hannibal. He was from the eastern shore of Maryland and had been brought away from his family and his friends halfway across the American continent and sold. He was a cheery spirit, innocent and gentle, and the noisiest creature that ever was, perhaps. All day long he was singing, whistling, yelling, whooping, laughing—it was maddening, devastating, unendurable. At last, one day, I lost all my temper and went raging to my mother and said Sandy had been singing for an hour without a single break and I couldn't stand it and *wouldn't* she please shut him up. The tears came into her eyes and her lip trembled and she said something like this:
>
>> Poor thing, when he sings it shows that he is not remembering and that comforts me; but when he is still I am afraid he is thinking and I cannot bear it. He will never see his mother again; if he can sing, I must not hinder it, but be thankful for it. If you were older, you would understand me; then that friendless child's noise would make you glad.

As a writer, the mature Mark Twain continued to "return" to his boyhood, most notably in his masterpiece, *Adventures of Huckleberry Finn.* Long after he had started working on the book, he described it in a notebook as "a book of mine where a sound heart and a deformed conscience come into collision and conscience suffers defeat." That important book raises profound questions about the unjust institution that exploited African Americans. When he became materially successful, Mark Twain never went back to live in the South, yet he recognized a duty to do what he could to make restitution to African Americans. He spoke of "the reparation due from every white to every black man," and showed what he meant. He read at African-American churches and came to the aid of Frederick Douglass with President Garfield. At his own expense, he paid for the education of a young black man at Yale University.

Like other members of his family, notably his father and his older brother, Mark Twain had trouble resisting speculative schemes. Sometimes these rewarded his risk. Early in his career, for example, right after the death of his only son, he came up with a clever innovation about which he wrote his brother. The idea was to make a scrapbook whose pages had a coating which could be wet to make things stick easily. Clever enough to patent what he named "Mark Twain's Self-Pasting Scrapbook," he sold in some years more copies of it than of books he had written. But later in life, that same taste for risk cost him his fortune.

Tired of being abused by greedy, dishonest publishers, Twain believed only one solution could end the mistreatment; he had to avoid publishers altogether and print books for himself. According to Twain, James W. Paige's typesetting machine would save him, partly because it was such a marvel in itself, easily overshadowing other inventions. (Considering what nineteenth-century inventions were, Twain was making an extravagant claim for the apparatus.) At first he remained a silent, invisible, financial backer. After five years he stepped forward to be its primary sponsor, expecting not only to print his own books but to realize huge profits from the investment. In fact, he lost everything that he risked in what turned out to be a ruinous venture.

The setback of failed expectations and financial ruin did not arrest Twain's progress as a writer. Quite the opposite, the loss of these hopes corresponded to the years of some of his best-known achievements. *Adventures of Huckleberry Finn* (1884) showed more depth and a far more developed moral awareness than *The Adventures of Tom Sawyer* (1876), written before the disaster of the Paige typesetter. Twain's great financial loss helps explain the pessimistic view in the works he produced next, such as *A Connecticut Yankee in King Arthur's Court* (1889) and *The Tragedy of Pudd'nhead Wilson* (1894).

Even after achieving financial recovery Twain suffered new loss when his daughter Susy died in 1896. More personal loss darkened his energetic wit when his wife of thirty-four years died in 1904, and in 1909 his daughter Jean died. Throughout these later years Twain, a success and a celebrity, continued extensive lecture tours both in the United States and overseas. An award which especially pleased him in his old age was the honorary degree given him by Oxford University in 1907.

In his seventies, in an era when the average man could expect to live to age sixty-two, Mark Twain began to be bothered by his "tobacco heart." Cutting down from forty cigars a day to just a few made little difference. Chest pains and dizzy spells slowed him down, but only a little. In 1910 he sailed to Bermuda yet knew once he arrived that his lack of strength would make the voyage home risky. A friend from Connecticut went to Bermuda to accompany Twain home. Not long after he completed the journey, Twain lapsed into a fatal coma.

By the time he died, Mark Twain had seen America healed; only a few years later Southerners would go to war, fighting alongside Northerners to defend the Union, a nation without slavery. At the end of his life in 1910 Mark Twain left many manuscripts which had not been published. *The Mysterious Stranger* appeared in print in 1916. His autobiography, so full of cussedness, crankiness, and contradictions that it inevitably inspired scholarly controversies, may have been his parting joke.

QUESTIONS FOR THOUGHT AND DISCUSSION

1. Why did Mark Twain, in his early journalistic career and in his published works, become the master of the hoax and satire? What made that style so popular to Americans in the "Gilded Age"?

2. As Twain's literary career progressed, he was increasingly associated with the American South, though he had left it behind permanently. Why was this so?

3. Though a success as a writer and as a lecturer, Twain struggled financially throughout his life. Why?

4. To many British audiences, Twain came to symbolize the brash, iconoclastic American. Was Twain a representative American?

SUGGESTED READINGS

Budd, Louis. *Our Mark Twain: The Making of His Public Personality.* Philadelphia: U of Pennsylvania P, 1983.

Darbee, Henry. "Mark Twain Moves to Hartford." *American Heritage.* December 1959, 66–80.

Kaplan, Justin. *Mr. Clemens and Mark Twain: A Biography.* New York: Simon, 1966.

Lennon, Nigey. *Mark Twain in California: The Turbulent California Years of Samuel Clemens.* San Francisco: Chronicle, 1982.

Neider, Charles, ed. (1917) *The Autobiography of Mark Twain.* Harper: 1966.

Sanborn, Margaret. *Mark Twain, The Bachelor Years: A Biography.* New York: Doubleday, 1990.

Taper, Bernard. "Mark Twain's San Francisco." *American Heritage.* August 1963, 50–94.

2

Sitting Bull

Culture, for nineteenth century Americans, came from the East and was brought along by pioneers who headed past the western edge of civilization, which by the middle 1800s had spread all the way to Minnesota. When Easterners loaded volumes of Shakespeare into the wagon along with cooking pots, they thought they guaranteed the transmission of culture. Europeans who sailed up the Mississippi and debarked at Keokuk for points west brought their Goethe for the same reason. But no Americans thought of the indigenous population as having anything like a culture because they had no Shakespeare. Americans, even those who had risked their lives or lost family members in a war to end slavery, moved west in the hope of clearing the land of these "savages." Like the buffalo, in white eyes, the Natives stood no hope against progress, the proof of culture.

THE NAME OF Tatanka Iyotanka ("Sitting Bull"), like every other significant part of his culture, referred to buffalo. The image of a bull buffalo on its haunches, having decided not to budge from the fight, depicts with uncanny accuracy the man who won that name for himself at age fourteen. The child born in 1831, by the most recently accepted estimate, to the elder Sitting Bull and Her-Holy-Door, belonged to the people who called themselves Lakota, and their particular tribe, the Hunkpapas. In the East, their kinsman, related by language and culture, designated themselves as Dakotas. Both groups taken together were called "enemy" by the Chippewa in a word that ended up as "Sioux" when outsiders tried to say it. As fighters and hunters, the Sioux followed the buffalo herd in a nomadic way of life that sustained them successfully even in the severe winter of the northern Plains. From the buffalo they counted on meat but also hides to make their tepees, clothing, shirts, leggings, moccasins, and even shields. Ponies, their transport and also their sign and measure of wealth, had let them go where the herds led, in a region covering six western states.

No one could have told a Plains boy born in 1831 that before he was fifty the buffalo would be practically extinct. The same changes that diminished the herds would destroy the Sioux—whites looking for gold after it was discovered in 1874;

the Northern Pacific railroad that set out to link Saint Paul and Seattle; and white forts penetrating more deeply into hunting grounds. In 1831, when the boy who would become Sitting Bull was born near the Grand River, the nearest whites were 500 miles to the southeast. The world he knew depended on hunting, a dangerous and essential undertaking that sometimes required making war on neighboring enemy tribes to preserve or win hunting ground. The winner stayed and hunted and the defeated side had to leave. That code organized the society of the Lakota and their neighbors, such as the enemy Crow tribe.

"Jumping Badger," the name given at birth to the elder Sitting Bull's son, did not suit the solemn boy whose father quickly renamed him Hunkesni ("Slow"). To succeed in a culture that depended on hunting as well as fighting to win, a child needed to be trained and encouraged in the direction of physical courage. To put your safety at risk proved bravery. Soldiers who would later berate the Sioux as "wild Indians" did not recognize the rules that warriors observed as they attacked. Nor did the soldiers know the consequences for warriors. In fighting bravely, Lakota men won respect within their tribe and more importantly, merit in the spirit world. But their spirit world did not mean "heaven" or any such unearthly remote place, as Christian soldiers would believe. For the Lakotas, like other native peoples, the spirits belonged to their daily world, inhabited every aspect of nature: the rain, the earth, the buffalo, and all the rest. Making war in the correct way assured the continuation of the tribe's way of life. Warriors learned to tell when they had fought enough. They stopped at that point and went back, either to dance and sing their victory into celebration, or returned in shame and in silence if they had not won, or had not had victorious moments. Lakotas did not fight to wipe out another tribe. Their developed and solemn notions about fighting made it impossible for them to understand the intentions of white soldiers who came west.

At age fourteen, Slow became Sitting Bull when he won his first "hit," or "coup," against an enemy. By Lakota protocols, any claim to have gotten the first (or any up to the fourth) strike touching the enemy with a special stick, had to be confirmed by witnesses from the tribe. In a code that upheld valor above mere survival, to kill or to eliminate an opponent did not automatically carry glory in itself. By these guidelines, to kill a man from far away never made a story, and did not enhance a warrior's reputation for bravery. The mutilating of bodies that sometimes took place in bitter fighting could also be explained in Lakota terms as a final revenge since a body that was disfigured could not easily pass to the spirit world. The Lakotas thought about fighting in the same way as the other Natives of the Plains whom they fought, such as the Crow. But the white soldiers, especially veterans of the Civil War, had seen carnage multiplied on a scale so immense that it brutalized them. In native terms, they did not fight bravely and did not know when to stop. They made no sense.

From his earliest fights, Sitting Bull stood out for his courage and strength. He fought well because he had developed the strength and skills that Lakotas respected: an unusually good rider, he could stay on his pony and "disappear" by hugging the mount from one side and holding its mane. Like other Lakotas, he rode without a saddle. He had won the distinction of first coup, marked by being given not a medal but an eagle feather, by arriving on the scene ahead of the other warriors.

Most eagle feathers went to braves who had gone out ahead and had fought away from their comrades, in other words without protection. Extraordinary risks of that order won respect in the style of fighting that Sitting Bull understood.

From boyhood games, Sitting Bull had become an excellent shot with a bow and arrow. At age ten, he killed his first buffalo. Everyone recognized that he would continue to distinguish himself by fighting. In Lakota culture, those accomplishments meant that he would be recognized as a leader, one chief among others in the tribe. Their social order, developed without reference to white ways, put men of ability in positions of respect, but no single person held unique or absolute authority. Leaders worked to achieve not dominance, but agreement so that the tribe could act in unity.

Inevitably, people who chose to expose themselves to danger got hurt. Early in his fighting career, Sitting Bull was hit in the foot, a wound that changed the way he walked for the rest of his life. That injury, because it did not change his way of riding, did not detract from his distinction as a fighter. Because he distinguished himself so precociously and advanced so easily along the path to a position of authority, it did not violate the normal course of tribal life that he would choose to add another domain to his achievements.

In addition to its warriors, the tribe gave respect to men with spiritual gifts such as the ability to foresee important events or to cure physically or spiritually troubled members of the community. In that light, Sitting Bull turned in the direction of becoming a medicine man. Part of the initiation to that special circle involved rites intended to tame the flesh by testing physical endurance. The Sun Dance was a grueling ceremony that made men stick pieces of buffalo bone through their flesh, on the chest and on the back. Long strips of stretched hide were attached to these pegs on one end with the other end lashed to the top of a pole. After fasting and remaining suspended by their own skin in this dramatic way, would-be medicine men had to "dance" and pull against their own flesh in hope of seeing some great spiritual truth in a vision. Men sometimes hung and waited for the vision for days, as eventually the flesh tore. Sitting Bull voluntarily went through this test more than once and had scars front and back to prove it. This gruesome rite makes mere racist prejudice of early biographical accounts that suggested that Sitting Bull was cowardly or deficient by choosing to become a medicine man. Some accounts suggest he lacked the courage to go on as a warrior when, in fact, he continued to fight.

Scant contact between Lakota and whites explains the ignorance with which each regarded the other side. Because he seldom saw whites in his youth, Sitting Bull knew almost no English for most of his life and later, as a matter of principle, he did not want to talk to these foreigners he learned to distrust. That reticent stance caused him inconvenience and later exploitation. Even without English (or French), Sitting Bull could deal with traders. These rough and colorful characters, often the offspring of French trappers and Indian wives, learned what merchants have always known, that commerce transcends language. In exchanges that could be as full of ritual as was hunting or war, the traders met with Lakotas in tepees set up for the purpose of exchange. Sitting Bull or other Lakotas would give buffalo hides and receive rifles and ammunition. By Lakota logic, the exchange made sense: weapons that they could not make given for hides they could not use. In the days of plentiful herds, trade extended the ways in which the buffalo hides motivated the economy of village life.

Very quickly, the reasoning and the rhythm of Lakota life exploded when technology came screaming out of the East. Railroad locomotives brought, first of all, noise louder than anything ever heard on the plains, noise powerful enough to frighten off and scatter buffalo herds. Before long, the trains also brought a new kind of white. Not traders, but tourists now came west and expected to kill a bison from wherever they got off the train. Another power totally outside the imagination of the practical Lakotas, fashion had created in the East an increased demand for buffalo hides. Before long, trains were bringing commercial hunters who could kill as many as 100 buffalo in an hour. Estimates put the number of buffalo killed between 1872 and 1874 at nine million. Their paths of migration also had to change with the advance of the railroad, one more force that transformed the opening West. Anything that radically altered the habits of buffalo dictated major change for the Lakotas.

Even before technology wrecked the ecosystem that rationalized the Lakota way of life, political events in the East changed how Washington viewed the Indians of the Plains. The Mexican War of 1846–47 had guaranteed the United States more territory as had the Webster-Ashburton Treaty of 1842 with Great Britain which opened up Oregon. By the summer of 1848, 1,000 covered wagons of whites were heading west along the Oregon Trail every week. When Lakotas and other tribes saw settlers in wagons who passed through their hunting grounds and drove off game, the Natives attacked as they would have fought off an encroaching enemy tribe. The United States government, wanting to protect its citizens, looked for a treaty to end the attacks. The first important treaty in Sitting Bull's lifetime, the Fort Laramie Treaty of 1851, attempted to make all the Plains Natives peaceful. Not only did the treaty require the Natives to stop attacking settlers, miners, and other whites headed west, it added the naïve provision that the Natives should stop fighting each other. In all likelihood the tribes who signed in 1851—which did not even include Sitting Bull's Hunkpapas—did not understand that they accepted the unthinkable condition of ceasing fighting their enemies. To add to the confusion, the United States Senate came up with changes to the treaty limiting the term of government payments, which were then "signed" by still another set of chiefs. The Sioux had begun to accept limits on their territory—on paper.

Back East, where distinctions between Indians did not exist, news changed what Americans in general believed about the Plains Indians. The Santee Sioux had seen their territory reduced to a ten-mile-wide strip that ran along the Minnesota River for about 150 miles. Fear distorted reports from that frontier on the way to Washington. In 1862 word reached the capitol that war had broken out between the Sioux and the white settlers. Unfortunately for the Sioux, the United States Army was already fighting a war. The commanding officer sent to Minnesota had lost the second Battle of Bull Run, where he saw 16,000 Union soldiers killed or wounded in two days. General John Pope looked for armed conflict of a kind the Sioux did not practice: "It is my purpose utterly to exterminate the Sioux," he said. His instructions to his men made clear that he knew everything he wanted to about the enemy: "They are to be treated as maniacs or wild beasts and by no means as people with whom treaties and compromises can be made." His forces, led by Colonel Henry Sibley, did capture 1,800 Sioux warriors. Pope wanted a mass execution of 303 Indians. Abraham Lincoln intervened and insisted on seeing the records of the court martials that had condemned them. In the largest public execution ever held in the United States, President Lincoln consented to the public hanging of thirty-eight Sioux. The public showed a strong and indignant reaction: why so few?

Only two years later, in 1864, Colorado militia had massacred 400 Southern Cheyenne at Sand Creek in Colorado. The band felt secure because they had been promised safety by the commander of a nearby fort. Their leader, Black Kettle, flew in front of his tepee an American flag which Abraham Lincoln had given him with assurances of peace when the chief visited Washington. Even the medicine of that flag could not protect the Cheyenne from Colonel John Chivington's command to "kill and scalp all, big and little." The native civilizations of the Plains were changing the way white soldiers fought.

A small number of generals understood that when the Natives fought they were reacting to unfair treatment. Generals George Crook and Oliver O. Howard tried to explain to politicians that treaties should offer some advantage to both sides and that promises had to be honored. Arguments by experienced generals could not reduce the gulf between two alien ways of thinking. Unfortunately for the Native Americans, the traditional white solution in dealing with them could no longer work. In the East, geography provided a false solution: send the Indians west. But in the West the continent was running out of "rug" under which Native Americans could be swept. By white reasoning, progress had to be acknowledged as irresistible. The Native Americans could not be allowed to continue living as they used to and wanted to. They would have to turn themselves in at Indian agencies, accept white education, and become white.

Sitting Bull never expected a treaty to do what it promised. If anyone had asked him, he knew exactly what he wanted for his people. Nothing could be simpler: whites should stop coming and scaring the game away and interrupting the paths of buffalo herds. If they did not, he would attack. The white settlers could remain as traders if they wanted but not go any further than they had gone. How arrogantly they behaved and what senseless demands they made. Some of the land they asked for the Lakotas had only recently won from the Crow. Now, without a fight, the "walking soldiers" expected them to hand it over. To a chief who had known the respect of his people his whole life, the idea of compromise and of giving up a little land spelled the beginning of dishonor. In the eyes of many of his people, he behaved with enormous integrity. True to his name, he had made up his mind and did not budge. To the United States he was labelled a "hostile," the name for Native Americans who were not willing to accept white civilization. Natives who cooperated they called "progressives."

In June 1868, a distinguished and courageous visitor arrived in Sitting Bull's Hunkpapa village on a peace mission that succeeded, according to some official accounts. Father Pierre-Jean de Smet, a Jesuit missionary known as Black Robe to many Natives of the Plains, brought a request for representatives to accompany him to a peace conference. He spent three nights staying with Sitting Bull, who received him as an honored guest. Politeness required all the hosts to listen with respectful attention. After the formal greetings and requests were presented, even after his own formal talk, Sitting Bull said what many of his tribe thought. The Lakotas wanted their land left alone. Whites should go back where they came from or expect to be attacked. When de Smet prepared to leave, he asked for some spokesmen of the tribe to accompany him to Fort Rice. Sitting Bull, because of his own reluctance to make any agreement, sent chiefs less important than himself. These Lakotas, including his friend Gall, did not grasp that what they told de Smet, and later the soldiers, had no relation at all to the paper they signed.

That document, which had originally been prepared as part of the Fort Laramie Treaty of 1851, contained a blueprint for the fate of the Sioux. Words they could not have comprehended, words like "reservation" and "annuity," described a way of life they could not imagine. Schools would be built, training would convert the Sioux from hunters into farmers. Until almost the end of the century, for thirty years the government would give the Natives food rations, give them clothing of the kind white people wore. Sitting Bull could not have understood these concepts either, but he knew that he had signed nothing. As a man of his word, he had a clean conscience. No one could expect to hold him to agreements signed by less important chiefs, he thought.

Sitting Bull continued to start fights with whites, as he told Black Robe he would. When the Lakotas around him saw that settlers had not stopped coming, they made a structural change in their tribal confederation in order to allow, for the first time, authority that surpassed one tribe. Four Horns, an uncle of Sitting Bull, wanted all the Lakota tribes and even some neighboring Native Americans to acknowledge a supreme commander, one leader who would speak for many tribes on the question of when to make war. The tribes chose Sitting Bull as that commander.

According to estimates, one-third of the Lakota followed Sitting Bull's leadership and beliefs. By fighting, they would keep whites away and guarantee the continuation of the way of life they knew. Because their attachment to the land rationalized that life, any loss of land, even by treaty, spelled humiliation in their terms. On his side, Sitting Bull had enormous credibility because he had fought so valiantly so many times and had already refused any compromise. In practical terms, he knew how to win, an art that depended on knowing when to make war. After 1870, Sitting Bull stopped making attacks on settlers and thought more of defending the land that his people already claimed. That policy let Sitting Bull satisfy his followers until everything changed, when a man ambitious for a reputation trespassed on a place that already had one.

Lieutenant Colonel George Armstrong Custer, identified by the Sioux as Long Hair, came West with the Seventh Cavalry in 1872. When he started an expedition into Paha Sapa (the Black Hills), he violated a Native-American taboo. The Sioux did not go there much, and seldom camped in the region that some feared and some spoke of as holy. Every Sioux understood that something made those hills unique. Leaders like Sitting Bull knew that even when game grew scarce in other places, the hills could be counted on for food and for tall, straight trees suited for the frames of tepees. Custer was hunting when he went there, but not for food.

Besides soldiers, Custer had miners and equipment with him. He wanted to be the man associated with confirming that the reports of gold in the Black Hills were true. The special status of Paha Sapa obliged Sitting Bull and the Lakotas to threaten to attack. But the Sioux did not fight Custer there in 1874. Government agencies had been increasing, and Sitting Bull added to his reputation as a "hostile" by refusing to go near any agency. When a fort was built as an agency for the Crow, the traditional enemy of the Lakotas, Sitting Bull attacked it.

The most famous Sioux victory, when they killed Custer near the Little Bighorn River in June 1876, did not deceive Sitting Bull. As a medicine man, he had predicted the battle as Custer's defeat and he participated in it by making medicine, not by fighting. When the battle ended, he also knew that whites would be ready for revenge and would be able to send enough soldiers to guarantee their success. Because Custer had hoped to be a candidate for President, news of his death appeared on page one of newspapers back East. That story shared the front page with a less dramatic historical event, the one hundredth anniversary of the United States.

Rather than stay and be forced into a fight that he could not win, Sitting Bull sought safety in flight rather than risk being taken to a reservation. With around 2,000 followers, Sitting Bull crossed the border to Canada in May 1877, expecting the protection of Queen Victoria, or "Grandmother," as he referred to her.

Besides peace, Sitting Bull also hoped to find food when he took his people to the new hunting ground north of the border, but the hunters stayed hungry, unable to find enough game. Canadian winters strained the Sioux capacity for misery and made some desert their leader. News of this hardship reached army forts to the South. In reply to an invitation from the government of the United States, Sitting Bull appeared at Fort Buford, Montana, where he used to go to trade, and he turned himself in along with his people in July 1881. As a chief, he made the hard decision for the well-being of those he governed, people who had become desperately hungry and demoralized in Canada. From what he knew of treaties and the worthlessness of their promises, Sitting Bull may have been less than surprised when he was taken prisoner even after he was promised a pardon. From Fort Buford he was taken to Fort Randall, South Dakota.

Because of his national reputation, Sitting Bull was given special permission to leave the reservation to go on a national tour. As he became more widely known, rumors spread fantastic notions about Sitting Bull. According to some, he was a West Point graduate. Others held that he could write in Latin. A new kind of reputation, unrelated to Lakota bravery, drew curious crowds who wanted to see the chief who did not fear the United States Army. When he headed East, he knew that he would not be paid for the tour but that he would be allowed to sell his autograph. As he traveled, Sitting Bull made speeches in theaters to audiences who did not understand anything he said but neither did he understand the translator who followed him. In Philadelphia, the audience included an English-speaking Sioux boy who recognized an unfaithful translation. In his speech, Sitting Bull announced he would see the "Grandfather," or President of the United States in Washington, D.C. (He never did.) He also said he was glad to know his children would be educated when he saw so many white people. "There is no use fighting

The Bettmann Archive

By the time Sitting Bull could be photographed, he knew that the Lakota way of life was doomed.

any longer," he went on. "The buffalo are all gone, as well as the rest of the game." The translator then explained to the audience that they had been listening to a gory description of what happened at the Little Bighorn from a chief who boasted that he personally killed Custer. The people who heard those false claims from the translator also saw the tired-looking warrior as he gave away money to hungry and filthy white children.

When he returned to the West to live on the Standing Rock Reservation (in present-day South Dakota), Sitting Bull had to deal with new deceptions. In the new style of trading, the Sioux faced government commissioners who offered money for land. Sitting Bull, predictably, did not want to give up even one Sioux acre, not until he could believe in promises from older agreements. Not wanting to come across as simply belligerent, Sitting Bull tried to explain the bond between the Sioux and their land. In frustration, he saw that the bored-looking commissioners were indifferent to his being a chief: to them, he was one more Indian.

One white man understood Sitting Bull's authority at the Standing Rock Reservation so well that he vowed not to defer to it. James McLaughlin, an Indian agent married to a Dakota woman, zealously set out to bring Sitting Bull to his knees, to persuade him that he could not hold out against progress. In an odd rivalry with his famous captive, McLaughlin exerted his authority in the hope of diminishing that of Sitting Bull. He had an opportunity to display his importance when William Cody (Buffalo Bill) wanted Sitting Bull to make a second tour, this time as part of his Wild West Show. Cody and Sitting Bull had become good friends during the first tour, a friendship sealed by Cody's gift of a trick pony. The proposition came to involve McLaughlin because as a reservation Indian, the Sioux chief could not leave without his permission. Seeing a chance to display his own importance, McLaughlin refused outright, maybe because he understood that by coming back with stories of his travels, Sitting Bull would enhance his standing on the reservation.

Another unseen outside force elevated Sitting Bull and bedeviled McLaughlin. Far more significant than Buffalo Bill's glamour, a native religious movement with an urgent spirit of revival was coming from the West. The movement was started by a Paiute Native of Nevada who had a mystical experience in which he saw salvation for all the Natives. Whites would leave and the forest would be full of game again because the Messiah was about to come, he predicted. According to the vision, the date would be the next year, in the spring of 1891.

As an aspect of native religion, the fact of that vision in itself did not necessarily threaten whites, but the medium which passed the news terrified them. The powerful message had to do with an ancient culture, it could not be forcefully transmitted if it were simply told. Words conveyed very little compared to dance as a means of demonstrating a truth of such magnitude for the community. The fervor attached to the news inspired a new dance, a revolutionary dance with Messianic overtones. The spiritual craze left dancers on the ground, some transported beyond their bodies into a mystical dimension in which they heard more recent news of the Messiah, whom the Natives pledged to treat decently—unlike what the whites had done. To outsiders, these spiritual rites looked hysterical partly because the Natives had just invented it, proof that they were lying about becoming white and were very dangerous. Dancers started talking about new medicine related to the "Ghost Dance," a shirt that protected its wearer from bullets and from white weapons.

When settlers got word of this cult, they asked the government in Washington for help against the wild fanatics they saw ready to start a war of religion. Government leaders in Washington, D.C., did not doubt the power of new medicine in North and South Dakota. The United States Senate voted to give each of those states guns and ammunition for citizens and citizen armies to protect themselves. The Secretary of War would authorize federal help, but first he had to convince the Secretary of the Interior, who argued that Washington should send food to the Indians, not guns to the whites. He argued that food already promised by treaties had never been sent, and even if Indians could not read, they could see that their rations were being cut down and that their children were getting sick. Shortages did not occur by accident. Leaders in Washington, D.C. believed that hungry Natives could be counted on to cooperate. Meanwhile, the Ghost Dance spread.

Sitting Bull lived at the Grand River Camp, on the vast Standing Rock Reservation, far away from James McLaughlin, who knew about the Ghost Dance and the magic shirt. Hoping to substitute a stabilizing fad for a disruptive one, he had already offered the reservation Sioux a shirt that gave worldly rather than mystical status. Blue army uniforms with shiny buttons transformed Sioux into Indian police, a force that helped McLaughlin spy on Sitting Bull and follow his movements.

Against the Ghost Dance, McLaughlin knew he was as helpless as the United States government. After all that they had given up, the Natives would not put up with whites meddling in their religion. Could the government hope to make a dance illegal? But McLaughlin knew that if he could take Sitting Bull out of the picture, the Sioux would lose interest in the dance, because they would lose all hope—including hope of a Messiah. While Sitting Bull dreamed of seeing the Messiah, McLaughlin worked on arresting Sitting Bull, his plan for shutting down the Ghost Dance.

Word had reached Sitting Bull that the Messiah would appear even sooner than predicted. In December 1890, the Messiah was expected at the Pine Ridge camp of Red Cloud, a longtime friend of Sitting Bull. To visit that camp to the east of Standing Rock, near the border of Nebraska, Sitting Bull needed permission from McLaughlin. He sent his written request to McLaughlin, who knew he wanted Sitting Bull to stay put. On December 14, 1890, the night before Sitting Bull expected to leave for Red Cloud's camp, McLaughlin sent, but did not accompany, forty-three Indian police to arrest Sitting Bull. By daybreak, the police reached Sitting Bull's cabin and told him he was under arrest. In the midst of anger and confusion that have never been completely untangled, one of his loyal friends may have fired the first shot on the Indian police. Minutes later, Sitting Bull lay dead and mutilated, shot in the chest. The fighting did not stop. As planned, soldiers from a nearby fort arrived with an automatic weapon, a Hotchkiss gun, which they fired into the camp. Outside, the pony given to Sitting Bull by Buffalo Bill repeated what he had done so many times in the Wild West Show. When he heard shots, he started his routine of stunts.

In February 1891, not even two months after the death of Sitting Bull, Lyman Casey, Senator of North Dakota, wrote from Washington, D.C., to the Indian

Office to take steps to negotiate with Sitting Bull's widow for the dead chief's belongings. Obliging the Senator, the state did get title to the cabin in which Sitting Bull had died. It appeared as part of the 1893 Columbian Exposition in Chicago in the exhibit from North Dakota, in commemoration of the four hundredth anniversary of the arrival of Columbus in the New World.

QUESTIONS FOR THOUGHT AND DISCUSSION

1. What sort of culture was practiced by Sitting Bull's native tribe, the Hunkpapa people? Could their way of life have somehow been preserved in the midst of the movement of American settlers from the East?

2. How did the U.S. government try to convert Plains Indians into "real" Americans? Do you think this attempt to Americanize was humanitarian or cruel? What does being an "American" mean to you?

3. In what ways was Sitting Bull converted into a commodity after he surrendered to U.S. government authorities? Can you imagine yourself in his situation or listening to him in an audience during his speaking tour?

4. After reading this sketch do you sympathize with Sitting Bull and the plight of the Plains Indians? Explain.

SUGGESTED READINGS

Billington, Ray Allen and Martin Ridge. *Westward Expansion: A History of the American Frontier.* 5 ed. New York: MacMillan, 1982.

Johnson, Dorothy M. *Warrior for a Lost Nation: A Biography of Sitting Bull.* Philadelphia: Westminster, 1969.

Milner, Clyde A. *et al. The Oxford History of the American West.* New York: Oxford UP, 1994.

Turner, C. Frank. *Across the Medicine Line.* Toronto: McClelland, 1973.

Utley, Robert M. *The Lance and the Shield: The Life and Times of Sitting Bull.* New York: Holt, 1993.

Vestal, Stanley. *Sitting Bull, Champion of the Sioux.* Norman: U of Oklahoma P, 1957.

3

Myra Colby Bradwell

After the Civil War Americans did not go back to the country they had left. The long absences from home had hardened many men through brutal fighting and whiskey, the battlefield anesthetic and cure-all. Back at home, women found that they had to keep family farms and businesses going, and that they could. Advances in weapons technology had made fighting more dangerous, but Northern factories had also produced lightweight farm machinery that women could operate. In this new style of agriculture, women found that stamina could be worth as much as brawn. In the North, where factories relied on machines, women composed one-third of the work force. When husbands returned home, women had already been emancipated from their pre-war dependence emotionally and economically. That same spirit inspired women in towns and cities who expected to hold on to at least some of the liberty—and cash—they had earned and were learning to enjoy.

Myra Colby Bradwell, the first woman licensed to practice law in the United States, fought for years to change laws and institutions in ways that would correct the official inequality of men and women in so many domains. Brilliantly successful at business and proud of her husband and family, she held back her endorsement and financial backing from Susan B. Anthony's suffrage forces. For that difference, Bradwell lost the approval of the author of the History of Women Suffrage *who hoped that to diminish Bradwell's place would diminish her importance.*

MYRA COLBY WAS taught as a girl that when extreme demands tested members of the Colby family, they became heroes every time in order to prove the family tradition. Colbys in America knew that they had ancestors who died at Bunker Hill whose memory the family preserved and honored. But when Myra Colby was born near Manchester, Vermont, on February 12, 1831, her parents already had plans of leaving New England. By the time Myra was two, her abolitionist parents had moved the family to western New York state and, after that, to Illinois.

Another hero, although not an ancestor, whose praises Myra heard from her parents was Elijah Parish Lovejoy, an abolitionist journalist and friend of the Colbys. He was killed by a mob in Illinois as he tried to protect his newest press. The imprint of those stories heard in girlhood would reappear in the linking of journalism and idealism that influenced the unexpected and brave path that Myra would first imagine and then pursue.

Like many other daughters of educated, middle-class parents, as a young woman Myra Colby went to a women's seminary for her education. For three years, typically, young women studied geography, history, English authors, and sometimes languages. Seminary training—in her case in Elgin, Illinois—did not direct young women toward life in a religious community. Yet their education carried a strong moral stamp, an emphasis that helped reinforce a view of women that most men and many women of the nineteenth century would not think to question: in terms of their morality, women stood superior to men. In the restricted and controlled sphere in which they lived their lives, women were expected to be considerate of others, kind, thoughtful, modest, and pious to a degree impossible for "the rougher sex." Since women did not go after and earn money, they remained untainted by greed and ambition; because their sensual desires did not go beyond the wish to reproduce, they functioned above lust. Like children, they needed the protection of men. And, as with children, no one demanded a great deal from women, nor were people supposed to take them seriously.

This concept of virtuous womanhood describes the cultural milieu of the early 1860s, a continuation of what Americans had believed for generations. The only ripple on that tranquil surface came from women who preached temperance and condemned demon rum. For women in general, the lasting importance of the temperance movement would be that it taught women to gather in large meetings organized around a shared idea. But during the Civil War, women's behavior had to change in the absence of their husbands' protection, a period of trial that would eventually force a hard look at old attitudes. Myra Colby, reared with pre-war beliefs, did not come into her own, either, until after the war, after the relations of men and women in society changed, but before people recognized the contradictions between what they believed and what they saw around them.

Myra Colby started to mystify and displease her family when she married James Bradwell. The Colbys had thought so well of their pretty, intelligent daughter's prospects that they would have chosen a more promising young man for her, if she had asked. The Bradwell family, unlike the Colbys, had not fought at Bunker Hill. They had only left England in 1830, when James was two years old, and had next to nothing to show for it. No one knows if Myra was looking for a husband who did not belong to the respectable class and who did not accept the same beliefs about women that a more suitable young man would have held. Whatever attracted their daughter so passionately and defiantly to young Bradwell remained an enigma to the Colbys, even in 1852 when Myra and James Bradwell eloped. Two years later they moved to Chicago after the birth of their first child, a girl named Myra.

From the beginning of her marriage, Myra Colby Bradwell knew two things: she wanted to use her education and she wanted to work alongside her husband. Throughout her life, especially when women began to insist on the freedom to follow any career they chose, she repeated her conviction that the most satisfying arrangement for a marriage allowed a husband and wife to work side by side. That belief shaped, but did not ultimately limit, her career plans and decisions.

The newly married Bradwells moved to Memphis in 1853 and started a private school where Myra taught, working with James at what turned into a successful effort. The school quickly attracted more and more students and held promise of continuing to grow. Showing the kind of courage that had enabled her parents to leave New England, Myra Bradwell along with James left the thriving school in Memphis to move to Illinois. James, with three years of college but no degree, turned out to have a drive for hard work that the Colbys had not noticed. While they were in Chicago, he studied law and in 1855 passed the bar, a career choice which would not necessarily have won over his in-laws, given the generally low estimation of lawyers. During those same years, Myra had three more children, Thomas in 1856, Bessie in 1858, and James in 1864.

When the Civil War interrupted all normal routines, Myra Bradwell put aside her lively intellectual interests and worked with local women as president of their Soldiers' Aid Society, helping organize sanitary fairs and contributing all her free time to the support and relief effort that claimed the energy of other educated women. Meanwhile her husband had set up a practice with Myra's brother who had finally gotten over his early prejudice against James Bradwell. The partnership grew, and in 1861 James Bradwell became County and Probate Judge for Cook County.

After the war, when her children were no longer babies—James had died in infancy in 1864 and her daughter Myra in 1861 at age seven—Mrs. Bradwell let her husband help in her new undertaking. With his guidance, she wanted to read law and then take the Illinois state bar exam. Bradwell saw herself as having the mental capacity for study and the advantage of a husband who found her plan sensible and possible, even if no other woman in Illinois had ever attempted what she now had in mind. In fact, nowhere else in the United States was there a woman attorney practicing the law. (In Iowa, Arabella Babb Mansfield passed the state bar exam in 1869, but never attempted to put her credential to use.)

Before long, every practitioner of the law in Illinois—lawyer, judge, law student, and many business people—knew the name of Myra Bradwell because in 1868 she started a weekly legal newspaper called the *Chicago Legal News*. At the outset she claimed that it would appear weekly on Saturday and would be four pages long. In her own words on the first page of the first collected volume it was "A Journal of Legal Intelligence containing cases decided in the various United States courts; the Supreme Court of Illinois, and other states; head-notes to important cases, in advance of their publication in the reports of the state courts; the public laws of Illinois, passed in 1869; recent English cases; legal information and general news."

Bradwell's judgment about the need for such a paper had been so astute that she regularly failed to keep it to four pages and soon had to increase its length to print all the advertising space that her paper sold. The news pages of the *Chicago Legal News* show the unusual cast of Myra Bradwell's mind, while the advertisements show the direction of growth in Chicago. Many notices appear with the names of lawyers, announcing their practices to the public. Alongside these are legal notices of the kind that still appear in newspapers, as well as new areas of business such as insurance companies from Connecticut and real estate brokers. Legal publishers claimed important space in the early issues and seem to have inspired Myra Bradwell because a short time after starting the paper she began her own legal publishing, printing, and binding company, the Chicago Legal News Company. Only by a special charter from the state was she allowed to be president of both the newspaper and the publishing company. State law dictated, however, that as a married woman she lacked the legal status to own a company.

Her practical nature let Myra Bradwell recognize needs that were not being satisfied, a category that included both the publication of new laws from the state capital, but also of standardized legal forms. Her newspaper became the source lawyers counted on for publishing new laws and her printing company provided them with the stationery they used. Whether or not her readers knew it, Myra Bradwell regularly went to the state capital at Springfield to get the text of laws passed by the legislature in order to print them before anyone else. Without that effort of hers, the public had to wait sometimes several months to see the new legislation in print. In the pages of the *Chicago Legal News,* only one name appears for the writing, the editorials, and the choice of material—Myra Bradwell.

The language of the *Chicago Legal News* conveys the energy of its author as it attests to the vitality of her interest in the law. If its pages are read closely, the choice of subjects implies a coherent point of view that is then reinforced more subtly in the arrangement of stories on the page. From the earliest issues, its columns assert "Now that there is so much talk in regard to the law relating to woman and her right to vote . . ." Whether or not that was true among the community of readers of the paper, when they read that the subject interested people, the claim became true. In other words, the paper was setting the agenda for discussion among its readers who included judges and legislators. When the paper started, James Bradwell himself was still a judge, but soon resigned in 1869. Through their relations with the judge, many of the paper's readers certainly had met the Myra Bradwell whose words they read and came to discuss.

In 1869, after Myra Bradwell had studied the law for several years, she passed her bar examination in a way that was called "most creditable." But the Supreme Court of Illinois denied her application, explaining that they had no choice but to say no because she was married, a state which constituted a "disability" for a woman in legal terms. Readers of the *Chicago Legal News* may have remembered the story that she had run concerning English common law according to which, when a woman married, her identity had no more independent existence apart from that of her husband. A married woman, for example, could not enter into a contract, could not own property, and could not act legally without the consent of her husband. In America, those concepts were accepted and made even more explicit. So unequal were husband and wife that in cases that required a woman to sign along with her husband, as in the transfer of real property, the wife had to be taken aside and asked to confirm under oath, out of the hearing of her husband, that she had not been forced into signing.

Myra Bradwell refused to let the court deny her on the grounds that she was married precisely because she wanted to force the judges to say what they really

Chicago Historical Society

In the decades after the Civil War, every lawyer west of Pittsburgh depended on Myra Colby Bradwell's legal weekly.

meant. She wrote a brief that destroyed their arguments and succeeded in requiring them to say more. The next time they wrote a refusal to Myra Bradwell, the justices said what she believed they should have stated first, namely, that she could not practice law in Illinois because she was a woman. In reply, Myra Bradwell prepared a request for the United States Supreme Court. No answer came back for several years.

The reasoning behind the Illinois decision reveals and articulates widely held beliefs about women, but again, beliefs that had been easier to defend before the Civil War changed the social environment for relations between men and women. To a great extent, the practice of the law appeared too rough a profession for women. No one on the court said that Myra Bradwell or women in general lacked intelligence, nor that the mental ability to study the law and master its subtleties lay beyond their possibilities. But many people, women included, believed that because women had smaller skulls than men, they were less suited for cerebral work. People had begun to use the phrase "strong-minded women"—not a compliment—to describe what some saw as a new kind of woman, one not satisfied with the stay-at-home role that had been seen as normal.

The problem with the idea of a woman lawyer had to do with public speaking and with the adversarial atmosphere of a courtroom. On the one hand, women did not speak in public, or should not, according to many men. To do so would mean a loss of feminine qualities such as passiveness. Imagining women in the courtroom as their opponents, many lawyers saw themselves at a great disadvantage against an opponent who could charm a judge or a jury. Such an inequality would put justice at risk, the reasoning ran.

After the second refusal, Myra Bradwell never asked again to be admitted to the Illinois bar, a silence that expressed a definite position, especially considering that in 1872 Illinois passed a law that allowed people to pursue whatever career they chose. But while she awaited a United States Supreme Court decision, the question Bradwell had raised invited talk and speculation precisely because it hung for so long without an answer. When the Supreme Court finally answered, in 1873, it upheld the decision of the Illinois court and suggested that the crux of the matter was states' rights.

Meanwhile, in the pages of the *Chicago Legal News,* a story appeared about a Mrs. Ada H. Kepley who had applied to the bar of Illinois after having passed her exam successfully. The point of the story, however, concerned another candidate who applied at the same time and passed, Mr. Richard A. Dawson, who was an African American. The headline made its point plainly, "The Negro Ahead of the Woman," as did its first witty sentence, "The woman, in the race to obtain the legal right to practice law in Illinois, has been distanced by negro."

The *Chicago Legal News* helped spread the name of its "editress," as some people called her (the paper listed her as "editor"). It circulated stories of what would be called today her "special interest" in the way that the law as an institution treated women. Because Myra Bradwell oversaw the composition of the paper, she could arrange stories in ways that made meanings on the overall page not explicit in any individual story. She could group a story about the status of women's citizenship alongside a story entitled "The Custody of a Child," linking the status of women and children. In another number, she put an item entitled "Woman's right to vote" next to a story on "Bankruptcy," a problem for many women because of the property laws they could not change without the vote. In another, she printed a story on "the Constitutional Convention" which argues that if women can be counted in calculations to decide the number of political representatives, they should be allowed to vote. Immediately after it, a title set off a story on the results of an election, "Cook County Officers." That is, in the layout of the page Bradwell invited readers to consider that different candidates might have won if women voted. (Her readers, no doubt, included candidates for state offices.)

Because she started the *Chicago Legal News* right after the Civil War, Myra Bradwell recorded the subjects that spawned the most confusion and controversy in that period of massive national reorganization. In much of the United States, inside and outside the South, Americans had to work out a way of dealing with freed slaves, a large population of newly liberated people, many of them homeless and many in need of training to develop new skills, especially if they attempted to leave the agricultural economy of the rural South. But at the end of the war, American women, who had not been legally emancipated, expected some compensation for the new roles they had taken during the war years. Myra Bradwell's desire to practice law fit into the huge social mosaic that Americans were attempting to reorder and make rational in a new design. When she printed her story entitled "The Negro Ahead of the Woman," she spelled out what puzzled and distressed many Americans. Women especially saw themselves in a contest with black Americans, black American men in particular.

East of Chicago, especially in New York state, women in favor of what was called "the woman suffrage question" worked to insure for women the right to register to vote. Susan B. Anthony, not the earliest but perhaps the best known today of these women, worked hard to address groups of women at large public meetings in the hope of changing their thinking. Many women, as well as men, resisted the idea of women voting. Even if women were allowed to vote they would not, many argued. Less hypothetical and more honest in a way, many men argued that if the law gave women the right to vote and thereby oppose their husbands, then harmony within the family would be disrupted forever. The most superficial and least convincing of the arguments pointed out that polls were rough places that women did well to avoid. Had women thought what it would be like to have cigar smoke blown in their faces?

In Myra Bradwell's way of thinking, which was the thinking of a lawyer, the question of woman suffrage had to be considered and analyzed carefully as a legal question. While she worked hard to bring out her paper every week with indefatigable energy, all the while upholding the obligation of the law to treat women justly in every domain of their experience, she kept her distance from the more strident feminists, with whom she differed on fundamental points. The unmarried Susan B. Anthony, for example, used passionate language to rouse rallies of women, to encourage them to see men as "tyrants." Anthony worked with women as her colleagues and constituents. Myra Bradwell, on the other hand, liked to point out that she was herself a wife and mother, and extremely fond of her family. Bradwell's commitment to equality of men with women helps explain her views: no one expected men to have to choose between professional life and family life. Why should women be expected to take only one over the other? Bradwell consistently pointed out other women like herself who had families and still expected to use their minds.

Myra Bradwell insisted on fairness, even when it stung. She took her professional commitment so seriously that she even printed articles critical of badly argued positions on the subject of woman suffrage. As she worked with men and wrote for men, Bradwell ran her business so skillfully that she succeeded better than most men. Myra Bradwell the newspaperwoman and publisher got rich. Leaders of the woman suffrage movement recognized her success with which they both wanted to associate themselves and wanted to claim a part to help their cause. Susan B. Anthony recognized that women needed examples of other women who had helped in their progress. Anthony believed that only by winning the right to vote could women change their old status as morally superior weaklings. Men could not be counted on to vote in legislative changes to help women, according to Anthony. Only by voting could women choose their political leaders and influence legislation in their interest.

While Myra Bradwell did not question suffrage as essential to women's needs under the law, she did see many avenues to achieving the prize of the vote. She worked in shaping political debate by keeping women's legal rights in the faces of judges who read her *Chicago Legal News*. Bradwell also tried to influence legislation in such areas as the property rights of married women. She worked to achieve a legislative change to have women elected to office on school boards in Illinois, then to other offices, such as notary public. But her general commitment remained to the law and to its application to guarantee equality.

Myra Bradwell and Susan B. Anthony could not agree on the most fruitful way to help women most in their race with blacks. After the passage of the Fourteenth Amendment, Susan B. Anthony made plain to her followers her indignant reaction at being expected to uphold the right of blacks to vote when women could not. Other women who had been allies of Anthony split at this point and issued a summons to form a new and different organization. Calling themselves the American Woman Suffrage Association, to be distinct from Anthony's National Woman Suffrage Association, the newly organized group met in Cleveland in November 1869.

After many years of working on the cause she considered her own, Susan B. Anthony edited the *History of Woman Suffrage* with two of her colleagues. That first volume reprints the entire text of the Supreme Court decision that refused Myra Bradwell the right to practice law and shows a portrait of Myra Bradwell, but says nothing about who Bradwell was nor any hint of her accomplishments as a publisher, a skilled business woman, and advocate of women. The reason for the oversight of such an important woman who had, after all, helped organize the first suffrage convention in the Midwest appears at the end of the volume. There, Anthony lists every contributor to her project, from the tiny number who gave the lavish sum of $100, to the lengthy list of one dollar contributors, all the way down to fifty cents, twenty-five, and even ten cents. The famous and well-off Myra Bradwell chose not to be part of that effort.

Politically, the question of allowing women to vote erupted in the years immediately after the Civil War when lawmakers finally acknowledged that times were changing. The Fourteenth Amendment, passed in 1869, said that Americans had to be allowed to vote despite "previous condition of servitude," the language that changed the life of former slaves. Then, in 1873, came the Fifteenth Amendment which changed the basis of political representation. Women who saw blacks being given political rights wanted to have that same opportunity, whether or not they found it fitting that African Americans should vote. Myra Bradwell, because of her conviction about equality and the need for the law to make equality real, wanted no part of proponents of woman suffrage who, like Anthony, refused to work for "Sambo." Unlike Susan B., as she was known, Myra Bradwell wanted legislation to usher in broader changes which would alter the political context and, indirectly perhaps, make woman suffrage inevitable.

In the pages of her extremely popular *Chicago Legal News,* Myra Bradwell wrote in favor of specific legislative changes, some of which she drafted and lobbied herself, often with the collaboration of her husband. Her efforts and writing carried the day to change the law concerning the property of married women. She wrote the sad and true account of a woman who worked because she had to, cleaning houses for the support of her children whose alcoholic father contributed nothing to his family. That same husband ran such a high tab at a bar that the tavern owner came after the couple for satisfaction of the debt, and was paid because a court ruled that any earnings of the wife belonged first to her husband.

As a mother, Myra Bradwell crusaded for the rights of the children who legally endured inhuman conditions at the Chicago Reform School. When a superintendent of the school wrote an irate denial letter to the *Chicago Legal News,* Bradwell printed his letter in full along with her own answer, saying that she stood by what she had written and dared the official to sue her for libel. Eventually the Chicago Reform School was abolished.

As the strong editor of a leading legal publication, Myra Bradwell fought for the right of women to be on school boards, then to vote for limited offices in limited cases. The use of the newspaper to achieve those ends was inspired because it changed the nature of political debate; readers noticed the inconsistency of allowing women to hold office before they were allowed to vote.

Because she stayed at the center of legal questions by making herself a source of fact—courts allowed her newspaper to be used as evidence—the whole issue of not allowing Myra Bradwell to practice law became a technicality. Maybe she did not stand before judges or plead cases on retainer from individual clients, but her writing put Bradwell's reasoning and agenda before judges, the legal establishment of Illinois, and the legal leaders of many other states every week.

An extreme test of Myra Bradwell's resilience and of her business sense came in 1871 when the Chicago fire destroyed a strip one mile wide and seven miles long in the heart of the city. The *Chicago Legal News* figured on the list of lost businesses. By happenstance, Myra's thirteen-year-old daughter managed to save the notebook that had the list of subscribers. Rather than collapse and use the disaster as an excuse to interrupt the publication schedule for even one week, Bradwell got on a train and went to Milwaukee, where she wrote that week's paper and had it printed. At that juncture, which could have been viewed as hopeless, Bradwell recognized a great opportunity for her enterprise. She reported to her readers that every lawyer in Chicago had lost his law library and would need to replace it. Since those lawyers were her readers, she also helped boost her own revenues when she encouraged publishers of legal books to advertise in her pages to help inform and guide lawyers who needed whole shelves of new books.

Although not a conventional lawyer, Myra Bradwell showed her powers of persuasion and her ability to make it harder for a man to use the law to treat a woman unfairly. The man she opposed was Robert Lincoln, Abraham Lincoln's only surviving child. He was a man motivated by greed, apparently, in his extreme cruelty to his mother, Mary Todd Lincoln, Abraham Lincoln's widow and Myra Bradwell's friend. As far as anyone can tell, in a case in which the documents have all been destroyed—as recently as the 1940s as a result of directions in wills—the conflict had to do with money.

Everyone who knew Mrs. Lincoln saw that the violent death of her husband traumatized her, especially because the deaths of her two other sons had left her in a state that people then called melancholy. One manifestation of her unhappiness was what people now call compulsive behavior, but in particular compulsive shopping. Because her tastes had always been luxurious, Mrs. Lincoln's shopping ventures cost her husband's estate a great deal. Her son Robert thought he had a good, if extreme, solution when he decided to have his mother put in an insane asylum to make her stop shopping.

To no one's surprise, life in the asylum in Batavia, Illinois, only made Mrs. Lincoln worse, and more melancholy. At age fifty-seven, she spent nine months there, from May to September of 1875. Through a vigorous campaign of writing letters— always that same belief in the power of rational argument—Myra Bradwell made the hospital director, Dr. Patterson, release Mrs. Lincoln. It did not hurt that the Chicago newspapers became involved, publishing what amounted to a debate. Bradwell even arranged to have a newspaper reporter come and interview Mrs. Lincoln without the consent of Robert nor of the doctor. But the trick worked. "She is no more insane than I am," argued Myra Bradwell, whose name was synonymous with clear-headed thinking.

Myra Bradwell's activities look like a catalog of every important issue in the history of the late nineteenth century. She worked hard on the committee that planned the rebuilding of Chicago after the fire, pioneering in concepts of zoning laws to control urban land use. She proposed ways to upgrade the standards of the legal profession, trying to make it necessary to attend law school. She worked to encourage states to establish bar associations, to raise the level of argument, and to increase professional awareness among lawyers. She worked to make the retirement of judges at age sixty-five compulsory. Her energy and efforts, including a trip to Washington, D.C., to talk to Congressmen, resulted in the choice of Chicago as the site of the 1893 Columbian Exposition.

But after being turned down by the Supreme Court in 1873, Bradwell never resubmitted her application to be allowed to practice law. She may have seen it as pointless to invite the same justices to turn her down again. Or she may have seen that the extent of her influence through the *Chicago Legal News* achieved far more reform than she might have realized as a courtroom lawyer. Then, without a request from her, the Illinois Supreme Court admitted Bradwell to the bar in Illinois in 1890, twenty-one years after her request. The language of the decision said that it was made *"nunc pro tunc,"* Latin for "now for then," being, in effect, a retroactive decision. Never before in the history of Illinois—and probably not since—had anyone been granted a license on the court's motion.

Myra continued to work on the *Chicago Legal News* until 1894, when she suffered from the cancer that claimed her life. Her daughter, also a lawyer of whom Myra Bradwell loved to tell people she was extremely proud, took over the *Chicago Legal News*, the most important legal newspaper west of the Alleghenies, exactly what Myra Bradwell had set out to make it.

QUESTIONS FOR THOUGHT AND DISCUSSION

1. What led Myra Colby Bradwell into the legal profession and how was she able to succeed in it without actually practicing as a lawyer?

2. Why did Illinois and other states deny women the right to practice law in this era?

3. Despite her differences with Susan B. Anthony, how did Bradwell strive to promote the cause of women's suffrage and female equality? Would you characterize her efforts as admirable or not?

4. Does the fact that married women enjoyed so few property or other civil rights at this time, a condition that did not change dramatically in many states until the 1960s and beyond, surprise you? Why do you think society has changed so dramatically in its attitude toward women's rights over the past 125 years? Has equality for all regardless of gender been achieved?

SUGGESTED READINGS

Baker, Jean H. *Mary Todd Lincoln: A Biography.* New York: Norton, 1987.

Flexner, Eleanor. *Century of Struggle: The Woman's Rights Movement in the United States* (revised edition). Cambridge, MA: Belknap, 1975.

Friedman, Jane. *America's First Woman Lawyer: The Biography of Myra Bradwell.* Buffalo, N.Y.: Prometheus, 1993.

Gale, George W. "Myra Bradwell: The First Woman Lawyer." *American Bar Association Journal,* Vol. 39, Dec. 1953, pp. 1080–ff.

Lerner, Gerda. *The Majority Finds Its Past: Placing Women in History.* New York: Oxford UP, 1979.

Neely, Mark E., Jr. and R. Gerald McMurty. *The Insanity File: The Case of Mary Todd Lincoln.* Carbondale, IL: Southern Illinois UP, 1986.

Notable American Women 1607–1950. Cambridge, MA: Belknap Press at Harvard Univ., 1971, pp. 223–225.

Smith-Rosenberg, Carroll. *Disorderly Conduct: Visions of Gender in Victorian America.* New York: Knopf, 1985.

Anthony, Susan B. ed. *History of Woman Suffrage,* 1881.

4

Andrew Carnegie

In 1859, the year Charles Darwin's The Origin of the Species *was published in England, twenty-four-year-old Andrew Carnegie became an executive with the largest corporation in the world, the Pennsylvania Railroad, at a salary of $1,500 a year, a handsome sum at the time. But the son of a threadbare, unemployed Scottish immigrant who had nearly starved when he landed in America only a decade earlier was already earning more than that from stock dividends. Before he was thirty, he was the equivalent of a modern-day millionaire, able to quit his post with the railroad and spend the rest of his long life amassing his fortune from investments, principally in his own Carnegie Steel Corporation, which would come to outproduce the entire British Empire. Carnegie's life was intertwined with the Industrial Revolution. No one could be more Darwinian than this real-life Horatio Alger.*

WHEN HE WAS an old man writing his autobiography, one of Andrew Carnegie's earliest memories was of the day his father, a master linen weaver, came home and announced to his family that he could find no more work. The textile mills of the Industrial Revolution had spread to his birthplace of Dunfermline, Scotland. Generations of skilled labor and a prosperous way of life for the Carnegies had come to an abrupt end.

The Scottish boy who would become, in his lifetime, the richest man in the world, the worker's champion, and then labor's most detested enemy, came to America like a million other Europeans who fled the Old World in the 1840s to avoid starvation. By his own account, Carnegie was born November 25, 1835, "of poor but honest parents" in "the attic" of a small, one-story house in the ancient town which had been the medieval seat of Scottish kings. As he grew up, he was steeped in Scottish folklore by his favorite uncle. When he was forced to leave Dunfermline to emigrate to America with his family in 1848, he could not possibly have imagined that he would return one day to build a castle of his own where his own bagpiper woke him every morning. All his life, Carnegie would be torn between the radical inclinations of his artisan ancestors—the urge to give away what he earned to ease the worker's burden—and amazing greed and ruthlessness that made him increase his riches relentlessly by constantly cutting the pay of those in his employ.

Carnegie's father, William, was well-known in radical circles in Scotland as an organizer of workers' marches against repressive English laws and active in the Chartist movement which would have democratized the British Isles by opening up Parliament to representatives of the working people. On his mother Margaret's side, Carnegie came from even more radical stock. Her father, a shoemaker by trade, was one of Scotland's most irrepressible labor agitators. A fiery and eloquent speaker, he campaigned for democratic elections, an English republic modelled on the United States to replace its monarchy, new factory laws, freedom of trade, destruction of hereditary privileges among aristocrats, and the abolition of kings and armies.

Andrew's free-spirited parents had lived only briefly in the one-story house where he was born. The damask weaving trade was booming for ten more years. His parents did not even insist that he go to school until he thought he was ready, which was at eight. He was free to spend his days wandering the surrounding hills and soaking up the history of his homeland. His tutor was his uncle, George Lauder, a dreamy romantic who operated a grocery store but preferred to spend his time teaching Andrew about flowers, music, and the poetry of Robert Burns and William Shakespeare. Meandering through the ruins where Macbeth and Malcolm had once drawn swords, young Carnegie learned about democracy as he memorized Burns's revolutionary verses. His uncle also taught him all he could know—and much that he imagined—about the United States, and about men such as Washington, Jefferson, and Franklin.

Even when his parents moved to a larger house where his father operated four looms and employed apprentice boys, there was little room at home for young Andrew. The downstairs rooms hummed with the activity of weavers all day, and were filled with the loud words of a workman designated to read aloud as the others shot the shuttles through the complicated warps and woofs. He was only seven when another uncle, Baillie Morrison, was arrested and jailed for his part in organizing the general strike of 1842. Seeing his uncle behind bars, Andrew learned to hate privileged institutions. "As a child," he wrote, "I could have slain king, duke, or lord and considered their death a service to the state."

Throughout his life, Carnegie believed that lack of political equality—not the collapse of obsolete trades—caused his mother country's social and economic woes and the conditions that drove his family out of their beloved Scotland. The family's decline was rapid and unexpected. In 1836, Will Carnegie had such a good year he bought a bigger house and three more looms and hired apprentices. Seven years later, a water-powered damask weaving mill opened in Dunfermline and he could never again find steady work. For five years they hung on, selling off one loom after another, letting the apprentices go, selling their house, and moving back into a one-room cottage where his mother learned to cobble shoes and ran a little drygoods store out of the living room. Finally, late in 1847, Will, a broken man at forty-two, told his son, "Andra, I canna get nae mair work." Andrew Carnegie never forgot that day: "I remember that shortly after this I began to learn what poverty meant."

It was Carnegie's gritty, determined mother who decided they must emigrate. Two of her sisters already lived in America: they would join them, and journey to the new industrial town of Pittsburgh, Pennsylvania. Borrowing passage money from relatives, the Carnegies embarked on a journey that took eleven weeks, the entire summer of 1848, by steamer, sailboat, and Erie Canal barge. They were so broke by voyage's end that they spent the last night of their journey sleeping on a wharf. The Carnegies, penniless, moved into two rent-free upstairs rooms in a grimy factory neighborhood called Slabtown. With the help of relatives and old friends who had also emigrated from Scotland, the entire family, except for five-year-old Tom, found jobs. At twelve, Andrew Carnegie had the thrill of earning his first wages. He went to work as a bobbin boy—oiling newly-made bobbins—in a cotton textile mill where his father worked. They left the house together before sunlight and, except for a forty-minute lunch break, worked until after dark. He liked the regular pay: "I was now a helper of the family, a breadwinner." After only three years, his formal schooling was over.

There had been no jobs in Scotland, yet there were jobs for everybody in boomtown Pittsburgh. Soon, another employer, also from Dunfermline, offered Andrew two dollars a week to work for him. It was an awful job, all alone in the cellar of a factory, where he ran a steam engine and fired the boiler that kept all the machinery working. The responsibility "was too much for me, I found myself night after night sitting up in bed trying the steam gauges." The employer's self-interest and Andrew's neat handwriting soon came to his rescue: he became a clerk in the office making out weekly bills, writing correspondence a few days a week, and dipping bobbins in preservative oil the other days. The smell of oil made him sick for the rest of his life. As much as he appreciated making more money, "I never succeeded in overcoming the nausea."

After only a few months, another opportunity opened up. This time, an uncle was playing cards with the manager of a new telegraph office, who said he needed a bright lad. As a telegraph delivery boy, Andrew now made two dollars and fifty cents a week. He was small (five feet three inches) and fast and learned the city quickly. He also developed the uncanny knack of "reading" the sound of the telegraph key by ear (he had taught himself Morse code) before messages could be printed out, one of only two people in America who could do this at this early date. He soon won promotion to telegrapher at a wage of four dollars a week. He had more than tripled his wages in one year.

By age sixteen Andrew Carnegie had earned a reputation as the best telegrapher in Pittsburgh just at the time the Pennsylvania Railroad was completed to the city. Its superintendent, Tom Scott, offered him a job as his personal telegrapher and private secretary at thirty-five dollars a month. Carnegie jumped at the chance. In one step, he left behind a world where he would always be an employee. As secretary to the superintendent of the nation's largest railroad he had a unique vantage point to study business. In twelve years with the Pennsylvania Railroad, Carnegie gained priceless experience: his jobs gave him managerial skills, a knowledge of economic principles, and a network of business colleagues. He was present at the creation of the most modern and efficient business system in the world as the railroads adapted traditional management and finance to fit their vast size and complexity.

A new kind of business, run precisely and profitably, emerged. Railroads demanded vast amounts of capital to expand: Carnegie learned that selling shares of corporate stock and bonds instead of borrowing at interest enabled this growth with less personal risk. But to pay regular returns to investors, railroads had to be run efficiently, with passenger and freight trains going in both directions around the clock, producing the cash to meet the dividends and pay salaries. There was no product other than efficient service. The railroad system that was emerging brought about a managerial revolution that rapidly changed how decisions were made. The railroad was the first business to adapt the military system of rank and discipline and perfect the first modern corporate bureaucracy to carry out complex and ceaseless operations.

Carnegie participated in the Pennsylvania's rapid growth as it became the largest private business firm in the world by the end of the Civil War, with 3,500 miles of track, 30,000 employees, hundreds of locomotives, and thousands of railroad cars. As Tom Scott's affable, young, right-hand man, he learned to deal not only with the new managerial class—he was a famous storyteller—but to earn the loyalty and hard work of the laborers. In his first year, he mastered the railroad's operations so thoroughly that he could take incredible risks. When a train derailed early one morning before his boss arrived, he telegraphed orders, signing them with Scott's initials, to burn the cars that were blocking the main rail line and get traffic moving again. This decision led to the hiring and training of full-time dispatchers with authority delegated from the top to keep the trains moving at all costs.

Scott repaid young Carnegie's brashness by giving him his first opportunity to invest money. He assured Carnegie that, if he bought five hundred dollars of Adams Express stock, he would prosper. But Carnegie didn't even have fifty dollars saved. When he reported Scott's offer to his mother, she unflinchingly asked an uncle for the money and mortgaged the house they had just bought. He began to receive his first dividends. When the first ten dollar check came, he took it to his friends and, showing off its fancy scroll, exclaimed, "Eureka! Here's the goose that lays the golden eggs!" Later, he wrote, "I shall remember that check as long as I live. It gave me the first penny of revenue from capital, something I had not worked for with the sweat of my brow." He soon was earning $1,400 a year on that first $500 of borrowed money.

As assistant to the railroad's operating executive, Carnegie seemed to be in the path of opportunities. He was riding the train one day in 1858 when a "farmer looking" man carrying a small green bag introduced himself as T. T. Woodruff and took out a small scale model of the first sleeping car. Impressed, Carnegie arranged a meeting with Scott. A grateful Woodruff offered to sell Carnegie a one-eighth interest in the new Woodruff Palace Car Company. A banker impressed with young Carnegie slapped him on the back and lent him a few hundred dollars that soon were yielding dividends of $5,000 a year.

When the Civil War broke out, Scott dispatched Carnegie with the first brigade of Union troops on a train south to Washington, D.C., to protect the Capitol. Scott became Abraham Lincoln's Assistant Secretary of War in charge of all military transportation, charged by Lincoln with organizing the Union's railroads. In turn, Scott put twenty-six-year-old Carnegie in charge of setting up a national telegraph system. After the first major battle at Bull Run, it was Carnegie who personally superintended the retreat by rail of the defeated Union forces from Virginia, loading train after train with the wounded. His work in the field throughout the war gave Carnegie a sunstroke: for the rest of his life, he had to spend summers in cool climates.

As a result of the Civil War, the American iron industry grew rapidly to meet the sustained demand for large amounts of iron for cannon, gunbarrels, bayonets, ironclad ships, and all of the other paraphernalia that depended on the once erratic supply produced by the iron masters of Pittsburgh. Carnegie saw firsthand the special need for iron railroad bridges to replace rickety makeshift wooden trestles so easily set afire by hot coals that spewed from the steam locomotives. He also foresaw the consequences of Union victory: the offer of millions of acres of free western land under the Homestead Act of 1862 would open up the West not only to veterans and millions of new immigrants but would make transcontinental railroads necessary to span the Mississippi, the Missouri, and the western mountains. He helped to organize the Keystone Bridge Company, the first successful manufacturer of iron railway bridges. This investment was soon yielding $15,000 a year (probably thirty times that amount in today's money). He also invested successfully in the newborn oil industry in western Pennsylvania at just the time when a process was developed to distill kerosene from crude oil, making whale oil obsolete for home heating and lighting. Carnegie used his Woodruff sleeping car dividends to buy 1,100 shares of the new Columbia Oil Company: eventually it earned him one million dollars.

By 1865, Carnegie's "side" interests were so lucrative that he decided to leave the railroad: he had been promoted to superintendent when Scott moved up, but Carnegie's $2,400-a-year salary paled beside his investment earnings, which were nearing $50,000 a year. At age thirty, he quit his executive job with the world's largest business to become a full-time capitalist. It was about this time that an old friend asked how Carnegie was doing. "Oh, I'm rich, I'm rich," he exclaimed.

Since he single-mindedly pursued riches for many years, Carnegie did not marry until his forties: "Nothing could be allowed to interfere for a moment with my business career." He broke ancient rules laid down for him as a boy. He borrowed to invest, almost never using his own money. He put everything on every roll of the speculative dice. His own dictum became, "Put all your eggs in one basket and then watch the basket." He expanded his businesses during depressions while others were cutting back so that he could cut prices and have material ready to sell when prosperity returned—which he never doubted would happen in the United States. He had incredible luck, playing out a Horatio Alger rags-to-riches story that could have landed him, as it did so many others, back on the street. There were no income or corporate taxes to diminish his gains, but there was also no insurance and no safety nets in case of failure.

Moving to New York City to pursue a wider range of business opportunities, he built on his railroad background. When George Pullman began to cut into the Woodruff sleeping car business, Carnegie confronted Pullman, pointing out to him that only the railroads would benefit from their competition. He proposed to a stunned Pullman that they combine their companies into a new one, then

The Bettmann Archive

Andrew Carnegie adapted the efficiency of the modern railroad to the corporation, raising billions of dollars with his personal charm and sharing little with his workers.

clinched the deal by flattery. He offered to name it the Pullman Palace Car Company. His shrewd use of psychology won over Pullman. Eventually, Carnegie owned most of the stock.

The growth of Carnegie's fortune parallels the rise of other millionaires of the new industrial age and his tactics were no better and no worse. At one time or another, Carnegie locked horns or interlocked interests with John D. Rockefeller, J. P. Morgan, Henry E. Huntington, Jay Gould, Commodore Vanderbilt, and

Henry Clay Frick. His process of financial growth employed every device of the rough-and-tumble unregulated business atmosphere of the times: mergers and acquisitions, pools and commercial piracy, even outright fraud in selling the U. S. government overpriced, substandard steel armor plate for the Navy.

Yet it was not chicanery or corruption that explained his phenomenal success. He was an astute observer of his times willing to take virtually any risk, and then a consummate salesman. He took annual trips to Europe, his briefcase bulging with bonds and prospectuses as he cashed in on his contacts with American tycoons by selling their securities to European investors. He earned large commissions, in one trip $150,000 (millions of dollars today). On one such summer visit to England, he saw for the first time the Bessemer process for converting iron into steel. He became instantly converted to the future of steel and dashed home to form his own steel firm. Carnegie, McCandless and Company, which later became Carnegie Steel, eventually would produce more steel a year than all of Great Britain, erstwhile world leader. Soon, Carnegie steel replaced iron in railroad ties, bridge construction, office buildings, ships, and machinery.

His secret weapon for expanding his steel industry was a team of brilliant managers he assembled and made partners. He spotted talent early, then pitted men against each other, buying their loyalty with shares of his company. Even a one-sixth of one percent share of Carnegie Steel eventually brought a partner fifty million dollars. Carnegie held fifty-eight percent of all stock and none of the partners could sell stock except to the company or each other. He rewarded men for cutting the costs of steel-making by pushing workers hard, and by inventing devices and processes that made skilled artisans obsolete and replaced them with lower-paid, unskilled workers.

In an atmosphere of ruthless corporate competition, the most ruthless accrued power. A case in point was Henry Clay Frick, the coal-field baron Carnegie chose as chairman of the Carnegie Steel board, the man on the embattled scene as, more and more, Carnegie absented himself from day-to-day operations to pursue capital in New York and Europe. Carnegie had built a reputation as a friend of labor—a bad reputation among businessmen, but something like hero status among his own workers. Nothing prepared his workers for the worst labor confrontation of the 1890s.

Shortly after Frick, known for using strikebreakers regularly in his own coal mines, took control, he vowed to break the power of the Carnegie Steel craft unions. Carnegie had acceded to a generous increase for workers at his most modern steel plant at Homestead, Pennsylvania, linchpin of the fifteen-mile long belt of Carnegie plants from Pittsburgh south to Braddock, Pennsylvania. Privately, Carnegie was pressuring Frick to cut wages by twenty percent. Publicly, in two magazine articles in 1886, Carnegie had proclaimed pro-labor sentiments. Especially denouncing strikebreaking, he coined an Eleventh Commandment for labor: "Thou shalt not take thy neighbor's job."

The contract between steelworkers and management at Homestead was to expire on July 1, 1892, shortly after Carnegie sailed to his summer home in Scotland. When talks broke down in late June, Frick declared he would close the mill on July 1 and reopen five days later, admitting only nonunion men, thus eliminating the unions. He built a huge fence around the entire plant down to the Monongehela River, then secretly hired 300 armed Pinkerton detectives to steam upriver at night and occupy the plant. When the barges tied up, gunfire immediately broke out. An all-day battle ensued in which the strikers overwhelmed the strikebreakers, finally forcing them to run a gauntlet of screaming, club-wielding workers and their wives. Three Pinkertons and ten strikers died that day but Frick refused to yield; 8,000 National Guardsmen were called in to lock out the workers. Eventually, forty percent of the men were rehired after the union gave up its five-month strike. The unionization of Carnegie and the American steel industry was set back forty years.

Carnegie was roundly condemned by the press for staying out of reach in Scotland even after an anarchist attacked, shot, stabbed, and nearly killed Frick, who still insisted, "There is no necessity for you to come home." Carnegie knew that, if he came home, Frick would resign. The day after the pitched battle, he cabled Frick, "All anxiety gone since you stand firm. Never employ one of these rioters. Let grass grow over works." When workers cabled, pleading with "Dear Master" to intervene, he refused to answer them. Had he been on the scene, he probably could have settled the strike, but his executives believed him likely to weaken again and begged him to stay away. Carnegie was stung badly by the public outcry. "This is the trial of my life," he wrote his friend, British Prime Minister William Gladstone. Frick's insistence on hiring strikebreakers was "a foolish step." It was "expecting too much of poor men to stand by and see their work taken by others." His pain, he wrote, "increases daily." The Homestead works "are not worth one drop of human blood. I wish they had sunk." He set up a pension fund for widows, orphans, and workers who had lost their jobs.

The Homestead debacle seems to have been the catalyst that led Carnegie to pursue a philosophy of philanthropy that he had already proclaimed in 1889 in his book, *Gospel of Wealth*. Even as his company became the largest steelmaker in the world, its profits reaching forty million dollars a year by 1900 (two-thirds of that amount going to Carnegie), he began to speak of himself as only a "steward" of his wealth. The life cycle of a rich man, he wrote, should be divided into acquiring and distributing wealth. A "man who dies rich dies disgraced," he wrote. He did not believe in hereditary wealth. He had one daughter, but never considered her his heiress. He believed that the accumulation of enormous wealth had the potential for enormous evil—unless the rich man personally gave away his riches. In the late 1880s, he began an unparalleled program of benefactions.

Selling out his controlling interest in Carnegie Steel in 1901 for $480 million, he endowed the Carnegie Corporation of New York with $125 million. He founded two Carnegie universities, in Pittsburgh and Washington, D.C., built Carnegie Hall in New York City, and endowed the Carnegie Hero Fund and the Carnegie Awards for Excellence in Teaching. He had cranky pet charities. He sent off $10,000 to buy a dinosaur skeleton for one of his museums and thus triggered a major archaeological dig in Wyoming that led to the discovery of a previously unknown late Jurassic species of dinosaur, named *Diplodocus Carnegii* in his honor. He thought it was more important to build public baths than churches, even though he donated 7,000 church organs. He also crusaded for a simplified form of spelling that triggered an uproar when President Theodore Roosevelt, a convert to the idea, gave secret orders for the Government Printing Office to use Carnegie's list of shortened, more simply spelled words. After the British expressed outrage, Congress defeated the notion of reform, and Carnegie abandoned the idea. His favorite and most far-reaching philanthropy was the building of some 2,509 libraries all over the English-speaking world, 1,679 costing forty million dollars in the U.S. alone. He built the entire twenty five-branch system in Philadelphia and all the branch libraries of New York City, yet he concentrated most of his library grants in small towns and cities in the West and South, where few libraries existed. The very first library he built was in his native Dunfermline. He rode there with his mother in a coach-and-four to the cheers of his fellow Scots.

In his final years, Andrew Carnegie advocated world peace and arbitration of national disputes even as he saw a great conflagration approaching. He built the Hague Peace Palace in the Netherlands and visited Kaiser Wilhelm II in 1907 in Germany. When World War I broke out in August, 1914, he supported Great Britain's declaration of war and American preparedness, but his health rapidly declined as the steel he had grown rich producing was turned into weapons of mass destruction. Prevented by the German submarine blockade of the British Isles from reaching his beloved Scotland, Carnegie grieved and died in 1919, at age eighty-four. He had kept far less wealth than most people thought: he had given away ninety-five percent of his money. By his own definition, Carnegie had narrowly avoided disgrace.

QUESTIONS FOR THOUGHT AND DISCUSSION

1. To what would you attribute Andrew Carnegie's rapid rise from penniless young immigrant to the richest man in America?

2. Was Carnegie at fault for not intervening personally in the Homestead Strike? Were Henry Clay Frick and Carnegie's other lieutenants pursuing legitimate business practices or unconscionable union bashing in the Homestead affair?

3. Carnegie made his vast personal fortune at a time that there was no personal income tax in the United States. Is a progressive income tax (where the wealthy pay a higher percentage of their income) fair? Why or why not?

4. Why did Carnegie spend nearly all of his wealth prior to his death? Was his life, taken altogether, a noble one?

SUGGESTED READINGS

Carnegie, Andrew. *Andrew Carnegie Reader.* Ed. and Intro. by Joseph Frazier Wall. Pittsburgh: U of Pittsburgh P, 1992.

Hacker, Louis M. *The World of Andrew Carnegie.* Philadelphia: Lippincott, 1968.

Hendrick, Burton J. *Life of Andrew Carnegie.* Intro. by Louis M. Hacker. New York: Harper, 1969.

Livesay, Harold C. *Andrew Carnegie and the Rise of Big Business.* Ed. by Oscar Handlin. Boston: Little, 1975.

McCloskey, Robert Green. *American Conservatism in the Age of Enterprise.* Cambridge: Harvard UP, 1951.

Swetnam, George. *Andrew Carnegie.* Boston: Twayne, 1980.

Wall, Joseph Frazier. *Andrew Carnegie.* New York: Oxford UP, 1970.

5

Thomas Alva Edison

While the United States still lagged behind England and Germany industrially at the start of the Civil War, the spirit of Yankee inventiveness was already legendary. Samuel F. B. Morse had stitched the vast continent together with his telegraph lines; Robert Fulton had connected it to the rest of the world with his steamship; and arms factories in New Haven had combined research, skilled labor, and precision machinery to produce what the London Times by 1857 was calling the "American way" of manufacturing. For sheer inventiveness, the thirty years following the war have rarely been matched. In 1893 alone, the U. S. Patent Office granted more than 500,000 patents, more than it issued during the entire decade of the 1850s. Most of the American inventions had been the handiwork of individuals working sporadically until Thomas Edison systematized research and produced the research laboratory that helped him obtain 1,093 U.S. patents. His spirit of invention had much to do with the fact that, by 1900, the manufacturing output of the United States exceeded the combined output of Britain, France, and Germany. Brought about by the marriage of American inventiveness and a massive growth in capital investment, technological developments in manufacturing, mining, agriculture, transportation, and communication changed American society.

ON JULY 4, 1876, Americans celebrated their first century of independence with a giant exposition in Philadelphia's Fairmount Park. Under a city of iron and glass exhibit halls covering thirteen acres, the exposition paid scant attention to the past and focused on the present and the future. There was a Japanese teahouse to celebrate new trade ties with Asian countries and a women's building where women artists displayed their paintings and their sculptures and where women operated long rows of textile machines.

Exposition-goers saw the first public demonstrations of the typewriter, the Otis elevator, the Westinghouse railroad brake, the high-wheeled bicycle, and even the "floor covering of the future"—linoleum. After gazing up at the four-story-high Corliss steam engine that powered the other 8,000 machines on exhibit and dwarfed everything else in Machinery Hall, the most popular building, they could stroll along the West River Drive and sip a new drink, root beer, served by a young druggist, Charles Hires, or munch for the first time on an exotic banana.

Americans seemed most impressed by the giant Corliss steam armatures, which seemed emblematic of their sprawling young world power, but foreigners were awed by smaller, more revolutionary devices. While long lines waited, the Emperor of Brazil tested Alexander Graham Bell's new telephone, exclaiming, "My God, it talks!" As he listened to the voice of a nearby demonstrator, he was holding in his hand the black carbon receiver that had been devised by the man who had more inventions under the great glass roof than anyone else, twenty-nine-year-old Thomas Alva Edison.

That centennial year, Edison had just opened the nation's first research laboratory at Menlo Park, New Jersey, promising to produce "a minor invention every ten days and a big thing every six months or so." He was to keep this extravagant promise, in the next decade alone inventing the phonograph, the incandescent light, the dictaphone, the mimeograph machine, the electric power plant dynamo, motion pictures, and electric transmitters. Only half a dozen years later, he invented the first electric company, with its Pearl Street generating station supplying electrical power for the illumination of New York City in 1882. In another six years, he founded the Edison General Electric Company to mass produce light bulbs which eventually lit up seventy percent of all American homes and virtually all the businesses. By century's end, there were 3,000 Edison power plants illuminating America.

The man who not only did as much as anyone to invent modern America also was the first to popularize science in America and to turn from manufacturing for other industries to produce innovations for the home, inventing mass production for the consumer. His labor-saving devices changed the way people worked, traveled, communicated, studied, and entertained themselves. By the time of the World's Columbian Exposition of 1893 in Chicago, when visitors filled out a questionnaire that asked what American would be best remembered a hundred years later, the majority answered, "Thomas Edison." At that 1893 fair, which celebrated the four centuries of change since Columbus's first landings, the Corliss engine was as obsolete as the steam power it had generated, the innovations of 1876 were the commonplaces of American urban life and everything at the vast fairgrounds was powered by Edison's electrical inventions, including 5,000 arc street lamps and 100,000 incandescent bulbs. Edison more than anyone else had prompted the U.S. commissioner of patents to proclaim that "America has become known the world around as the home of invention."

Thomas Alva Edison was born on February 11, 1847, in Milan, Ohio, the seventh and youngest child of Samuel and Nancy Elliott Edison. A powerful myth was fabricated by an admiring press that Edison, like Lincoln, was a poor boy who lived in a log cabin. In fact, his father for a time was a successful businessman until he lost most of his money when a railroad bypassed his business. The Edisons came from an old colonial American family, but what was unusual about them was that for generations they had been dissenters, outsiders, and mavericks. Thomas Edison's great-great grandfather, John, was a Loyalist who took the British side in the

American Revolution. He left his substantial farm in Caldwell, New Jersey to go through the British lines in 1776 and acted as a guide when British commander Sir William Howe invaded New Jersey. Captured by the revolutionaries and condemned to death for treason, he was held in chains in the Morristown jail for a year before he was exchanged for a British prisoner. His property was confiscated and he had to migrate to Nova Scotia at war's end, where he settled at Digby.

His son, Samuel, Sr., the inventor's grandfather's father, grew up in Ontario province, Canada where his family migrated in 1811 after John Edison received a land grant for his services to the British Crown for fighting against the Americans during the Revolution. His son, Samuel, Jr., became a Canadian militia captain who also fought against the Americans in the War of 1812. By 1837, however, Samuel Edison, Jr., was eager to join a revolt against the British, secretly forming a revolutionary militia for the Mackenzie uprising. The plot was discovered and Samuel Edison had to flee on foot, running for three days as he was pursued by British redcoats, Indians, and dogs. He found refuge in Port Huron, Ohio. His wife, Nancy Elliott, later escaped with their children, and the family moved to the new canal town of Milan. There Samuel Edison established a successful business manufacturing wood shingles and selling lumber and grain. The family fortune collapsed as the Grand Trunk Railroad bypassed Milan and eighty percent of the people left.

Two of Nancy Edison's children had already died by the time she gave birth to her seventh child, a small boy with a very large head whom neighbors thought was hydroencephalitic. Alva, they called him, or Al, was frequently in trouble for his mischievousness and inquisitiveness. When he was only six his father whipped him in the town square as neighbors watched because he had set a little fire inside his father's barn "just to see what it would do." The flames had spread rapidly and burned the barn down. A high wind was blowing and the whole town could have burned so no one intervened when his father invited them to the public flogging. Edison still remembered it vividly sixty years later when he wrote his memoirs.

If Edison resented his father humiliating him, he never said so, but he never said anything flattering about his father, either. Only rarely did he mention his father. "My father thought I was stupid and I almost decided I must be a dunce."

He had a lonely childhood—his brother and sister were much older—and he played alone much of the time. Even more than most children, he asked a lot of what his father called "foolish questions," usually of his mother. For example, he wanted to know why their goose squatted on her eggs. When his mother patiently explained, Edison disappeared. "We missed him and called for him everywhere," his brother, Marion, attested. His father found him in a neighbor's barn, "curled up in a nest he had made filled with goose and chicken eggs." He was trying to hatch them.

Alva also liked to draw, and at age five he sketched pictures of all the craft signs in Milan. In later years, he would sketch all of his inventions. By the time he was seven, the town began its swift, steady decline and the nomadic Edisons had to move again, this time to Port Huron, where Samuel Edison used what he had garnered from selling his house and granary to set up another lumber, grain and feed store. There was rarely any money now beyond the rent for a house. The story of

Edison's schooling is murky. It appears that at about this time Edison suffered from a serious case of scarlet fever which damaged his hearing, and that recurring ear problems left him increasingly in a silent world.

When his parents finally sent him to school at age eight, his teacher, a Puritan clergyman who reinforced his lessons with a leather belt, decided that young Edison was "addled." Little was known about hearing loss or physical handicaps at the time. Edison's memory of his brief education remained painful: "I remember I used never to be able to get along at school. I was always at the foot of the class. I used to feel that the teachers did not sympathize with me." When Edison overheard the schoolmaster describing him as "addled," he ran home and refused to return. His mother, who had taught school in Canada, kept him home and educated him herself, but what seems clear is that the Edisons couldn't afford to pay his tuition any longer.

Summer and winter, young Edison studied. His mother taught him not only the three R's but "the love and purpose of learning." A very fast reader, he read world history, Shakespeare, and Dickens, but his mother also made a chance discovery. She found a copy of an elementary science book, R. G. Parker's *School of Natural Philosophy*, which described scientific experiments that could be performed at home. This was "the first book in science I read," Edison recalled, "the first I could understand." Learning now became a lifelong "game" for him, he said. At nine, he read and tested every one of *Parker's* experiments. His mother found him an old *Dictionary of Science* and, before age ten, he had discovered a passion for chemistry. He gathered jars and bottles in the basement and mixed his own chemicals and marked them all "poison," which set the neighbors' tongues wagging, and while his father continued disapproving, his "mother was the making of me, she understood me, she let me follow my bent." She also overlooked the mess, which included chemicals in his bedroom and spills of sulfuric acid on furniture and floors that only stopped when young Edison secluded himself in the cellar with his batteries and bottles.

To Edison's father, though, it was a shame he never read any serious literature or learned to spell or play with normal boys and girls: "Thomas Alva never had any boyhood days, his early amusements were steam engines and mechanical forces." His father did not understand Thomas's excitement when he was able to verify experiments made by earlier scientists, in particular when he tried to prove the existence of static electricity after reading Benjamin Franklin's *Autobiography*. He tried rubbing together the fur of two big tomcats whose tails he connected to wires. There were no sparks, but ten-year-old Edison was badly clawed for his efforts.

Edison's father was quick enough to exploit the arrival of the telegraph line in Port Huron by seeing that young Edison had his own telegraph set and began to learn Morse code. Here was a trade the boy could learn, even if he was hard of hearing. He could hear and feel the clicking of the telegraph key—and pretty soon he was stringing his own homemade telegraph line to a neighbor's house. "It worked fine," Edison later remembered, not at all impressed by his boyhood achievement. By the time the Grand Trunk Line was being completed from Detroit to Port Huron in 1859, the elder Edison was ready to put his twelve-year-old son to work on it. He found there would be a job for a fulltime newsboy on the train who would receive no wages but could earn a profit from selling newspapers he bought in Detroit and selling food to passengers. There was to be no more thought of an education for Thomas Edison. At twelve, he began to ride the rails, sleeping in the baggage car and hawking his wares, calling out "Newspapers, apples, sandwiches, molasses, peanuts," and bringing the money home to help his family. "Being poor," Edison recalled, "I already knew that money is a valuable thing."

In Detroit each day, Edison loved to explore. "The happiest time of my life was when I was twelve years old," he wrote. "I was just old enough to have a good time in the world but not old enough to understand any of its problems." He was still too young to fight when the Civil War broke out but he quickly observed that newspaper sales jumped when there was a battle.

One day in April 1862, the first accounts of a great battle at Shiloh reached the office of the Detroit *Free Press* by telegraph. Young Edison made it his practice to go to the composing room to see what headlines were to appear on that day's edition so he could estimate his need for papers. Learning of Shiloh, he saw "a chance for enormous sales, if only the people along the line could know what happened. Suddenly an idea occurred to me. I rushed off to the telegraph operator." He offered newspaper and magazine subscriptions to the Detroit telegraph in exchange for a short bulletin wired to railroad stations along the train route, to be chalked up on bulletin boards, telling briefly of the great battle. Then he talked the *Free Press* managing editor into letting him have 1,000 copies of the paper. With the help of his young assistant, Edison lugged the papers to the station. Gradually, he charged more for the papers. "I raised the price from ten to fifteen cents" at early stops. At Port Huron, "I was met by a large crowd. I then yelled, 'Twenty-five cents, gentlemen—I haven't enough to go around'. . . It was then it struck me that the telegraph was just about the best thing going. I determined at once to be a telegrapher."

With a $150 clear profit (several thousand dollars in today's money) from the "extra," Edison also decided to publish his own newspaper. He purchased a small second-hand printing press and 300 pounds of old type and taught himself to type and print a small local newspaper, the Port Huron *Weekly Herald*. It was probably the first newspaper in the world printed on a train. The trainmen had allotted him a corner of the baggage car where he had been carrying out his chemical experiments. Clearing them away, he began recording the births of station agents' children or the names of Union Army recruits between lofty philosophical editorials. But there were soon problems: Edison could not spell and some of his local society tidbits were a bit too private. One subject of a news story tracked Edison down and threw him into the St. Clair River! Edison's newspaper career ended abruptly. It was at this time, however, that he saw the three-year-old daughter of the stationmaster playing on the main track in the path of an approaching train. He dashed toward the child and snatched her up. The grateful father rewarded Edison by teaching him how to be a telegraph operator. He invited fifteen-year-old Edison to board free and take meals at his house for three months while he studied under the night telegrapher.

Showing up for the first lesson with a set of telegraph instruments he had fashioned himself at a gunsmith's shop, Edison learned what was then a new and respectable craft. For the next two years he was to wander all over the eastern United States as a tramp telegrapher, a member of a dapper, carefree brotherhood. He learned to work on the night shift, a lifelong habit, devoting his days to reading scientific and technical books, sleeping and eating little, and spending most of his pay on books, chemicals, and metal for his experiments in a succession of rented upstairs backrooms in rundown boarding houses from Memphis to Boston. To gain more time to read, he invented labor-saving processes and telegraphic devices. He was often fired for ignoring office discipline, letting messages pile up while he worked on his experiments. Many of his inventions over the next twenty years were to result from these attempts to develop equipment that worked faster and cheaper. He devised a duplex machine that could send two messages at once, then began a long quest to pioneer a quadruplet that could send two messages in each direction simultaneously over the same wire.

He also learned to take down press copy over the wire at great speed so that he was able, despite his long hair, baggy pants, and plug of chewing tobacco, to land a job at Boston's main Western Union office in 1868 at age twenty-one despite his hearing difficulties. He used a skill common among hearing-impaired people called "filling the gaps," or guessing. Telegraph operators routinely used this technique to finish interrupted or incomplete messages. He was assigned to the Number One New York wire to receive press copy for the Boston *Herald*—with the fastest New York operator at the other end.

With his wages, Edison bought books, including Michael Faraday's two-volume *Experimental Researches in Electricity*. Like Edison, Faraday had been poor and self-taught. Later, Edison was to praise Faraday's "selflessness" as he devoted himself to science without concern for money or titles. He had found a role model to emulate. Working all night at Western Union, he began reading Faraday at 4 A.M. and often worked all day without sleep, studying and duplicating the master's experiments. To his roommate he announced his intentions: "I am now twenty-one. I may live to be fifty. Can I get as much done as he did? I have got so much to do and life is so short, I am going to hustle."

He set to work with a large induction coil, intended to be part of his planned multiple-message telegraph, once nearly electrocuting himself. The June 1868 *Journal of the Telegraph* announced his first invention at age twenty-one, a "mode of transmission both ways on a single wire . . . which is interesting, simple, and ingenious." A firm believer in self-promotion, he wrote the piece himself and signed his roommate's name. Then he sent copies to telegraphers around the country who had mocked his boardinghouse experiments.

Offered capital to go on with his experiments, in January 1869, he decided to quit his job and experiment full-time. With a $500 advance, he set to work to improve his "double transmitter," offering copies for sale at $400 each, but he lacked the money to patent the device. He also attracted another investor so he could begin his first patented invention, a telegraphic vote-recording machine which he demonstrated before the Massachusetts Legislature and a committee of the U.S. Congress. A forerunner of the modern voting machine, it was met with yawns by politicians who didn't want to vote faster and lose their ability to filibuster. He returned chagrined from Washington, vowing henceforth to invent products that had a certain "commercial demand." Developing a gold price indicating machine that transmitted numerals as electronic impulses, he took it to New York City in 1869, only to learn that Samuel S. Laws had invented a similar machine and had grown rich using it for several years on the New York Gold Exchange. But he was allowed to sleep on a cot in a basement battery room and spend his days studying the technology in the main telegraph room. He was there one day when the central telegraph device broke down completely. As Laws, his men, and three hundred messengers sent by angry, anxious dealers all over Wall Street looked on, Edison was able to fix the complicated machine. Laws hired him the next day and put him in charge of maintenance. He was soon promoted to general manager at a handsome $300 a month, very high pay for the times.

That same year, Edison launched a partnership with F. L. Pope and J. A. Ashley: Pope, Edison & Company described themselves as "electrical engineers," inventing a new professional term and offering to design instruments, test materials, build telegraph lines, design fire alarms, and make experimental apparatus. In less than one year, Edison had made so many improvements to stock ticker equipment that the firm was bought out by the Gold and Stock Telegraph Company for a handsome $40,000. With his profits, Edison set up the first commercial research laboratory, an "invention factory," as he called it, staffed with fifty skilled technicians under Edison's constant supervision.

Devoting the next five years to improving telegraphy, by 1874 Edison had accomplished his longtime goal of perfecting the quadruplet, making telegraphy far more efficient and profitable. Instead of a single message passing on the wire, now four could be transmitted at the same speed. Edison's reputation as an inventor skyrocketed. In the spring of 1876, Edison hired his father to supervise construction of a laboratory complex at Menlo Park, New Jersey, in the hills twenty-five miles south of Newark. With financial backing from Western Union, Edison pioneered in systematic research on the eve of the Centennial Exposition in nearby Philadelphia.

Shortly after Alexander Graham Bell patented the telephone in 1876, Edison perfected a superior transmitter that made a speaker's voice louder and clearer over the telephone: it was used for a hundred years. That year, too, he worked on experiments for recording and playing back messages sent over the telegraph and the telephone. They led to Edison's invention of the phonograph, his most original scientific breakthrough. To record messages, he attached a needle to a diaphragm, a metal disc which vibrated in response to the sound waves of the human voice. The needle rested against a rotating cylinder wrapped in tinfoil. When the disc vibrated, the needle made an impression in the foil. To reproduce this sound, a second needle was connected to a diaphragm and a funnel-like horn. This second needle followed the grooves in the foil. Edison demonstrated his phonograph in December 1877, to the editors of the prestigious journal *Scientific American* and, the following spring, to President Rutherford B. Hayes. So magical did the device seem that Edison was dubbed by the press "the Wizard of Menlo Park."

In 1878, Edison began research in electric lighting. Experiments had been made over the past four decades in England and the United States, but Edison's improvements, especially his decision to make a filament out of slightly-burned

UPI/Bettmann

*So deaf in his old age that he had to bite a piano to feel it play, Thomas Edison pop-
ularized science and invented a new way of life.*

carbon (he experimented with 6,000 different fibers) made the incandescent light
bulb cheap and practical for production. He then turned his mind to the complex
problem of a central power source for his lights and other electrified apparatus—
an immense engineering achievement. By 1882, with the financial backing of J. P.
Morgan, his system was put to work in New York City. Edison built the Pearl Street
Power Station, a steam-driven electric power plant near Wall Street, soon providing electricity to thousands of customers. Over the next ten years, he expanded his

operations and moved to a large new complex, ten times the size of Menlo Park in West Orange, New Jersey, his home for the rest of his long life. Edison, often working all night and not leaving his laboratory for months on end, developed all the equipment needed to generate electricity on a large scale: generators, power cables, electric lamps, and light fixtures. Spawning a series of companies to manufacture his products, he gradually combined them into the General Electric Company, with its manufacturing centered at Schenectady, New York. Not until then was Edison, now forty-five, ever free of financial worry.

Changing the direction of American manufacturing, Edison produced goods and services for the consumer, not other producers. He was so far ahead of his time that his ideas often outstripped available technology and practical applications. He discovered radiotelegraph sound waves twenty years before the radio receiver was invented; he plunged one million dollars into developing separators for low grade iron ore just as cheap, abundant high grade ore was discovered in the Mesabi Range. Always resilient, he converted this technology to cement manufacture and recouped his losses. His favorite invention was the phonograph, and when others learned how to make phonograph records, he bought them out and made another fortune in the record business. He could be incredibly wrong-headed and miserly when he wasn't convinced an idea's time had come.

It was a wager by California railway tycoon, Leland Stanford, that launched the motion picture. Stanford bet $25,000 that a horse had all four feet off the ground at a given moment. Eadweard Maybridge set up twenty-four still cameras with wires tripped by the horse as it passed. In February 1886, the photographer had the bright idea of interesting Edison in motion photography: the camera could boost sales of his phonograph. By 1888, Edison's assistants at West Orange had produced a cylinder that revolved around a peephole, its figures in a photographic groove half an inch high. "Everything should come out of one hole," instructed Edison, trying to imitate his phonograph. When George Eastman began to manufacture his photographic emulsion on a cellulose base in 1889, Edison could buy a fifty-foot strip of film for two dollars and fifty-cents. "That's it!" said an excited Edison when he was shown the long film strip in his Room Five laboratory. "We've got it! Now work like hell!"

Edison already had patented a rapid-fire shutter. He assigned an assistant, William Dickson, to the problem of moving film through the camera: he punched holes along the film's edges so a sprocket could synchronize each frame with the lens shutter. The first films ran horizontally through the movie camera, like the modern still camera. On October 6, 1889, three and a half years after Maybridge's first approach, Dickson made a dramatic demonstration to Edison and his wife, just returned from a vacation in Paris. Dickson appeared on a screen. He bowed, he talked: "Good morning, Mr. Edison. Glad to see you back. I hope you are satisfied with the Kinetophonograph" (his name for the camera). Talking motion pictures made their debut that day. But the first public demonstration was not until April 1894, in a penny arcade at 1155 Broadway in New York City. Crowds poured pennies into his arcade peep shows, as one person at a time watched. Yet Edison did not immediately go the next step to throw the image up onto a screen for a mass audience. Only after Thomas Armat produced the mechanism that enabled the modern projector did Edison buy it and begin to corner the patents and produce the machines that gave his company a virtual monopoly on film-making in America for many years. By the mid–1890s, Edison would only invest $637.67 to build a tiny studio on the back lot at West Orange. The studio was an ugly, oblong affair that looked like a police wagon known as a Black Maria. The studio revolved on tracks to follow the sun. Inside, before a one-ton camera that looked like an upright piano, Annie Oakley shot clay pigeons, Buffalo Bill fired his rifle, and Sioux Indians did their Ghost Dance. Edison cornered the patents on the technology of movie making. But Edison was too frugal to spend an additional $150 to file international patents. "It isn't worth it," he said.

He made science popular and the scientist virtually a cult hero in early twentieth century America, but his personal life was far less successful. Days, months, and years in the lab spelled neglect for his family. His most productive experimental years coincided with his first marriage to Mary Stilwell, one of his employees, who died in 1884, leaving him three children he hardly knew. After Mary's death he chose to court an eighteen-year-old socialite, Mina Miller. Edison tapped out his marriage proposal in the palm of her hand in Morse code and they married in 1886. Mina was a great beauty who fortunately had her own charitable and social activities. But his closest friends were probably Henry Ford and Harvey Firestone. The three great industrialists liked nothing better than to drive out into the woods, live under canvas tents, tell each other tall stories, and dress up like cowboys.

While Edison worked hard and grew rich, he was not especially impressed with his own genius. "Genius," he was fond of saying, "is one percent inspiration and ninety-nine percent perspiration." He died at age eighty-three after a life of hard work. On the night of his funeral, President Herbert Hoover requested that at the White House and in homes and businesses all across America, the light be dimmed in honor of the man who had almost single-handedly invented modern life.

QUESTIONS FOR THOUGHT AND DISCUSSION

1. What was the driving force that pushed Thomas Alva Edison to devote his life to scientific experimentation?

2. How was Edison able to achieve the success he did with his inventions? What was the personal price he paid? Was it worth it?

3. The nickname "Wizard of Menlo Park" suggested that many found Edison to be nearly super-human. Was he? Was he a genius?

4. In what ways was Edison personally responsible for hastening the modernization of American society? Was this modernization an improvement?

SUGGESTED READINGS

Baldwin, Neil. *Inventing the Century: Thomas Edison.* New York: Free Press, 1995.

Clark, Ronald W. *Edison: The Man Who Made the Future.* New York: Putnam, 1977.

Friedel, Robert D. *Edison's Light Bulb: Biography of an Invention.* New Brunswick, NJ: Rutgers UP, 1986.

Gessner, Robert. "The Moving Image." *American Heritage.* April, 1960, pp. 30–35, 100–104.

Josephson, Matthew. *Edison: A Biography.* New York: McGraw, 1959.

_____. "Last Days of the Wizard." *American Heritage,* October, 1959, pp. 32–45.

Millard, A. J. *Edison and the Business of Innovation.* Baltimore: Johns Hopkins UP, 1990.

6

Louis Sockalexis

During the final decade of the nineteenth century, as Carnegie and Frick, Rockefeller and Edison struggled to impose order and system on industry and the workplace, sports, too, became organized and, more and more, came to resemble other aspects of an emerging corporate America. "Baseball," wrote Mark Twain, "is the very symbol, the outward and visible expression of the drive and push and struggle of the raging, tearing, booming nineteenth century." Professional baseball had much in common with the new American landscape. It was urban, its seasonal labor took place between the planting and harvesting times, its intricate schedules depended on cheap, predictable transportation over great distances, and above all, its motivation was less and less pure sport and more and more consolidation to yield higher profits to its owners and investors.

While its green playing fields and timeless games retained traces of country life, they were merely symbolic: Ebbets Field was built over a Brooklyn landfill; Cleveland's League Park was completely surrounded by rail yards, smoky foundries, and locomotive works. But, most of all, team managers were like shop foremen enforcing the wishes of management that bound players to a harsh regimen for the good of the team. As sports reinforced teamwork, Pinkerton detectives if not teammates were used to enforce vestigial Victorian values, such as sobriety, punctuality, and hard work six days a week for low pay. League Park was hardly the place one would expect to find a full-blooded Indian only six years after Sitting Bull's murder and two years after Geronimo and his Apaches were finally confined to a reservation.

BY THE TIME Louis Francis Sockalexis was born on October 24, 1871, on Indian Island in the Penobscot River off Old Town, Maine, the professional sport of baseball had already come of age. Making use of the just-completed transcontinental railroad for the first time, the Cincinnati Red Stockings in 1869 made a coast-to-coast tour, playing other professional teams from New York City to San Francisco while winning fifty-seven games, losing none, and tying only once. More than 200,000 spectators paid (and nobody knows how many didn't) to see the triumphant Cincinnati team, including cigar-chomping President Ulysses S. Grant in Washington, D.C., and some 23,000 fans in New York City in a single six-day week (Sunday baseball was forbidden).

The Red Stockings' tour dramatized not only the possibility of a professional national baseball league, but its potential for profit. Here was a game that could earn millions of dollars if only it could be harnessed and controlled. By 1876, as Sitting Bull and Red Cloud sent their warriors to facilitate Custer's Last Stand on the Little Big Horn, and Thomas Edison threw a light switch at the Philadelphia Centennial Exposition, five-year-old Louis Sockalexis was learning to skip a stone over the Penobscot. Meanwhile, also in 1876, William A. Hulbert and several farseeing business associates were forming the National League, which was organized not around free-spirited athletic players, but around owners and club franchises in a system that encouraged monopolies. In each designated city, competition was eliminated not only for profit, but for players who were sold for cash by owners and had no right to refuse transfers, and in fact, had nothing to say at all about their purchase or sale.

By the time Louis Sockalexis was finishing his studies at the French-Canadian Roman Catholic mission grammar school on the shores of the Penobscot, baseball had become incontestably "the national pastime." The New York Mercury seems to have coined this phrase in its December 5, 1856, edition: by this time there were fifty baseball clubs in Manhattan alone. According to one theory, it had been founded by Abner Doubleday when he laid out the first diamond-shaped field at Cooperstown, New York, in 1839, on the site of today's Baseball Hall of Fame. Some historians dispute this notion and point out its resemblance to the ancient English game of rounders, a game that was transported to America by the time of the Revolution. Still others equally hotly insist that if any one person "invented" baseball, it was Alexander Joy Cartwright, Jr., a New York City stationer who wrote the first baseball rulebook in 1845. The game really began to flourish during the Civil War, when players North and South, even in prisoner-of-war camps, distracted themselves between battles with bats and balls. By 1865, baseball had followed Cartwright and his rulebook all the way to Honolulu, Hawaii, where he still had the original baseball he had thrown on Murray Hill.

Somehow, baseball was as much made for a young Penobscot Abenaki Indian as he was for it: the game took great vitality, an accurate hurling arm, a sharp eye, and an ability to thrive in a group of equally able men. Moreover, as a Penobscot Indian, he was peculiarly suited to pursuing a new path to integrate himself in what had already become an all-white sport. Of all the native tribes in the Northeast, historically the Penobscot branch of the Abenakis had attempted more than any other to assimilate with their white neighbors. Fishermen, hunters, and expert woodsmen, they had volunteered to fight in the American Revolution on the side of the revolutionaries, only to have their original offer rebuffed by George Washington. When Benedict Arnold led an expedition through Maine to attack Canada in 1775, Penobscots had shadowed the starving Continentals, killing game and placing it with other food in the path of the soldiers. When Arnold's army became hopelessly lost in the swamps, the Abenakis appeared in their camp, led them to safety, and then fought at their sides in the attack on Quebec. One Abenaki woman had even eloped with Arnold's aide, Aaron Burr, only to be killed by a sniper's bullet as she fetched water for him.

Throughout the nineteenth century, Penobscots from Indian Island including Louis's father, Chief Sockalexis, acted as skilled Maine guides who led wealthy summer vacationers on hunting and fishing trips and then went into the woods every winter to earn money hunting game for loggers. A boy's life on Indian Island had changed only slowly. Every boy had his own gun, his dog, and his birchbark canoe. He learned to construct his canoe with great care, forming the thin struts of wood and then covering them with birchbark sewn with the roots of spruce trees. The canoe could carry four people, but was light enough for the young Abenaki to carry alone. Louis learned that in a downpour he could take shelter under it. He also learned to make snowshoes of birchwood and elk gut, and to smear himself all over with deer or beaver fat to ward off black flies and mosquitoes. He was taught to survive on the juice of spruce, sugar maple, or birch trees. Long ago converted to Catholicism, the Abenaki children were educated by French-speaking priests and nuns.

By the time Louis was thirteen and able to throw a baseball across the Penobscot, he was already fascinated by the game sweeping every New England town. For a short while, there had been no color line in baseball, at least in the North. The first African-American professional baseball player was hired by a major league club. Moses Walker, black son of an Ohio clergyman and an Oberlin College graduate, was the first African American to make the majors, joining Toledo as a catcher in 1884. He immediately encountered cries from a teammate to "get that nigger off the field." When Toledo traveled to Richmond, Virginia, Walker received a death threat from "seventy-five determined men" who threatened to mob him if he stepped onto the field. Sold to Newark, New Jersey, in the International League, Walker was a favorite with the fans, even though a sportswriter for a rival city called him "the coon catcher." One player confessed to a reporter for the *Sporting News* that "about half the pitchers try their best to hit these colored players." Southern-born ballplayers in particular had trouble with the idea of playing with blacks. Two Syracuse Stars teammates of black pitcher Robert Higgins refused to sit for a team picture with him. One told a reporter, "I am a Southerner by birth and I tell you I would rather have my heart cut out before I would consent to have my picture in the group."

By 1887, there was organized resistance to black ballplayers in the majors. A majority of players for the St. Louis Browns refused to play even an exhibition game against a black club and sent this petition to management: "We the undersigned members of the St. Louis Baseball Club do not agree to play against negroes tomorrow." No player was more adamant than Cap Anson, veteran manager of the Chicago White Stockings, who made it clear that neither he nor any of his players would consent to go on a field with a black player. By 1887, major league owners made a "gentleman's agreement" to hire no more blacks, despite the objections of fans and the press. Mourned the *Newark Call*:

> If anywhere in this world the social barriers are broken down it is on the ball field. There, many men of low birth and poor breeding are the idols of the rich and cultured; the best man is he who plays best. Even men of churlish disposition and coarse

habits are tolerated on the field. In view of these facts the objection to colored men is ridiculous. If social distinctions are to be made, half the players in the country will be shut out. Better make character and personal habits the test.

There were sporadic attempts to reintroduce blacks to the majors as the nineteenth century ended. John McGraw tried to introduce a black second baseman named Charlie Grant to the roster by calling him a Cherokee and renaming him Charlie Tokahoma. "If he really keeps this Indian," said Charles Comiskey, president of the Chicago White Stockings, "I will get a Chinaman of my acquaintance and put him on third." The use of "Chinaman" was typical of derogatory terms used about Asians in this very race-conscious age.

By the time he was old enough to go to school, Louis Sockalexis was already learning hunting and fishing along the Penobscot, which abounded with salmon, from his father, the Abenaki chief, who was an expert outdoorsman who also excelled at sports. Forays into the forests with his father produced bear, moose, and deer that provided food and clothing, including shirts, shoes, leggings, fur-lined coats, and hats. Undoubtedly a good shot, he learned to run with the deer that his father taught him to track and kill. But there was the tug of the white culture all around his poverty-stricken island village, especially in the summers when wealthy New Yorkers and Bostonians came Down East to their "camps," as their elaborate summer houses were called. Not that eastern Maine was devoid of victims of the baseball fever that was spreading in the 1890s. Bangor, the logging capital of the world then, was only twelve miles away, and Louis would go there to watch the muscular loggers and shipbuilders take on challengers from all of New England. All over Maine, college boys came to play baseball. It was probably at one of these games that Louis made his college "debut."

As he traveled around Knox County playing ball for whatever money they would pay him (the going rate was ten dollars a game), Louis caught the eye of Maine journalist Gilbert Patten, who, after putting the Camden newspaper to bed at night, banged out short stories and "dime" novels that he would mail off to New York City. Patten liked to play baseball, even if he had never made the first string of anything. His publisher was looking for a fictional hero for a series of "dime" novels, until then based on Western gunslingers, but this time to be about a paragon of Victorian virtue and robust good health. Rejecting a purely English schoolboy model, Patten, who had seen Sockalexis play, came up with a new character he named Frank Merrywell. "The name was symbolic of the chief characteristics I desired my hero to have—*Frank* for frankness, *merry* for a happy disposition, *well* for health and abounding vitality," Patten wrote in his memoirs. The first of 648 Merrywell paperbacks appeared in 1896: in all 500 million copies of his "dime" novels would make their clean cut, polite, athletic hero the model for three generations of American boys, outselling any other American book ever published. Among the boys it influenced were Woodrow Wilson and Babe Ruth.

A catcher for Holy Cross College, Michael "Doc" Powers (who later played for the Philadelphia Athletics), came to play ball in Maine in the summer of 1895 and was impressed by Louis Sockalexis's great accuracy in throwing a ball with his right hand, his great speed in the outfield, and his powerful left-handed hitting. That autumn, Powers took his friend Louis aboard the steamboat from Bangor for

National Baseball Library, Cooperstown, NY

The first Native American to play major league baseball, Louis Sockalexis died clutching the press clippings of his brief but memorable career in Cleveland.

Boston, and then traveled by rail west to Worcester to try out for a scholarship at Holy Cross. Louis was impressive: nearly six feet tall, he could run a hundred yards in ten seconds in his spiked shoes. At twenty-five, he became a college student and a collegiate baseball star. The Holy Cross coach, Jesse Burkett, signed him up. The "Crusaders" became one of the best teams in the East the next two seasons. Louis played the outfield and pitched three no-hitters. He batted .436 and .444. In a game against Harvard, Louis made a lightning throw to the catcher to prevent a runner from scoring. Two Harvard professors measured the distance and announced that Sockalexis had set a world record of 138 yards. Coach Burkett was offered a better job as the Notre Dame coach in South Bend, Indiana—just so long as he brought his star outfielder with him.

In the summer of 1896, Louis traveled to New York with the Holy Cross team to play an exhibition match against the New York Giants at the Polo Grounds. Louis hit an inside-the-park home run, streaking around the bases before the Giants could make the play on him. The Giants' manager, John Ward, immediately wrote to Patsy Tabeau, the player-manager of the Cleveland Spiders (Holy Cross coach Burkett played third base for the Spiders during the professional season). Tabeau offered Louis a job as soon as he finished college. In the fall of 1896, Louis and his coach boarded a train west, all his belongings stuffed into a cardboard suitcase.

At Notre Dame, Louis became one of the most talked-about players. The tall for those days (5′11″), stocky (185 pounds), fast outfielder had another fabulous season. By April 1897 Louis had become one of the most talked-about players in college baseball. The talk wasn't always friendly. In a savage new kind of journalism, sports writers attacked the reputation of a rival player to build up the home team. By the time Louis left South Bend, the pundits were writing that he and a teammate had been expelled from Notre Dame for breaking up a brothel in a drunken binge, the two key elements of scandal that would be hurled at him again and again. Fortunately, there are record books that prove quite the opposite, that Sockalexis quickly became Notre Dame's best athlete with no hint of misbehaving marring his outstanding record at the college.

After the 1897 collegiate season, Louis borrowed the money from Coach Burkett to take the train to Cleveland, where he had been offered a major league tryout. Manager Patsy Tabeau offered him a place on the roster of the Cleveland Spiders, always a pennant contender in the National League and runner up the year before. Louis's eyes must have grown big as he ran out onto the field at League Park in his new blue and white uniform of a professional ballplayer for the first time on April 22, 1897. The first Native-American professional athlete (and for several years the only nonwhite in the majors), made such an impression that *Sporting Life,* the national weekly sports magazine, ran a two-column line drawing of him on page seven in the 1897's season's first edition, introducing him in an essay-length caption:

> Sockalexis, the Indian Ball Player now Playing with the Cleveland Club. Sockalexis is not a well-greased Greek, notwithstanding the Hellenic hint his name conveys. He is a well-educated Indian. Furthermore, he is a professional baseball player, and during this season he will travel through the country playing right field . . . Of course, the "rooters" will have no end of fun with his name . . . as he merrily chases the ball over the field or legs it for bases. Captain Tabeau of the Cleveland nine counts himself a fortunate man in having him on his team . . . .

The elongated caption went on to describe Louis's background, pointing out that "his origin shows clearly enough in his dark complexion, straight black hair" and in his "somewhat modified but still noticeable high cheekbones . . . . He is over six feet tall, of powerful physique and noted as a hard, reliable and safe hitter . . . . He is nimble and fleet-footed in the field . . . he throws as straight as a rifle shot." The long-winded description ended with an aside, that Sockalexis was also a formidable handball player who had even beaten Captain Tabeau, "a remarkably alert player."

Louis Sockalexis left no record of his impressions of his teammates or of the city of Cleveland, so far from the Maine woods, where he now found himself. But few places in North America could have been more antithetical than Cleveland to his Old Town. Cleveland in 1897 was already nearing a population of 400,000, having tripled in only twenty-five years as it became the great, sooty, grimy center of oil refining in the United States and a crossroads for shiploads and rail cars of iron ore bound from Lake Superior to the iron foundries of Cleveland and the steel mills of Pittsburgh. The sky was a perpetual yellowish-gray from burning soft bituminous coal, yet pollution was the hallmark of employment for the thousands of Hungarian, Lithuanian, Polish, and Russian immigrants arriving to seek jobs every year.

There were few outlets for relaxation for the workers in the few hours they had to unwind from the urban drudgery of their jobs. Louis could not know that he had walked into a crossfire of controversy over which fans were to be allowed into League Field to see the pennant-contending Spiders play. The city of Cleveland had a strict ban on Sunday baseball. In the era before electrified night games became possible, this all but shut out the workers, who toiled every day but Sunday. Attendance rarely hit 5,000 for a Saturday game, when the fans were virtually all middle or upper class gentlemen. As a further disincentive, the National League ticket price was fifty cents a game at a time when only skilled workers earned ninety cents to one dollar a day. There were a few twenty-five cent seats but, as one sportswriter put it, "they were in Erie (about 100 miles away)." On average, there were only about 800 fans at a Cleveland home game, a small percentage of the league average.

At a time when the game was rough and umpires could expect to be crippled by the spikes of disapproving ballplayers, umpires were the favorite targets of abuse and could also expect to be pelted by fans with trash, garbage, and sometimes stones. Player managers were selected for their lung power and their ability to hurl verbal abuse more than any managerial skill. Yet Louis Sockalexis could hardly have been luckier than in having third baseman Patsy Tabeau for his player-manager. The two became not only handball partners but close friends. He also was fortunate in having a tall farm boy, Denton Tecumseh "Cy" Young, the leading pitcher in baseball, as his teammate and friend. Young had joined the team so poor, one sports historian notes, that "his sleeves failed to cover his wrists and his trousers appeared sawed off at the ankles." The manager had to buy him "a complete new outfit" so he "would not be ridiculed."

Quiet, smiling, and determined, Louis Sockalexis came to the plate of his first major league game on April 22, 1897, batting third in the lineup, to the warwhoops of the fans, a sound he would hear over and over that season. The jeers lasted until he swung. Time after time, his wooden bat connected solidly in those opening weeks, usually for a double, a triple, or a home run. The unfortunately named Spiders surged ahead into the league lead, winning eight of their first ten games. Like his fictional counterpart, Frank Merrywell, Louis became famous for game-winning ninth inning homers with a man on base. Four times in nine games in late May, he made such dramatic finishes.

There was, as a sportswriter covering Cleveland for *Sporting Life* saw clearly, enormous pressure on Sockalexis. After he made his first error two weeks into the season, Elmer E. Bates, author of the regular weekly column *Cleveland Chatter*, observed:

> All eyes are on the Indian in every game. He is expected not only to play right field like a veteran but to do a little more batting than anyone else. Columns of silly poetry are written about him; hideous looking cartoons adorn the sporting pages of nearly every

paper. He is hooted and howled at by the thimble-brained brigade on the bleachers. Despite all this handicap, the red man has played good, steady ball.

When Cleveland made its first grueling month-long railroad trip east, playing from Pittsburgh, to Washington, D.C., to Boston, sports writers were waiting for him, with their poisoned pens ready. The New York *Tribune* predicted that the Giants' fireball king, Amos Rusie, would strike out Louis in his first trip to the plate at the Polo Grounds. As the fans warwhooped and yelled "Ki-yi's," Louis quietly demolished Rusie by sending the first flying fast-breaking curve ball flying over the centerfield fence for a home run. Nearly half a century later, Giants manager John J. McGraw, there that day, still ranked Sockalexis as the number one ballplayer of all time. After feeding Louis several such pitches for the Philadelphia team that year, Andy Coakley echoed McGraw's accolade. "He had a gorgeous left-hand swing, hit the ball almost as far as Babe Ruth," recalled Coakley, who coached baseball at Columbia University for many years. In four consecutive games before July 4, 1897, Louis hit eleven times out of twenty-one at-bats. "He was faster than Ty Cobb and as good a base runner. He had the outfielding skill of Tris Speaker. He threw like Bob Meusel, which means that no one could throw a ball farther or more accurately." The years of hurling a baseball across the Penobscot from the island to the mainland were paying off. Players and fans were astonished at Louis's speed and his accurate throwing. Few baserunners dared run on him. His batting average rose to .386 by May 17, and then to .413 by July 31.

Handsome, "with a perfect Indian profile," and his long black hair streaming after him as he ran, Louis Sockalexis became the baseball sensation of the 1897 season. Today, he would be paid millions: at the time, the top salary was $2,000 and he did not make that. He gloried in the adulation of the fans and he clipped all the newspaper articles and carried them with him. One sportswriter wrote a poem in Hiawatha-like meter about "Sockalexis, Chief of Sockem." The barbs of rival writers cut deeply and the hard life of cheap boardinghouses and endless train trips began to take a toll. After an all night Fourth of July party with his teammates, Louis began to slip out his hotel room window at night to drink bourbon with friends. He had never had anything stronger than milk before leaving Old Town. After that holiday binge, Louis could not play for two days.

When he returned to the lineup, he made only two hits in each of the next three games. Then he began to stagger and make errors in the outfield. In mid-July, Coach Tabeau assigned another player to room with him to make sure he did not go out at night. One night, as Louis tried to elude his wards, he climbed out his second floor hotel window and jumped or fell to the ground, severely injuring an ankle. He played one game a few weeks later, was suspended for drunkenness, benched for another month, and then made two errors in the final game of the season. He ended the season with a .331 average for sixty-six games.

The newspaper pundits showed no mercy. Some insisted that he had hurt himself while jumping out of a brothel window; others, that the injury followed "a tryst with a pale-faced maiden" as well as a "dalliance with grape." *Sporting Life* came to his defense: its Cleveland correspondent wrote that

> much of the stuff written about his dalliance with grape juice and his trysts with pale-faced maidens is pure speculation . . . Too much popularity has ruined Sockalexis . . . . It is no longer a secret that the Cleveland management can no longer control Sockalexis.

Louis's friend, Captain Tabeau, did not give up on him. He told *Sporting Life* that Louis would be back the next season at the top of the lineup. He belatedly had an x-ray taken of Louis's injured foot and announced to the press that it wasn't broken, only badly inflamed. Nevertheless, Louis was lame.

There were other factors at work over the winter that neither player nor manager could understand. Cleveland's owner, trolley car magnate Frank DeHaas Robinson, had been waging a legal battle all season to open up League Park for Sunday games, a move that he predicted would quadruple attendance—and his profits. Robinson was a visionary businessman who had resuscitated the team after it had failed in the 1880s, and now he wanted to make money. When city fathers fought him to a legal stalemate on Sunday games, he won league approval to change the rule forbidding interlocking boards of directors and he bought another team, the St. Louis Browns, the worst team in baseball.

When the 1898 season began, Louis Sockalexis returned from Maine to find that all of the best players, including Cy Young and his close friend, Patsy Tabeau, had been shipped to St. Louis and the St. Louis lineup and manager shuttled to Cleveland. Further, owner Robinson put the Cleveland team on the road far more that season where he could make more money in cities where he divided a larger gate. The home fans deserted League Park and gave the Spiders a few nicknames such as the Cleveland Misfits, the Exiles, and the Wanderers. The hapless new manager, Lave Cross, confronted owner Robinson and begged for help. "I need about five players to have a pretty good team, Mr. Robinson. A couple of pitchers and a shortstop would help." Robinson stared at the man and answered, "I'm not interested in winning games here." The Spiders were headed for the worst season record in the history of baseball, winning only twenty games and losing 134.

Louis, increasingly lame, could no longer race across the outfield and was used only as a pinchhitter. In 1897, he had batted 278 times in sixty-six games; in 1898, only sixty-seven times in twenty-one games. Instead of ninety-four hits, he connected only fifteen times for a .224 batting average. Lonely and dejected, he began to drink more. But there was less and less press interest in an alcoholic ballplayer. There was all the excitement of the outbreak of the Spanish-American War and few people other than the astute *Sporting Life* correspondent Elmer Bates wrote about Louis Sockalexis or his "fall from grace." Lave Cross was not allowed to transfer Louis to St. Louis to rejoin his friends. When Louis returned to Cleveland for his third and last season in 1899, the stands were virtually empty and there were no warwhoops as he posted his worst record, producing only six hits in the seven games in which he was allowed to play. His major league career was over with the nineteenth century. In all, in his three-year major league career, he had chalked up 115 hits (including three homers), stolen sixteen bases and played in ninety-four games, with a solid .313 career batting average.

For the next three years, Louis played minor league ball in New England, drifting down to Hartford, Connecticut, then to Lowell, Massachusetts, but his alcoholism led one manager after another to drop him. Sick from his addiction, and once again as poor as all his neighbors, he rarely left Indian Island after 1903 except to pull the ferry across the Penobscot, and, when the river froze over, to go deep into the winter woods, as his forebears had done, to hunt and trap on snowshoes. In the summers, too, he taught young Indians on the island how to play baseball as his father had done, teaching them they must learn to excel at the white man's game. As the snow piled up in the winter of 1913, Louis went into the winter woods one last time. He died on Christmas Eve at the age of forty-two, clutching the press clippings that he had always carried tucked inside his shirt. He was buried beside the other tribal chiefs on the shore of the Penobscot. Two years later, the Cleveland fans were asked to choose a permanent name for their team, which now played to tens of thousands on Sundays. They remembered Chief Louis Sockalexis's meteoric career. They named the Cleveland Indians in honor of his memory.

QUESTIONS FOR THOUGHT AND DISCUSSION

1. Why would a Penobscot Indian from Maine want to achieve success in professional baseball? In what ways was Louis Sockalexis following in a long tradition of Penobscot relations with the dominant American culture?

2. Why were African Americans banned from professional baseball in 1887? How did this reflect other limitations imposed on black Americans in the late nineteenth century?

3. Was it personal weaknesses that cut Sockalexis's career short? In what ways was he burdened by his background? Would today's sports system save him?

4. As a tribute to Sockalexis, Cleveland renamed its baseball team the Indians. Are sport team names based on Native Americans (e.g., Indians, Seminoles, Chiefs, Braves, Redskins, Aztecs) and the war whoops or tomahawk chops that their fans use to reflect the team's name any more offensive than team names like the Vikings, the Fighting Irish, the Pirates, or the Cornhuskers?

SUGGESTED READINGS

Alexander, Charles C. *Our Game: An American Baseball History.* New York: Holt, 1991.

Angell, Roger. *Season Tickets: A Baseball Companion.* Boston: Houghton Mifflin, 1991.

Holway, John B. *Voices from the Great Black Baseball Leagues.* New York: Dodd, Mead, 1975.

Rader, Benjamin G. *Baseball: A History of America's Game.* Urbana: U of Illinois P, 1992.

Seymour, Harold. *Baseball: The Early Years.* New York: Oxford UP, 1960.

Smith, Robert M. *Baseball.* New York: Simon, 1970.

Ward, Geoffrey C., and Ken Burns. *Baseball, An Illustrated History.* New York: Knopf, 1994.

7

W.E.B. DuBois

When Reconstruction ended in the South in 1876, Northerners abandoned any pretense of protecting the rights of the nation's four million freed blacks. As Mark Twain observed, in the early 1880s you couldn't go five minutes in polite conversation in the South without the subject turning to the Civil War, while, in the North, you could go all day. Southerners were left to settle their own race relations. Even former champions of black rights such as The Nation *magazine doubted whether former slaves could participate "in a system of government for which you [the Northern reader] and I have much respect."*

A fierce debate developed among emerging black leaders over what course to follow in the face of Northern indifference. Booker T. Washington, a former slave turned educator in Alabama, won the support of many blacks and whites by abandoning the quest for black seats in Congress in favor of teaching blacks how to farm, build houses, and work machines. W.E.B. DuBois wanted blacks, especially the "talented tenth" with the intellectual ability, to pursue leadership roles that would win equal rights and opportunities. The lines were drawn for a long struggle.

IN JUNE 1896, William Edward Burghardt DuBois, a twenty-eight-year-old classics professor at all-black Wilberforce University, received a telegram from the provost of the University of Pennsylvania offering DuBois a position there as a sociology field researcher at the munificent sum of $900. Young Dr. DuBois's first year as a college professor had been frustrating. He was miserable at the backwater Ohio school, in part because he had jumped at the first offer and missed the opportunity to teach at Booker T. Washington's famous school, Tuskegee Institute, in Alabama. "President Washington, Sir! May I ask if you have a vacancy in your institution next year?" DuBois had written to Washington, the most famous black leader in America in the late nineteenth century. By the time Washington wired back to offer DuBois a job teaching mathematics, the versatile DuBois had, only eight days before, accepted the Wilberforce job and was on his way west.

Unable to accept the religious zealotry that then permeated rural Wilberforce University, DuBois was also obviously ill at ease in the rural isolation of northern Ohio after years of studying at Harvard and at the University of Berlin. As the first black American Ph.D., he jumped at the one-year offer to live in urbane Philadelphia and hurried there with Nina, his bride of three weeks. For one thing, Philadelphia boasted the largest and most sophisticated black community in the United States.

In the summer of 1896 when DuBois arrived at the University of Pennsylvania to take up his $900-a-year position as a Penn "assistant in sociology," he found that he had been given no office, no classes to teach, and was not even listed on the faculty roster. "My name never actually got into the catalogue," he wrote in *Dusk of Dawn*. It was not until he had nearly finished his monumental Philadelphia study that the 1897–98 catalogue announced a "special sociological investigation of the condition of Negroes in Philadelphia," misspelling his name and adding that his work would conclude January 1, 1898. So strong was racial segregation on the Penn campus that no one seemed to have thought of keeping DuBois on the teaching staff. DuBois didn't dare think of it either—it "didn't occur to me," as he later said.

Yet the work DuBois did in the Seventh Ward slums of West Philadelphia was to set him on his course as the most militant black leader in a century. The newly-wed DuBois found a one-room apartment above a cafeteria at 700 Lombard Street and made it his home and office as he surveyed door-to-door the largest black community in the North. Unknown to him, DuBois had been hired by the Penn provost to gather data documenting crime and corruption in the black community that was to be used against the city's Democratic machine, which derived crucial support from blacks. The city's reform-minded Republican elite had, according to biographer David Levering Lewis, hatched the scheme of documenting the alarming moral and social conditions among them in order to mount a more effective campaign to recapture City Hall.

A block from the DuBois apartment stood Mother Bethel African Methodist Episcopal Church, soul of the city's once proud free black community, founded at the end of the Revolution when Richard Allen and James Forten with their followers, walked out of St. George's Methodist Church because the seating was segregated. For more than a century, proud, civic-minded, free black merchants, caterers, and servants in the nearby grand Society Hill redbricks had been listened to, but not heeded, by the whites who controlled the city. But as the city's mills, foundries, and construction sites pulled in more and more unskilled white immigrants, Philadelphia's blacks became caught in a crossfire between their exploitation by white political leaders and the hatred of working class whites competing for once black jobs. As white historian Edward Turner was to write in 1911, "The history of the relations between the Negro and white man in Pennsylvania is largely the history of increasing race prejudice."

From their window on the crowded, crime-ridden Seventh Ward, the DuBois-es saw and heard the terrible sights and sounds of a black ghetto crammed with nearly 10,000 of the city's 40,000 blacks: DuBois would verify the existence and living conditions of 4,501 black men and 5,174 women during that year of door-to-door interviews, making detailed notes on cards that formed the basis for his classic book, *The Philadelphia Negro*.

The Seventh Ward was "the bane of respectable Philadelphians," writes black historian Lewis, "because so many lived there, because many of them were so poor, because many had recently arrived from the South, because they were responsible for so much crime, and because they stood out by color and culture so conspicuously in the eyes of their white neighbors." In the grimy slum streets, blacks were dangerous to each other and posed a threat to their gentrified Society Hill neighbors. Eight out of ten blacks, DuBois concluded, were already excluded from jobs by the color bar and left to idle in smoky, honky-tonk bars and crowded rowhouses where, all too often, fights, robberies, and murders led them to be carried dying or maimed to the swamped emergency rooms of Pennsylvania Hospital, two blocks away.

What DuBois saw and heard in his eighteen months in Philadelphia would anger and motivate him for many years. The year in the Quaker City was to prove pivotal in the life of the first militant black American leader, the man who would live for nearly the entire post-Civil War century, helping to found the NAACP and then, near the end of his ninety-five year life, despairing of America, finishing his days an avowed Communist in exile in Ghana, where he helped found the Marxist Pan-African Movement. The story of the life of W.E.B. DuBois is not only his own story but that of the African-American race in the near-century between the euphoria of Emancipation in the 1860s and the frustration leading through decades of Jim Crow segregation, Marcus Garvey's back-to-Africa movement, thousands of lynchings, and finally, the civil rights movement of the 1960s.

Born three years after the Civil War ended, DuBois died in Africa on the day before Martin Luther King, Jr. delivered his famous "I Have a Dream" speech during the Freedom March of August 1963. While the news of his death in exile was broadcast to 300,000 Freedom Marchers and spread worldwide by news media, his birth was in absolute and unpromising obscurity. Born in 1868 in the virtually all-white Berkshire Mountain milltown of Great Barrington, Massachusetts, Willie DuBois, as he was nicknamed, was the illegitimate son of an illegitimate son who was an itinerant mulatto barber with Huguenot French and Haitian ancestors. His father, Alfred, "gay and carefree," as DuBois later described him, "refusing to settle long at any one place or job," was, at various times, a baker, a barber, an Albany, New York, hotel waiter, and a deserter from his Civil War unit of the 20th New York Regiment Colored Troops. His mother, Mary Silvina Burghardt, was a melancholic woman "of infinite patience," DuBois wrote, which she especially needed after her husband deserted her and their infant baby. Mary Silvina did a lifetime of domestic work in the big houses of Great Barrington and encouraged her son to get the best possible education.

A star student in an otherwise all-white public school, DuBois at first aspired to the life of an educated, white, New England gentleman. Neighbors helped him find odd jobs so he could buy books; high school teachers helped DuBois prepare for Harvard. But Harvard at first wouldn't have him, so DuBois went South to the abolitionist-founded American Missionary Association-funded Fisk University in Nashville, which was still using converted Union Army barracks. During summers, he confronted his black roots by teaching in a rural school in East Tennessee set up for the children of freed slaves. Finally admitted to Harvard with the class of 1890, he was only the college's sixth African-American student. There, DuBois soaked up the friendship, social theories, and values of philosopher William James, who introduced him, among others, to Helen Keller at her nearby institute for the blind.

After graduating Harvard *cum laude,* DuBois won a traveling scholarship to the University of Berlin. He was already steeped in the writings of Marx and his teacher, Engels, and he now imbibed Hegel as he studied for his doctorate in Berlin. One semester short of completing his dissertation, he ran out of money and had to return to Harvard without the German doctorate he so coveted. His Harvard Ph.D., the first ever granted to an African American, came as a consolation prize. As a Harvard undergraduate, DuBois had been anti-labor, berating in a paper the "ignorant lawlessness" of the Haymarket rioters. By the time he left Berlin at age twenty-four, he had written most of his seminal work on the history of the American slave trade, the first of his path-breaking studies on African-American life.

Back in America, where he was to write in 1903 in *The Souls of Black Folks,* DuBois began to feel more and more his "twoness—an American, a Negro." He felt increasingly walled off by the emerging American apartheid, and he looked back fondly in later years on his years in Europe, where he felt exceptionally free and more liberated than he ever would again. After teaching for one year in increasingly segregated Atlanta and one year in rural isolation in Ohio, he came to Philadelphia in veritable flight from the loneliness and Bible-beating of black revivalism. No matter that Penn offered him no office, no listing on the faculty roster, nor the promise or possibility of future employment, he was convinced that his labors in the Philadelphia ghetto would launch him as a sociologist. Sallying forth each day in his elegant celluloid-collared white shirt and dark suit, flicking the cane with the gloves he had learned to affect in Berlin, he stepped off briskly for eight hours of knocking on doors. He devoted an average of twenty minutes to each interview, patiently guiding often suspicious, barely literate subjects, many of them former slaves, through his series of questions, in all canvassing 2,500 African-American households that summer of 1896. What emerged were the life historie's of the entire black population of Philadelphia's teeming Seventh Ward—the first scientific urban study of African Americans.

It was while DuBois was a faculty adjunct at Penn that he began to emerge as a national spokesman for black Americans. On March 5, 1897, the American Negro Academy held its first formal session in Washington, D.C. DuBois was elected first vice president. He presented a paper, "The Conservation of Races," that helped to establish his position as the leading young black intellectual in America. He argued that blacks had to reject the goal of racial "absorption" and assimilation into white American society:

> . . . Their destiny is not a servile imitation of Anglo-Saxon culture but a stalwart originality which shall unswervingly follow Negro ideals. . . . We are Negroes, members of a vast historic race that from the very dawn of creation has slept, but half awakening in the dark forests of its African fatherland. We are the first fruits of this new nation, the harbinger of that black tomorrow which is yet destined to soften the whiteness of the Teutonic today. We are that people whose subtle sense of song has given America its only American music, its only American fairy tales, its only touch of pathos and humor amid its mad, money-getting plutocracy. . . .

DuBois's resounding prose, his cadences so evoking the preaching of black clergymen, brought him into sharp conflict with the prevailing message of assimilation and accommodation espoused by Booker T. Washington, the black spokesman favored by white American politicians. In the spring of 1897, DuBois's rewritten version of the Washington speech was accepted for publication by the *Atlantic Monthly.* "Strivings of the Negro People" was his first article to receive a national audience. It enunciated the central theme of DuBois's intellectual life, his theory of a "double consciousness" which separates blacks from other Americans:

> One ever feels his twoness—an American, a Negro; two souls, two thoughts, two unreconciled strivings; two warring ideals in one dark body whose dogged strength alone keeps it from being torn asunder.

At the age of twenty-nine, DuBois found himself caught between two conflicting black political and cultural positions. Frederick Douglass, the central black leader of the abolitionist era, had finally accepted the goal of black assimilation into white society but fought for full democratic rights. Other black leaders since Paul

AP/Wide World

Author of the controversial "gifted tenth" theory, W.E.B. DuBois clashed with Booker T. Washington on how best to improve the lot of American blacks.

Cuffe in the early nineteenth century had espoused the resettlement of America's blacks in Africa. DuBois argued that the "general emigration of American Negroes to Africa is neither possible nor desirable." He took a dim view of returning to the African "fatherland" for practical reasons:

> There was no proper preparation, no equipment or tools or capital, no proper idea of the country and climate—simply an indiscriminate invitation to the lazy, vicious, and ignorant to go to a land of milk and honey.

DuBois did not feel comfortable with the role at first, but he was emerging, not as a messianic figure prophesying change for blacks but as a combination philosopher and chronicler of black grievances seeking pragmatic solutions to short-term problems.

His increasingly outspoken stand brought him into direct conflict with Booker T. Washington, unlike him born a slave and the founder of Tuskegee Institute in Alabama's Black Belt, who had established his rural school as a major center for technical and agricultural education. By 1901, Tuskegee had 109 full-time faculty and 1,095 pupils. Many of black America's leading researchers and scholars worked at the Institute, including the great agricultural chemist, George Washington Carver. Washington, an effective orator, was no "Uncle Tom;" during the 1880s he openly condemned racial segregation laws on public transportation, and as late as 1894 encouraged blacks to boycott Jim Crow-restricted streetcars.

Washington had suddenly emerged as a major political figure in September, 1895, when he gave a short speech in Atlanta which DuBois later criticized as the "Atlanta Compromise." He noted that one-third of the South's population was black and so any "enterprise seeking the material, civil, or moral welfare" of the South could not ignore blacks, who should remain in the South. "Cast down your bucket where you are," he said. "Ignorant and inexperienced" blacks had tried to start "at the top instead of at the bottom" by pursuing seats in Congress prematurely instead of seeking "real estate or industrial skill." At Atlanta, Washington pledged the fidelity of his race, "the most patient, law-abiding, and unresentful people that the world has seen," reducing race relations to a simple metaphor:

> In all things that are purely social we can be as separate as the fingers, yet one as the hand in all things essential to mutual progress . . . The wisest among my race understand that the agitation of questions of social equality is the extremist folly.

Many white Americans responded enthusiastically to Washington's Atlanta speech. President Grover Cleveland saw "new hope" for black Americans. Booker Washington was to become the advisor on racial matters to Presidents Cleveland, William McKinley and Theodore Roosevelt.

At first, DuBois was sympathetic: "Let me heartily congratulate you," he wrote, "upon your phenomenal success in Atlanta—it was a word fitly spoken." It was shortly after this that he had applied for a job at Tuskegee. Even after his research in Philadelphia, DuBois, accepting a teaching post at all-black Atlanta University, in 1899 urged black entrepreneurs to create Negro Business Men's Leagues with a strategy of "Negro money for Negro merchants." Washington espoused DuBois's suggestion and established the National Negro Business League in 1900. That year, when the post of Superintendent of Negro Schools of

Washington, D. C. became vacant, Booker Washington lobbied to get him the job, which DuBois declined. DuBois decided to stay on in Atlanta, where he had gone after his Penn research and where he remained from 1899 to 1909. He did accept Washington's invitation to visit him at his West Virginia home in the summer of 1901 and shortly after that Washington generously praised DuBois for his research "on the condition of the public schools in the South. . . . I know it is hard work."

By 1901, when Washington published his famous memoir, *Up from Slavery,* the two were good friends. Both believed that the future for blacks should be trusted to the guidance of a small, well-educated black elite, what DuBois would later start calling the "talented tenth" of the black population. He was, at this time, in accord with Booker Washington ideologically: both believed in racial self-sufficiency, education as the means of upward mobility, black cultural pride, and entrepreneurism. DuBois also at this time accepted property and literacy qualifications for the right to vote in Georgia in order to save the franchise for a minority of blacks. By 1903, the majority of black Americans accepted Booker T. Washington's vision of a separate, all-Negro society where the emphasis was on learning skills, getting jobs, buying property, and aspiring to the middle class.

But a growing number of radical black intellectuals, especially northern black journalists, began to criticize Washington's "accommodationism:" William Monroe Trotter of the *Boston Guardian* described him as a "coward" and unprincipled "self-seeker." When DuBois reviewed *Up from Slavery* for *Dial* magazine in July, 1901, he publicly criticized Washington's educational and economic principles for the first time. A little more than a year later, he explicitly rejected Washington's accommodation politics in "Hopeful Signs for the Negro." He insisted that there were blacks like himself who would not "abate one jot" from their "determination to attain in this land perfect equality before the law." Washington responded by making a series of lucrative job offers to DuBois in late 1902. A wealthy Tuskegee trustee invited him to New York City for a conference on "the condition of the colored people" there. DuBois drew up a detailed proposal for a Philadelphia-style social study, but his host was really bent on recruiting him for Tuskegee: DuBois could name his own salary. DuBois traveled to Washington, D.C., where he twice met with the Tuskegee founder. All he would agree to do was to lecture in the summer session of 1903 at the Alabama school and participate in a private conference with a group of black leaders.

At this same time, however, a Chicago publisher invited DuBois to collect several of his essays: he added a new chapter, "Of Mr. Booker T. Washington and Others" in which he gave a "frank evaluation" of the Tuskegee philosophy. Published in 1903 as *The Souls of Black Folk,* it has become a classic, graceful and powerfully written. Several years later Henry James, writing in *The American Scene,* commented about it, "How can everything have so gone that the only Southern book of any distinction published for many a year is *The Soul of Black Folks?*" It immediately sparked a debate among black intellectuals. DuBois called Washington "certainly the most distinguished Southerner since Jefferson Davis, and the one with the largest personal following." DuBois dissected the Tuskegee "Gospel of Work and Money" that had obscured "the higher aims of life." Washington's call for industrial training jeopardized black higher education. Washington's rise to national political prominence had intimidated and all but silenced his critics. Firmly rejecting "Mammonism" and renewing Frederick Douglass's call for democratic protest, DuBois publicly broke with Washington. No book had had such an effect on African Americans since *Uncle Tom's Cabin,* fifty years earlier.

Stunned, Washington allowed DuBois to give his summer course at Tuskegee, but his followers counter-attacked. The *Outlook* declared that DuBois was "half ashamed of being a Negro." The *Colored American* urged the president of Atlanta University to curb the "ill-advised criticisms of the learned doctor." But events were overtaking both camps. On July 30, 1903, while Washington spoke to 2,000 blacks and whites in Boston, radical journalist Trotter disrupted the meeting and police were called. Trotter spent a month in jail, the maximum sentence. When he was released, DuBois visited him as a house guest. Booker Washington had come to believe DuBois was behind a "conspiracy to riot," he wrote to a major financial backer of Atlanta University. Other white philanthropists cut off their gifts to DuBois's employer, despite his denials that he had instigated the "riot."

The so-called Boston Riot of 1903 was a turning point for African Americans. DuBois began to proselytize his "Talented Tenth" theory that only segregated black colleges, not Tuskegee, could produce a black elite. Black America could only be "saved by its exceptional men," they must "guide the Mass away from the contamination and death of the Worst, in their own and other races." Between Washington's 1895 "Atlanta Compromise" speech and 1903, as segregationist Jim Crow policies had been applied and tightened in the South, DuBois had come to believe he must openly protest for full democratic rights for blacks. Going on the stump himself for the first time in Baltimore, Maryland, in December 1903, DuBois declared that black Americans had "the right to know." Washington's "sneers at Negro colleges," his "exaltation of men's bellies and depreciation of their brains . . . becomes a movement you must choke to death or it will choke you."

Over the next half dozen years, more and more liberals, confronted with the evidence of worsening conditions faced every day by blacks, came to realize that a nationwide campaign for black civil rights was needed. In June 1905, DuBois secretly circulated a call "for organized determination and aggressive action on the part of men who believe in Negro freedom and growth." Fifty-nine African Americans signed the agreement. In July, they met at Fort Erie, Ontario—outside the United States—and decided to form a militant civil rights organization to be called the Niagara Movement. Their goals included "freedom of speech and criticism," "manhood suffrage," and "the abolition of all caste distinctions based simply on race and color." DuBois was elected general secretary.

DuBois later said he did not like having to become a political figure. "My career as a scientist," he complained, "was swallowed up in my role as a master of propaganda." He did manage to keep his research and writing alive, next producing his favorite work, a biography of abolitionist John Brown in 1909. In 1904, he also published poetry, his *Credo,* a prose-poem, and *The Song of the Smoke* in 1907. He had become the leading black American writer.

DuBois could not ignore worsening racial violence. The worst of the violence was right in Atlanta, where a series of inflammatory newspaper articles in September 1906, depicted an imaginary attack by black males against white women that revived the Ku Klux Klan and led to widespread attacks on blacks. A black shoeshine boy was beaten to death; black laborers were thrown out windows; black-owned shops and restaurants were destroyed, with white police joining the rioters. Booker T. Washington's leading supporter in Atlanta, J. W. E. Bowen, was beaten over the head by a policeman with his rifle butt. As DuBois and the Niagara Movement held whites accountable, Washington proclaimed Atlanta as safe as New York.

By 1909, there were more than 100 branches of the Niagara Movement. By mid–1909, the movement had gained the support of prominent white liberals. Among its backers now were writer William Dean Howells, social activist Jane Addams, and the editor of *The Nation,* Oswald Garrison Villard, grandson of abolitionist journalist William Lloyd Garrison. In 1910, black and white leaders of the Niagara Movement decided to form the National Association for the Advancement of Colored People (NAACP). DuBois was the only black officer: he was elected NAACP Director of Publicity and Research.

At first he was reluctant to sever his ties with Atlanta University, which had so long supported him. But in August, 1910, he moved to New York City and went to work full time for the NAACP, founding and editing its new journal, *The Crisis.* By 1917, he had built its circulation to 70,000. For the next twenty-four years, he would write its editorials, taking as his central political theme the relationship between racism and American democracy. He became famous not only for upholding black civil rights, but for attacking what he saw as wrongheaded policies of other black leaders.

By 1914, a "Back to Africa" movement once again was gaining widespread support among blacks, organized by Jamaica-born Marcus Garvey. The Red Scare of 1919 produced fresh attacks on blacks, especially black workers who had been recruited to work in northern cities to free whites to fight in Europe. A gifted orator, Garvey was catapulted into national prominence by his outspoken belief that blacks would never receive justice in countries where most of the people were white. By the early 1920s, Garvey had an estimated two million followers in the United States sending him many thousands of dollars to support his various organizations—the Black Star steamship line, the militant Universal Negro Improvement Association, and its newspaper, the *Negro World.* Garveyism grew just as fast and at the same time as the Ku Klux Klan. At first, DuBois kept quiet about Garvey in *The Crisis* even as he attended its 1920 national convention. Privately, he was describing Garvey as a "demagogue," and his supporters "the lowest type of Negroes." But his suspicions of Garvey were confirmed when Garvey denounced the NAACP's call for social equality. In a February 1923 essay, "Back to Africa," DuBois called Garvey "a little, fat black man, ugly, but with intelligent eyes" whose back-to-Africa movement was doomed by his "pig-headedness." He further denounced Garvey as "a liar and blatant fool" deluded into thinking that the Ku Klux Klan would finance his Black Star Line. DuBois received death threats from Garveyites that only stopped when Garvey was convicted of mail fraud and sent to federal prison in 1925. Before Garvey was deported in 1927 to Jamaica, DuBois attacked him bitterly in *The Crisis,* calling him "without doubt the most dangerous enemy of the Negro race in America . . . . He is either a lunatic or a traitor."

DuBois's denunciation of Garvey and the back-to-Africa movement was to prove the central irony of his long life. Quarreling with other NAACP leaders over policy in 1934, he returned to the University of Atlanta, where he taught for the next ten years. During this time, his political views were shifting farther to the left. A member of the Socialist Party briefly, he had become a Democrat in 1912 to support Woodrow Wilson. He became critical of the Democrats as Franklin Delano Roosevelt rose to power, calling him "impudent" and a lackey in the *Crisis* in 1920; by 1931, he wrote that Roosevelt "is about to buy" the presidential nomination. During the Depression, DuBois, who was writing a syndicated *Pittsburgh Courier* column with a wide national audience, criticized the New Deal for doing "nothing for the tenant farmer and sharecropper," but he also sharply attacked 1936 Republican nominee Alf Landon. "If Roosevelt is defeated it will be because of his championship of organized labor and the Negro." As Fascism spread in Europe, DuBois made a seven-month tour spending much of his time in Nazi Germany and the Soviet Union. He wrote in his *Courier* column that he was astonished by the social progress there and he began to espouse making "common cause" with the working classes of Europe, Africa, and Asia. He also became more sympathetic to the American Communist Party, by 1938 writing privately, "I am not a communist but I appreciate what the communists are trying to do."

In 1944, he resigned again from Atlanta University to work for the NAACP as its director of research. Four years later, after another policy dispute, he left for good this time, dismissed for his increasingly leftist views. He became president of the Council on African Affairs. By 1947, DuBois was writing a torrent of books and articles calling for world peace and redistribution of wealth. In one year, he wrote fifty-one essays on African politics. He was also preaching a pan-African movement: "the emancipation of the black masses of the world is one guarantee of a firm foundation for world peace." At the same time, he lobbied for the abolition of the House Un-American Activities Committee in Congress, just beginning its investigations of Communist infiltration of American institutions. He labeled President Truman's Marshall Plan an attempt to establish American corporate domination over post-World War II Europe. In 1949, he became chairman of the Peace Information Center in New York. At the height of the Cold War in August 1950, United States Secretary of State Dean Acheson denounced the center as a Communist front: it was helping the Soviet Union to wage a "peace offensive" against the United States.

The year 1950 was another turning point in DuBois's long life. In July, his wife, Nina, long an invalid, died. He buried her beside their only child in Great Barrington. In August, even as Acheson denounced him, the American Labor Party asked DuBois to run for the United States Senate from New York. Laughing about it at first, he decided his candidacy would be an opportunity to speak out against increasing anti-Communist repression. With almost no budget and the press virtually boycotting his campaign, he addressed mass meetings in Harlem, the Bronx, Brooklyn, and Queens. Seventeen thousand came to hear America's leading black intellectual at Madison Square Garden. On August 11, the Justice Department ordered the Peace Information Center to register "as an agent of a foreign principal"; the center was dissolved on October 12, 1950, during DuBois's senatorial campaign. A federal grand jury in Washington, D. C., indicted DuBois and four other center staff members for "failure to register as agent of a foreign principal." His passport was suspended, he was barred from leaving the country, and his NAACP pension was cut in half. Prestigious journals and book publishers began to refuse his work. Although he was later acquitted after a federal trial, DuBois became embittered about American politics.

Nevertheless, his international reputation only grew. In 1952, he received a Grand International Prize of $7,000 from the World Peace Council that helped support his writing of *In Battle for Peace*. He had become increasingly dissatisfied with the slow progress of race relations in the United States and came to regard Communism as a solution to the problems of blacks. In the late 1950s, he traveled extensively in the U.S.S.R. and Communist China. In 1958, on his ninetieth birthday, he was honored in Peking by a celebration hosted by Premier Chou En-lai. In 1959, he received the Soviet Union's Lenin Peace Prize in Moscow "for strengthening world peace." In the United States, he was the first black elected to the National Institute of Arts and Letters.

On a visit to Ghana, where he was planning to edit an African encyclopedia, he was offered citizenship by President Khame Nkrumah. In 1961, at age ninety-three, he renounced his U.S. citizenship, became a member of the Communist Party, and moved to Ghana. In his application to join the Communist Party, he wrote that he had been "long and slow" in deciding to give up on progress for blacks in America. Nearly forty years after denouncing Marcus Garvey, W.E.B. DuBois left the United States and moved to Accra, where he lived for four more years. He died at age ninety-five on August 27, 1963. His death was announced the next day from the podium in Washington, D.C., at the high point of the Freedom March. After Roy Wilkins, executive director of the NAACP read the announcement of DuBois's death and there was an ovation from the throng, Martin Luther King, Jr. stepped to the microphone and delivered his famous, "I Have a Dream" speech. Faraway, in Accra, Ghana, the U.S. Embassy did not even lower its flag to half-mast and the U.S. ambassador spurned the funeral.

QUESTIONS FOR THOUGHT AND DISCUSSION

1. Given his upbringing in a virtually all-white Massachusetts town, and his graduation from Harvard with a Ph.D., was W.E.B. DuBois a fitting champion of racial equality in the United States? In what ways was his idea about the "talented tenth" a reflection of his own achievements?

2. Why did DuBois ultimately reject the accommodationist approach to race relations put forth by Booker T. Washington? What was DuBois's alternative?

3. On what grounds did DuBois criticize Marcus Garvey and the Back to Africa movement which had such strong appeal in the late 1910s and early 1920s?

4. Why did DuBois himself eventually sour on America and the hope for racial equality in the United States? Did DuBois give up too soon, or was he all too accurate in his ultimate pessimism?

SUGGESTED READINGS

Clarke, John E., ed. *Marcus Garvey and the Vision of Africa*. New York: Random House, 1974.

Cronon, E. David. *Black Moses: The Story of Marcus Garvey and the Universal Negro Improvement Association*. 2nd ed. Madison, Wis.: U of Wisconsin P, 1968.

DuBois, W.E.B. *Writings*. New York: Library of America, 1986.

Harlan, Louis R. *Booker T. Washington: The Making of a Black Leader, 1856–1901*. New York: Oxford UP, 1972.

Lewis, David Levering. *W.E.B. DuBois: Biography of a Race, 1868–1919*. New York: Holt, 1993.

Marable, Manning. *W.E.B. DuBois, Black Radical Democrat*. Boston: Twayne, 1986.

Rudwick, Elliott. *W.E.B. DuBois, Voice of the Black Protest Movement*. Urbana: U. of Illinois P, 1960.

8

Eugene V. Debs

*T*he year 1912 marked a turning point in American history. Only a year earlier, a catastrophic fire at the Triangle Shirtwaist Company in New York City had caused the deaths of 146 men and women locked in to keep out union organizers. The tragedy galvanized public opinion against unsafe working conditions as little else in the thirty-year struggle for labor reform had done. The Progressive Era and its accompanying spirit of reform was sweeping the country, touching most Americans in some way. Progressives set out to humanize living and working conditions, which had grown increasingly harsh over a half-century of industrialization and urbanization.

There was a fundamental optimism about the possibilities of sweeping reform in the air: progressives believed that if they learned about a problem, informed the public about it, and brought pressure on government, they could find and enforce a solution. Believing that the world could be made better for most people, the progressives, appealing to the great mass of farmers, workers, and the growing middle class, swept everything before them.

By 1912, a Progressive tide overwhelmed the Democratic National Convention: after forty-six ballots, reform Governor Woodrow Wilson of New Jersey was nominated over machine politician Champ Clark. The Republican Party was split in a desperate fight between incumbent President William Howard Taft and former President Theodore Roosevelt, who formed a third party, the Progressives, or Bull Moose Party. The Socialists would draw a million voters away from traditional parties as labor leader Eugene V. Debs won the support of factory workers, disillusioned Populists, socialist intellectuals, tenant farmers, lumberjacks, and coal miners. With Socialist mayors in thirty-three cities, the Socialist Party had increased its votes tenfold in twelve years. Not content with the Victorian notion of human progress to bring about reform, the Socialists, sparked by their firebrand orator, Eugene V. Debs, were calling for radical changes that would redistribute wealth among the workers.

EUGENE VICTOR DEBS, the son of Alsatian immigrants who came to America immediately after the suppression of the Socialist revolts all over Europe in 1848, was born in Terre Haute, Indiana, on November 5, 1855. His parents, the French-born Jean Daniel and Marguerite Marie Debs, named their first son after two Romantic Era literary figures, Eugène Sue and Victor Hugo. And all through his childhood, young Debs loved to listen as his father read aloud to him from the works of Romantic writers such as Goethe and Victor Hugo, with their emphasis on individual, objective experience as the way to truth.

As a leader of Socialism who had already run for the Presidency at the beginning of the twentieth century and was to make it the strongest third party up to that time, Debs was to acknowledge his debt especially to Hugo, whose immortal *Les Misérables* and the *Hunchback of Notre Dame* had stressed the struggle of the oppressed against tyranny and injustice. "Victor Hugo prophesied that the present century (the twentieth) would abolish poverty," Debs wrote in 1903. "He foresaw the day when all the earth would be fair and beautiful and all mortals brethren." It was Debs' assuming the mantle of the dead Romantic literary hero that so vexed other reformers as, with fiery words and jabbing finger, he crisscrossed the United States for thirty-five years, stirring the social conscience of the Industrial Age to action.

Born to a life in his father's grocery business in Terre Haute, Debs never knew the poverty he preached against. His parents loved learning, and Eugene was known even as a child for his generosity and his readiness to help others. While he was well-liked, he was not interested in school, much preferring his father's readings of Hugo, Goethe, Racine, and Corneille, writers who strongly influenced not only his social conscience but helped him develop his great oratorical skills and gave him a larder full of literary references for his speeches and writings.

Bored by the rote teaching of the "Three Rs" in school, he also found working after school in his father's store stultifying. Like many boys his age, he was attracted to the romance of the railroads. At age fourteen, he left school and made his bookish parents unhappy by taking his first (and thoroughly unromantic) job on the Vandalia Railroad. It was his job to clean the grease from the trucks under passenger cars for fifty cents a day. Within the year, the hard-working, cheerful Debs was promoted to painter and then, in 1873, at only seventeen, he became a fireman, riding the rails and shovelling coal into the locomotive boiler all day. When he experienced his first and only layoff, the nightmare of the workingman, that year in the Panic of 1873, he left home and went to St. Louis, Missouri, where he found a job as a fireman. It was a dangerous job and, when a friend died under a locomotive's wheels, Debs finally listened to his mother's pleading and went home to Terre Haute, in 1874. He had seen not only hard work but, especially in St. Louis, poverty and suffering in urban squalor for the first time.

Reluctantly returning to the grocery business, Debs, now nineteen, worked as a billing clerk for the largest wholesale house in the Midwest. He hated the job and kept up his friendships with railroad workers. When the head of the national Brotherhood of Locomotive Firemen came on a union-organizing trip to Indiana, Debs joined the Brotherhood and was elected secretary of the newly-formed Terre Haute lodge, at age twenty beginning his half-century association with the labor movement. He also kept up his lifelong habit of reading late in the night. He founded a weekly debating society, the Occidental Literary Club, which sponsored the visits of famous guest lecturers who were to have an impact on his thinking, including the poet James Whitcomb Riley, who became his friend, and the agnostic orator Robert G. Ingersoll.

Debs' popularity in Terre Haute led in 1879 at age twenty-four to his first brush with politics when he ran for and won the post of city clerk on the Democratic ticket. Reelected in 1881, he campaigned successfully in 1885 for the Indiana state legislature on a platform promising new laws to protect workers, but when he sponsored a bill requiring railroads to compensate workers for on-the-job injuries, he failed. So discouraging was his brief experience in Indiana's thoroughly pro-business legislature that Debs declined to seek a second term.

Burning midnight oil, he had kept his political job while rising in union ranks, becoming assistant editor of the *Locomotive Firemen's Magazine* in 1878, and editor two years later even as he became secretary-treasurer of the national union. He attained high union office in 1880 just as most of the Brotherhood's delegates to the national convention were about to give up. Promising to expunge the union's debt, he urged the union to give him one more year to reenliven the Brotherhood. Debs and his fellow officers succeeded, increasing membership, eliminating the debt, and making their magazine nationally read and respected. The tall, good-looking, friendly, twenty-five-year-old unionist was well on his way to the forefront of the labor movement.

At first an opponent of strikes, the idealistic young Debs predicted their number would decline and eschewed violence, in his magazine writings declaring "we do not believe in violence and strikes as means by which wages are to be regulated, but that all difference must be settled by mutual understanding arrived at by calm reasoning." He also opposed the use of the boycott, "a terrible weapon to be used only when a terrible wrong exists." He believed workers would prevail "by logic and law and by the intelligent use of the ballot." After the failure of the Chicago, Burlington, and Quincy strike of 1888 in which his union participated, he tempered his pacifism, now declaring the strike "the weapon of the oppressed." By the mid-80s, too, he came to espouse unions that included all the various trades within one industry as opposed to the craft unions of the time. Craft unions were made up, like medieval guilds, only of the master craftsmen in one plant and excluded all less-skilled workers and other work sites within the trade, the prevailing style of union at the time. By 1886, he was calling editorially for "unity of action," for the "engineer and fireman [to] stand together side by side."

The fear of many union members at the time was that they would be "amalgamated," swallowed up by such nationwide giants as the Knights of Labor. But that did not bar federations of unions. "If labor is ever to reach the goal of equality with capital in shaping policies," he editorialized in 1887, "it will have to federate." After the collapse of the Chicago and Burlington strike, Debs saw the need for labor federations as urgent: "If corporations and the press confederate to overwhelm workingmen when they demand redress of grievances, they too must federate." He still believed the strikes could be avoided: "Instead of a strike there would be arbitration." In June 1888, he called on all labor organizations in the United States to form a federation: "They would exert a moral power which would bear down all

UPI/Bettmann

A fiery orator who supported himself with his socialist writings, Eugene V. Debs made his fifth run for President from federal prison in 1920.

opposition." By June 1893, his efforts had led to the formation of the American Railway Union, of which he was elected president at age thirty-eight. The union had its first victory in late 1893 over the Great Northern Railroad. But within a few months this early success led to utter failure in the great Pullman strike of 1894.

Workers of the Pullman Palace Car Company, because it operated a few miles of track near Chicago to switch its equipment, were eligible to join the new union. After the Panic of 1893, Pullman tried to cut workers' wages, which were already so low workers could hardly pay rent in company-owned housing and food in company stores. When Pullman workers struck, Debs ordered a sympathy ARU strike: 100,000 railroad workers nationwide refused to handle Pullman cars. A general railroad strike resulted. Declaring that the strikers were interfering with the United States mails, which traveled by rail, President Grover Cleveland sent in Federal troops. When they arrived in the Chicago area, violence erupted and much railroad property was destroyed over several days' time. Crowds of rioters gathered and fought with soldiers: several rioters were shot and many injured as hundreds of boxcars burned and railway switches were smashed.

After Debs ignored a Federal court injunction to end the boycott of mail-bearing trains, he and other ARU officers were arrested and charged with conspiracy to obstruct a mail train and contempt of a Federal court order. He was convicted of the contempt charge and jailed for six months in Woodstock, Illinois, where he was held in the home of the sheriff. His arrest had ended the Pullman strike and his imprisonment shattered the ARU. His jailing at age forty made him a national union hero and he received hundreds of letters a day and large crowds of visitors. He also had time to write a weekly article for the Chicago *Evening Press* and edit the ARU's *Railway Times*. At this time, too, he announced his conversion to Socialism. It had not been a sudden conversion, however; as early as 1884, he wrote, "To take a man's money out of his pocket is larceny" and "it should be made impossible for one man or a few men to control the property and happiness of thousands of their fellow creatures." The Pullman strike and his arrest obviously precipitated Debs' public announcement. A decade later, in 1903, Debs wrote of his "blissful ignorance" and "utter failure to grasp the significance, scope, and character of the Socialist movement." Released from jail, Debs received a hero's welcome from a crowd of 100,000 in Chicago.

Abandoning the Democratic Party over Grover Cleveland's handling of the Pullman strike, Debs was very nearly nominated as a presidential candidate of the new People's Party in 1896 and gave many speeches supporting it. Enormously popular, he was also coming to be considered a threat at this time by other union leaders, especially Samuel Gompers, president of the American Federation of Labor. Gompers had taken a strong dislike to Debs. In October 1897, he wrote to another union leader,

> There can be no denying that Debs can say most pleasing things to one, and, yet, a short time before and after ascribe to that same person the most malevolent of designs, and even with all that he is not a bad fellow, I firmly believe, but brainy, bright— but the apostle of failure.

As Debs spoke out against craft unions in late 1897, Gompers again criticized him to a Boston labor leader for advocating "so very many different things."

What Gompers could not yet grasp was that Debs was in the process of transforming what was left of the American Railway Union into the Social Democratic Party of America. By the 1900 presidential election, Debs made his first of five unsuccessful bids for the Presidency, polling 96,116 votes. In 1901, he formally founded the Socialist Party of America; in 1904, it nominated Debs for President and he polled 402,321 votes, four times the 1900 total. He campaigned on the Red Special, a rented train that carried him to small towns and large cities nationwide. His "whistlestop" tour turned out enthusiastic crowds to see and hear the now-famous orator as he leaned far out toward the crowd, jabbed with a forefinger and berated the wealthy for the conditions the poor lived in. But his campaign war-chest was usually so low his train nearly became stranded on the West Coast.

Between elections, Debs spent much of his time now in Girard, Kansas, waiting and editing the Socialist weekly, *Appeal to Reason*. Running again in 1908, he disappointed Socialists by receiving only 420,793 votes, half what they hoped for. By 1912, the party was split and its right wing tried to block his fourth bid, but he prevailed and conducted a vigorous campaign. His fiery reform-minded oratory may have turned out more voters for the liberal Democrat Woodrow Wilson and the Progressive "Bull Moose," Theodore Roosevelt, but when the votes were counted, Debs received 897,011, or six percent of the votes cast, the highest proportion of votes ever polled by an American Socialist candidate.

Nearly sixty now, Debs decided to retire and live from the income of his writings. He settled into a large house he had built many years earlier, where his wife had often lived alone while he barnstormed the country. His retirement lasted two months because he couldn't stand it. He took a job writing for the Socialist monthly, the *National Rip-saw.* As the United States invaded Mexico in 1914, Debs condemned President Wilson's policies; when World War I broke out in Europe that same year, he called for complete neutrality. Debs declined to run for President in 1916 at the peak of the Progressive era reform tide, tacitly supporting Wilson, who promised neutrality. But when Wilson brought the United States into the war, Debs called for a general strike.

The manifesto of a Socialist national convention in April 1917 denounced the war and urged party members to oppose it by any means in their power. This bold attack on U.S. entry was enthusiastically endorsed by Debs, and reflected similar opposition to the war by European socialists. As the government carried out widespread arrests of pacifists and labor union members under a new Sedition Act, Debs, at a Socialist state convention in Canton, Ohio, on June 16, 1918, bitterly attacked the Wilson Administration. Four days later, a Federal grand jury in Cleveland indicted him for violating the Espionage Act. On September 14, 1918, he was convicted, after a trial that lasted only four days, and sentenced to ten years in prison.

Debs did not try hard to win acquittal. There was not much in the Canton speech he hadn't said over and over for years. He had mentioned the war only once, but to speak out in opposition against the war at all had been declared seditious treason and that was enough to give the government the case it wanted. His position in court was that the speech was not a criminal act, that the Sedition Act itself violated the First Amendment guarantee of freedom of speech. But Debs refused to recant his speech and he called no defense witnesses. He told a packed courtroom:

> From the beginning of the war to this day, I have never by word or act been guilty of the charges embraced in this indictment. If I have criticized, if I have condemned, it is because I believe it to be my duty, and that it was my right to do so under the laws of the land. This country has been in a number of wars and every one of them has been condemned by some of the people, among them some of the most eminent men of their time . . . .

The United States Supreme Court rejected Debs's appeal in March 1919, and he was imprisoned in April at Moundsville, West Virginia, where he was assigned to work in the prison hospital. Transferred to the maximum security Federal penitentiary at Atlanta, Georgia, he worked in a prison clothing warehouse. The Socialists again nominated him to run for President in 1920; it was the first presidential campaign conducted behind bars. But the Socialists had split—the left wing supporting the Russian Revolution. Debs refused to join the Communists. He received 919,000 votes, only 3.5 percent of the total vote, even though women were voting for the first time. Nearly one million Americans had voted for a jailed radical, yet President Wilson refused a recommendation by his own attorney general to commute Deb's sentence.

When President Warren G. Harding took office, he used his first Christmas pardon to commute Debs' sentence; he also freed twenty-three other political prisoners, but he did not restore Debs' citizenship. As he left the Atlanta prison, the other prisoners roared their support of him. In *Walls and Bars,* he wrote:

My own heart almost ceased to beat. I felt myself overwhelmed with painful and saddening emotions. The impulse again seized me to turn back. I had no right to leave. Those tearful, haunting faces, pressing against the barred windows—how they appealed to me—and accused me!

In his last five years of life, Debs championed prison reform, became national chairman of the Socialists in 1923—the first time he had accepted a paid party post—and became the American champion of the underdog. One of his last lost causes was the Sacco and Vanzetti case: with many others worldwide, he believed Nicola Sacco and Bartolomeo Vanzetti had been condemned to death because of their political beliefs. He called for "a thousand protest meetings" and "a million letters of indignant resentment."

But his years in prison had weakened him and his wife's health, too. They sailed to Bermuda in March 1926, to recuperate. But his worries about their health only made matters worse and, on October 20, 1926, he suffered a fatal heart attack. The Chicago *Evening Post* put it for many of the wealthy and the poor who flocked to his funeral: "He loved his fellow man. We did not agree with him, but we could not help admiring him . . . He thought from the heart and his heart was always moved by the suffering and misfortunes of the underdog."

QUESTIONS FOR THOUGHT AND DISCUSSION

1. How did Eugene Victor Debs become committed to the Socialist cause? How would you characterize his commitment?

2. In what ways did the Pullman Strike transform Debs? Why were more traditional national labor leaders like Samuel Gompers not impressed with him?

3. Does it surprise you that Debs won six percent of the popular vote (nearly one million ballots were cast for him) for President in 1912? Why do you think the Socialist Party never grew any more successful than that in the United States?

4. What caused Debs to be imprisoned in 1918? Do you sympathize with him for the statements he made during his trial?

SUGGESTED READINGS

Currie, Harold W. *Eugene V. Debs*. Boston: Twayne, 1976.

Debs, Eugene V. *Letters of Eugene Debs*. Urbana: U of Illinois P, 1990.

Debs, Eugene V. *Writings and Speeches of Eugene V. Debs*. New York: Hermitage Press, 1948.

Ginger, Raymond. *Eugene V. Debs: A Biography*. New York: Collier, 1962.

Morgan, H. Wayne. *Eugene V. Debs*. New York: UP, 1962.

Salvatore, Nick. *Eugene V. Debs: Citizen and Socialist*. Urbana: U of Illinois P, 1982.

9

Woodrow Wilson

Few leaders in American history have presided over as much change as Woodrow Wilson. His two terms in the White House linked the immigrant farmer epoch with the modern urban state. During his tenure, city-dwellers became a majority in the United States for the first time, and skyscrapers began to rise over them. When Wilson began campaigning from the rear platform of a train, only 500,000 Americans owned automobiles; by the end of his second term, a rapidly-expanding network of roads were jammed by eight million cars. The electrical industry rapidly illuminated homes, businesses and factories for seventy percent of the nation's population. Rapid industrialization only accelerated with American entry into World War I; government became more centralized and industry more standardized. Scrapping the Monroe Doctrine, Wilson brought the United States out of its isolation and sent a military expedition to Europe after a sustained, vast, military intervention in Mexico.

Just how this unlikely world leader, ranked by historians as one of the most effective Presidents, came to power and ushered America into the modern age is itself the story of the United States in transition.

THOMAS WOODROW WILSON's earliest remembrance (he dropped the "Thomas" when he got to college) was the outbreak of the Civil War. It was on a day in November 1860, and, at four years old, Tommy Wilson was swinging on the gate of his father's house in Augusta, Georgia, where his father was the minister of the First Presbyterian Church, across the street from the imposing red brick parsonage. The little boy saw two men meet on the sidewalk and heard one of them say shrilly, "Lincoln is elected and there'll be war!"

For most of the war, Augusta stayed safe, its gray-uniformed companies of men marching off to a war that seemed foreign. Most of its 15,000 people were associated with manufacturing for this faraway struggle. Augusta was a center for rolling mills, furnaces, railroad shops, and cotton spinning mills. Yet Tommy Wilson saw enough during his boyhood to make him loathe war—wounded soldiers in his father's church, Yankee prisoners confined in a nearby stockade, terrifying rumors of William Tecumseh Sherman and the approach of his bloodthirsty "bummers" on their murderous march through Georgia.

He was never to forget all Augusta's men riding out to resist Sherman, and especially of one particular troop of men in every sort of clothing riding past the house one day to join the Confederate army and of bravely yelling at them, "Go get your mule!" He remembered years of scarcity, of less and less food as the war dragged on, of his mother's necessary frugality, making soup from cowpeas ordinarily only fed to cattle. And he remembered the anxiety of all the women and children of Augusta as the men remaining in town armed themselves and marched valiantly in the direction of Sherman. That night, as the town kept vigil with Reverend Joseph Wilson in the church, all the gaslights blazed all night in the parsonage, but Sherman never came. Young Wilson was nine when the war ended and Federal troops did march in to occupy it through Reconstruction.

Tommy was a boy who always ran everywhere. He was thrilled when the first streetcar came to town and he made friends with the drivers, sometimes working the brakes and the switches. He also learned to ride his father's big, black, buggy horse. Since he had a horse, his father's big house, stable, barn, and walled-in grounds to play in, he got to be a natural leader. He also became a storyteller, delighting in reciting James Fenimore Cooper's *Leatherstocking Tales* and acting out the parts of lurking Indians.

His father, a learned, wise, and determined man, patiently taught Tommy himself. Not understanding that his son suffered from a form of dyslexia, he kept him home from school, which was haphazard in the wartorn town anyway. The boy's mother and sisters took turns reading aloud to him from Sir Walter Scott and Charles Dickens. On weekends, the father took Tommy on tours of Augusta's factories—a corn mill, a munitions plant, and an iron foundry—and taught him to write up reports, explaining clearly what he'd seen. His father was a master of the English language and insisted on no less from his son. Mainly, Reverend Wilson taught his son to fight his handicap, and every day, the family read the Bible aloud together. Later, Wilson acknowledged that his father was the strongest influence on his life.

Reverend Wilson was something of a missionary, a Scots Irishman born in Ohio who spent his entire working life in the South. He had taught at Hampden-Sydney College in Virginia as a young theologian, then had been a pastor in Staunton, Virginia, in the Shenandoah Valley, where Tommy was born on December 28, 1856. A year later, he had brought his growing family to Augusta. A noted, if quarrelsome, theologian, he was Stated Clerk of the General Assembly of the Presbyterian Church in the United States from 1865 to 1898. Mixing sternness, satire, and affection in educating his own children, he was, his son later said, "one of the most inspiring fathers that a lad was ever blessed with."

When Tommy was fourteen, his father became a professor in the Presbyterian theological seminary at Columbia, South Carolina, and the family moved again, this time to a war-ravaged city slowly rebuilding. Wilson saw the devastation wrought by Sherman's army, which had burned the once beautiful city to the ground.

After three years of being privately tutored in Latin and Greek, in 1873 Wilson enrolled in Davidson College, at Davidson, North Carolina, also still suffering from the effects of war. He had to carry his own water and firewood and perform other chores. Wilson did well in his first year away from home; he liked college, but his health was poor, and it forced him to go home for a year. His father, after a bitter feud at the seminary, resigned and took the family to a new ministry in Wilmington, North Carolina. Brilliant in isolation, Reverend Wilson did not work well with others.

In the year he had to stay home, young Wilson decided he wanted to go to Princeton University. He spent his time preparing himself, teaching himself shorthand, and studying Greek and Latin. He also began writing articles and publishing them in the *North Carolina Presbyterian.* Taking the train north in 1875 as so many other Southern boys had done, he found Princeton an exciting new world where he made lifelong friends. An A-student, he was enthralled by the lectures of the reform-minded president, James McCosh. Wilson had never been out of the South until age nineteen and would spend most of his first thirty years there, but at Princeton, a traditional meeting ground between North and South, he formed a strong nationalism. He found he had a powerful intellect and devoted much of his energy developing it, not only in studying history, politics, and literature, but in student activities as well. He became Speaker of the Whig Society, founded the Liberal Debating Club, became managing editor of the *Princetonian,* and president of the baseball association. He discovered that his passion was politics, vowing with a fellow student to "acquire knowledge that we might have power." He also basked in the honor of having his first article, "Cabinet Government in the United States," published in a national magazine, *International Review,* his senior year. In 1879, he graduated thirty-eighth in a class of 106, intent on public life.

That October, resisting pressure from his father to go into the ministry, he enrolled at the University of Virginia Law School, and began signing himself T. Woodrow Wilson. Once again, he became a prominent debater. He fell madly in love with a young cousin, Hattie Woodrow, proposed, and was rejected. Overdoing every aspect of his law school life, he became ill and had to go home early in 1880. For a year and a half, as he recovered, he studied law, history, and literature. Admitted to the bar, he moved to Atlanta, heart of the new South, and set up a law partnership with a University of Virginia acquaintance. Because they attracted few clients, he had plenty of time to study the South's political problems and write newspaper articles. His sole act of distinction in Atlanta was to testify before the United States Tariff Commission, which published his report. After less than a year, he abandoned the practice of law and renewed his studies at Johns Hopkins University in Baltimore, Maryland, which was just embarking on the German system of graduate teaching of history.

For nearly the next thirty years, Woodrow Wilson was a distinguished scholar, earning honors enough to have earned a place in the history books even without entering politics. At Johns Hopkins, he came into contact with brilliant men pioneering in professional studies of history. He worked hard and honed his writing style. In 1883, on a summer break, he visited Rome, Georgia, where he met Ellen Louise Axson: they were married June 24, 1885. She became the most influential person in his adult life, appreciating his greatness and sympathizing with his ideals.

The year they were married, Wilson published his first book, *Congressional Government, A Study in American Politics.* The book, an instant success, was widely praised and Johns Hopkins accepted it as his Ph.D. thesis. It was a critical analysis, about which he had been thinking for at least a decade, and it was not friendly to Congress. He had been an observant boy during the impeachment of President Andrew Johnson, and a thoughtful college student of English and American history during the scandals of the Grant administration, when the president's congressional associates were implicated in corruption. He had watched President Garfield start to crack down on the spoils system and he had studied the tariff system, advocating (as he would in his own presidency) reducing the tariff even as President Arthur ran into stiff opposition on Capitol Hill. Young Wilson struck a popular note when he wrote "the prestige of the presidential office has declined with the character of the Presidents . . . and the character of the Presidents has declined as the perfection of selfish party tactics has advanced." Like his other early writings (he wrote a series of biographical sketches and speeches), this book revealed Wilson's admiration for great statesmen such as Washington, Lincoln, and Jefferson. He believed in America and in the orderly, steady growth of American institutions. He feared the unregulated growth of corporations and had disdain for Congress and congressmen. He preferred the British system of cabinet government. The book also revealed his fear of the tide of recent immigrants and the radicalism he saw coming with them from Eastern Europe. Most of all, it revealed his yearning to see the nation ruled by a wise, eloquent teacher figure and national leader who would "master multitudes" while instructing them how to "keep faith with the past" by espousing "the progress that conserves." There can be little question he already could imagine himself in that role.

In autumn 1885, Wilson became an associate professor of history at Bryn Mawr College, an all-women's school on Philadelphia's Main Line. Three years later, he became professor of history and economics at Wesleyan University, in Middletown, Connecticut, where he also successfully coached football. He preached to his players his own personal dogma: "Go in to win. Don't admit defeat before you start." At Wesleyan, he published *The State,* one of the first textbooks in comparative government. In 1890, his *alma mater,* Princeton, offered him the post of professor of jurisprudence and political economy. For the next twenty years, he would stride the tree-lined walkways interlacing the rural New Jersey campus as he became one of America's best known historians. A popular lecturer, in 1902 he became the first layman elected president of the all-male college.

In his eight years as president, he made Princeton one of the preeminent American universities. He introduced a new method of teaching, the praeceptorial system, which broke large lectures down into small discussion groups presided over by faculty members, including the college president. No professor was allowed to remain aloof from students. He also did battle with the private eating clubs, Princeton's fortresses of snobbism. In addition, he pioneered the Quad Plan, which set up separate colleges, each arranged in a quadrangle around a central court with its own dining hall, dormitories, master, and tutors. Favored by students, the plan was opposed by many alumni who enjoyed coming back to their dining clubs for football games and reunions. Finally, the trustees asked him to withdraw his plan, which was later adopted by Harvard and Yale. He also ran into stiff resistance over his proposals for a graduate school, which he tried to integrate with the college as the center of the campus's intellectual life.

Modern medical detective work has shown that Wilson may have suffered from a massive stroke in 1906 during these academic controversies. Only his sheer will and determination helped him recover. He kept his illness secret but he emerged less tractable and less willing to compromise. For years, he battled Dean Andrew West. In the end, when an alumnus left a fortune to Princeton on condition Dean West remain in charge of the graduate school, the Dean won out and moved the graduate campus to the edge of town. Wilson retreated behind iron fences and gardens into Prospect Hall, a presidential palace.

His struggles at Princeton won Wilson wide publicity as a reformer fighting for democracy and against snobbery. New Jersey Democratic leaders saw him as a possible gubernatorial candidate who could campaign for the common people against the rich. By 1910, as the progressive reform spirit swept the state and the nation, the corruption-ridden city Democratic machines needed a squeaky-clean candidate. When party boss James Smith, Jr., and Colonel George B.M. Harvey, editor of *Harper's Weekly* and a Democratic power broker, approached Wilson, he readily accepted. Wilson decided he wanted to use the governor's office as a springboard to the White House. On October 10, 1910, he resigned his Princeton post to campaign for governor.

Wilson's eloquent Sunday-sermon oratory stirred large audiences and he was elected governor of New Jersey by a majority of 49,056 votes, the largest majority ever received by a Democrat. Putting together a coalition of reformers from both parties, he disavowed Smith's machine politics and, when Smith ran for the U.S. Senate, backed a rival candidate, who won. The national press came to watch the idealist from New Jersey who was pushing a series of reforms through its legislature. His campaign promises, for primary election reform, corporate holding company and public utilities regulation, a workmen's compensation law, and school and city government reforms, all passed. Seeking the support of individual lawmakers and attending their secret caucuses, he often appealed directly to the people, influencing public opinion through the press to keep pressure on legislators for his reform agenda.

By 1911, as the Democratic Party sought a replacement for the four-times failed presidential contender, William Jennings Bryan, Wilson seemed to the party's progressive wing the ideal flagbearer for the 1912 election. With his gray suits, ascetic leanness, *pince-nez* eyeglasses, and resounding rhetoric, he appeared the essence of no-nonsense, reform-minded father-figure and teacher to the nation. His public image was almost priestly: no journalist or ordinary citizen got to see him frolicking on the floor with his children or singing with his daughter, Margaret, old-fashioned Southern songs or Gilbert and Sullivan or "Old Nassau," his Princeton fight song, or his favorite hymns—"The Son of God Goes Forth to War" and "The Strife of Life Is O'er." Presidential campaigners had not yet learned to exploit their families or their private lives.

By 1912, Wilson was only a long-shot contender for the nomination as he started making speeches on national issues around the country. In Denver, Colorado,

The Bettmann Archive

Son of a minister, Woodrow Wilson preached a peaceful reform agenda, but author-
ized an invasion of Mexico and brought the United States into World War I.

he spoke on "The Bible and Progress"; at Harrisburg, Pennsylvania, on "Democracy's Opportunity"; in Lexington, Kentucky, on "The Lawyer in Politics"; and at Carnegie Hall in New York City on "The Rights of the Jews." He spoke on electoral reform, the tariff, on efficiency in government (a new idea), on government relations with business, and to one Democratic Party banquet in New York City speculating on "What Jefferson Would Do." By June 1912, he had won the confidence of Bryan, the official party leader, as he headed for Baltimore, Maryland. There Champ Clark, head of the St. Louis Democratic machine and Speaker of the House of Representatives, received a majority on the first ballot. But Wilson's progressive coalition did not desert him. On the fourteenth ballot, Bryan openly swung his support to Wilson, rising dramatically on the convention floor to announce that since Clark had the support of New York's Tammany Hall politicians, and he could not support anyone backed by Tammany Hall, he would have to switch to Wilson. On every ballot, Wilson gained more votes until he won on the forty-sixth. His campaign against renominated President William Howard Taft and "Bull Moose" third party candidate Theodore Roosevelt was no less dramatic. Wilson crisscrossed the country outlining his "New Freedom" liberal reform solutions to national problems. He won the popular vote by a landslide, receiving 435 of 531 electoral votes.

The first Southerner in the White House since Zachary Taylor, the fifty-six-year-old Wilson was the last president to ride to his inauguration in a carriage. He gave no inaugural ball, but gave the first presidential press conference, reasoning that the people had a right to know of his progress. For the first time since John Adams, he delivered his legislative proposals in person to a joint session of Congress, outlining his demand to lower tariffs and encourage domestic competition and world trade. This first reform passed six months later. He next proposed the most far-reaching reforms in American history to banking and currency laws to set "the business of this country free." He pushed creation of the Federal Reserve Board with twelve regional banks to assist the free flow of currency. As President, Wilson came to support many of the "New Nationalism" ideas Theodore Roosevelt had trumpeted in 1912, especially laws that increased government regulation of industry. Wilson's reforms included establishing the Federal Trade Commission to investigate and end unfair trade practices, the Clayton Antitrust Act to police big business dealings and promote competition, the Adamson Act to establish the eight-hour workday for railroad employees, and the Child Labor Act to limit children's working hours. Reviving the Internal Revenue Bureau and pushing through Congress a federal income tax law (actually already in motion when Wilson came in), he initiated heavy taxation of wealth. He also started programs to improve rural education and build rural roads. No president had ever brought about such sweeping reforms. Many traditional Democrats were upset because Wilson increased the power and scope of government, but most lauded Wilson's progressive use of the state to serve as a necessary check on business abuses. Under Wilson, the progressive spirit reached its zenith.

Yet Wilson was increasingly distracted from his domestic reform agenda by foreign affairs. When Victoriano Huerta seized power in Mexico and put to death his constitutionally-elected predecessor, Wilson told Congress that there could be no peace with Mexico while Huerta ruled. After failing to force out Huerta, Wilson allowed the dictator's rivals to buy arms in the United States. When Huerta forces arrested fourteen American sailors who had gone ashore in a launch in Tampico Bay, Wilson refused to accept Huerta's apology and demanded that he publicly salute the American flag. When the Mexican president refused, Wilson ordered the Atlantic Fleet to seize the main Mexican port of Vera Cruz. When Argentina, Brazil, and Chile offered to mediate, a truce was worked out and Huerta fled the country.

Peace might have survived if World War I had not broken out in Europe in August 1914. While Wilson declared a policy of strict neutrality, in fact he protected Mexico's oil supplies for the British (Mideast oil reserves were still distant mirages). The Royal Navy ran on fuel from the Tampico oilfields, making Mexico prey to intrigues by the European combatants. In the first oil war, Wilson intervened again in 1916 when the revolutionist Pancho Villa carried out a raid on the town of Columbus, New Mexico, sending in a large force under General John J. Pershing to pursue Villa deep into Mexican territory. The American incursion prompted the legitimate Mexican president, Venustiano Carranza, to warn that he would resist any further American invasion.

More than punishing a Mexican insurgent for a minor raid into United States territory, Wilson was actually protecting rich American interests. Americans had poured nearly one billion dollars (in late nineteenth century dollars) in capital to develop Mexican railroads, mines, oil, and ranches. American investment in Mexico accounted for more than half of all American investment in the Western Hemisphere and represented the largest United States investment in any foreign country. Continued tranquillity in Mexico to Wilson seemed crucial to continued American profits. By 1917, as U.S. involvement in the European war loomed, Wilson recognized the Carranza government. But U.S.–Mexican relations remained strained for many years.

At the outset of World War I, Wilson, reflecting public opinion and adhering to the Monroe Doctrine of noninvolvement in European affairs, declared the United States "must be neutral in fact as well as in name." But the German torpedoing of the British passenger liner *Lusitania*, which killed 128 Americans, enraged many Americans. Coolly, President Wilson secured a German promise not to torpedo neutral or passenger ships. In June 1916, Wilson won the renomination and campaigned on the Democratic slogan, "He kept us out of war." Despite early confusion over a slow vote count that made it appear Wilson had lost the election, he narrowly carried California (by 3,400) to win reelection by 277 electoral votes to 254 for his GOP opponent, Charles Evans Hughes of New York.

Even before he was sworn in for a second term, Germany chose to break its pledge and resumed unrestricted submarine warfare against merchant shipping, including the American ships that were largely benefiting England. Wilson quickly broke off diplomatic relations. British agents then revealed coded messages they said they had intercepted which revealed a German plot to arm the Mexicans in a war against the U.S. Finally, in March 1917, German submarines began to attack U.S. ships without warning. On April 2, Wilson went before a joint session of Congress and, his face ashen and his voice quivering, asked Congress to declare war against Germany: "The world must be made safe for democracy."

In stirring speeches, Wilson galvanized public opinion in a crusade that led to five million men enlisting to go "over there." Broadway musicals, Liberty Bond drives, films and popular songs all contributed to a frenzied war effort. Turning over most of the functions of government to his Cabinet officers and specially-created war boards, Wilson concentrated on statecraft. On January 8, 1918, in an address before Congress, he listed Fourteen Points as an outline for a peace settlement. Five points set down diplomatic ideals. Eight points touched on problems of territory and diplomacy among the European powers. The fourteenth point called for a permanent international organization to be set up—a League of Nations—to help prevent future wars. Wilson's list laid the foundations for peace negotiations that came only ten months later (after Russia withdrew from the war, caught up in its own revolution) and after millions of American troops began to bolster British and French forces on the Western Front. After an armistice was signed on November 11, 1918, Wilson became the first American president in office to travel abroad as he sailed on the USS *George Washington* to Europe to negotiate the Versailles Treaty.

Arriving to a tumultuous hero's welcome in Paris (where a boulevard was renamed after him), he also visited England and Italy, where he conferred with Pope Benedict XV (the first president in office to talk with a pope).

Wilson was less successful at Versailles, where he had to make concessions to the Allies that weakened his image at home as a peacemaker. He returned briefly in February, 1919, to confer with Congressional leaders: under the Constitution, the Senate has the right to approve or reject treaties. In his absence, a Republican majority had been elected in the off-year Congressional election. Wilson could not win Senate approval of the peace treaty without several amendments. He returned to France and won some concessions, then came back to the United States, exhausted, only to find stiffening congressional resistance to further American interference in "European affairs." Wilson decided to go around Congress by taking his case for the League of Nations directly to the people. On September 4, 1919, he began a long train tour through the Midwest and Far West.

But Wilson's popularity had waned as thousands of gassed and maimed veterans came home and as agents of the newly-created Federal Bureau of Investigation, unleashed by Attorney General J. Mitchell Palmer, had raided hundreds of union halls and radical meetings during the 1919–1920 "Red Scare." As the sixty-three-year-old Wilson, ignoring his doctor's advice, stumped hard for support of the League of Nations farther and farther from Europe, on October 2, 1919, he suffered a paralytic stroke. An invalid for the rest of his life, he refused to step down as President. Largely bedridden, he watched helplessly as Republican Senator Henry Cabot Lodge successfully led the opposition to the League, tacking on fourteen reservations that led to the defeat of League ratification in the Senate.

Although Wilson had wanted the League to be the central issue of the 1920 elections, it was not. Despite his very poor health, he wanted the Democratic Party to renominate him; it did not. The Republican candidate, Warren G. Harding, promising something he referred to as "normalcy," swept the Democrats from office. Wilson's rigid refusal to commute the sentence of Eugene V. Debs even after the war's end—and the nearly one million votes cast for the imprisoned

Socialist—undoubtedly further weakened the Democrats. Wilson received a Nobel Peace Prize for his efforts, but he was largely ignored as the increasingly isolationist Roaring Twenties began. Only partially able to use his arms and legs, he lived for three more years an invalid, able to go to movies and plays but unable to work. Once again, he was only able to listen as his family read books and newspapers to him. He died certain that he was right and that time and events would vindicate him. At his last public appearance, on Armistice Day 1923, Wilson said he could not refrain from saying that he had "the least anxiety about the triumph of the principles I have stood for." There had been "fools" before who had resisted God's will "and I have seen their destruction. . . . That we shall prevail is as sure as that God reigns." Three months later, Woodrow Wilson found peace. He died in his sleep on February 3, 1924.

QUESTIONS FOR THOUGHT AND DISCUSSION

1. How did Woodrow Wilson make a name for himself prior to his nomination by the Democrats for President in 1912? In what ways had Wilson already shown himself to be a progressive champion of his era?

2. What led Wilson to ask Congress to declare war on Germany and bring the U.S. into World War I? Was there sufficient reason to believe, as Wilson suggested, that the fate of democracy itself was on the line?

3. What was the significance of the Fourteen Points? Why did Wilson accede to the Versailles Treaty in spite of its deviation from his Fourteen Points peace program? Why did he fail to convince the Senate to ratify the treaty?

4. How would you rate Wilson as President? How does he compare with other presidents in terms of personal qualities, failings, and achievements? Should history treat him kindly?

SUGGESTED READINGS

Ambrosuis, Lloyd E. *Woodrow Wilson and the American Diplomatic Tradition: The Treaty Fight in Perspective*. Cambridge: Cambridge UP, 1987.

Blum, John Morton. *Woodrow Wilson and the Politics of Morality*. Boston: Little, 1956.

Bragdon, Henry Wilkinson. *Woodrow Wilson: The Academic Years*. Cambridge: Belknap, 1967.

Eisenhower, John S. D. *Intervention!: The United States and the Mexican Revolution, 1913–1917*. New York: Norton, 1993.

Ferrell, Robert H. *Woodrow Wilson and World War I*. New York: Harper, 1985.

Garraty, John. *Woodrow Wilson, A Great Life in Brief*. New York: Knopf, 1956.

Hecksher, August. *Woodrow Wilson*. New York: Scribner's, 1991.

Ions, Edmund S. *Woodrow Wilson: the Politics of Peace and War*. London: Macdonald, 1972.

Link, Arthur S. *Wilson*. 5 vols., Princeton: Princeton UP, 1947–1965.

_____. *Woodrow Wilson, a Brief Biography*. Cleveland: World Publishing, 1963.

_____, ed. *Woodrow Wilson: A Profile*. New York: Hill and Wang, 1968.

_____. *Woodrow Wilson: Revolution, War and Peace*. Arlington Heights, Ill.: AHM Publishing, 1979.

10

Theda Bara

At first, even the people with their hands on it could not recognize the newborn, freakish thing for what it was. How could they? Not for a thousand years had there been a new art and here it was, an art that would not stand still: moving pictures.

In the beginnings of the movie industry, the big picture was beyond everyone. Technicians, on the one hand, many of them trained by Edison, worked at solving strictly mechanical problems, such as how to move the film through the projector. But to have moving pictures to show, they needed the output of film makers, mostly technicians themselves trying to solve problems of art. David Wark Griffith, a rare early director who showed a poetic streak, made wild experiments as he moved the camera and manipulated light to set mood. For all his effort and artistic success, Griffith never saw movies as anything to be taken seriously. His work left him with no grand expectations about the future of moving pictures: "I give them a few years," he speculated.

Theda Bara, seen by 182,000,000 movie-going Americans in one year, understood that her work belonged to an irrational realm. The illusion of acting played a secondary role in her success. A reputation, what people had not yet learned to call her "off-screen" personality, fit seamlessly with her roles, they thought. Her story combines biographical fact and, of equal significance, America's reaction to a new species, the movie star.

WHEN THOMAS EDISON ran his kinetoscope for visitors to the Columbian Exposition in 1893, he celebrated his proof that pictures could be made to move. He could show small pictures, viewed through a peephole, in sequences as long as ninety seconds to people who lined up to view the wonder individually. Before long an enlarged version of that invention, now projected onto a screen, spread to many cities. It started to draw curious viewers, and changed America by making it possible to show the same picture to the masses at once, a first that would change art, politics, and ultimately imaginations.

By 1915, the year of *A Fool There Was,* Theda Bara's first film and her triumph, there were 13,000 movie houses in the United States. In New York alone there were more than 500. Those numbers radically changed the scale of an artistic reputation. Movies, more than theater, opera, or any existing art form, were big business. In 1915, the *New York Times* estimated that half a million people a day were seeing Bara's pictures. The profits on that first film alone were so great that her employer could take the important step of incorporating his vaudeville company into a motion picture production company and get his real start. Her employer was called William Fox.

Thanks to the stunning success of Theda Bara, the Fox studio prepared to turn out more films on the model of the one that had done the trick. Theda Bara agreed to work hard turning out films "like sausages," as she later said. Her plan at the outset was to star in films for five years, make a great deal of money, then quit. Fox paid Theda Bara $4,000 a week at a time when a good new car cost $400. For her part, the actress had to maintain a strenuous pace of work, and had to continue to play morally repulsive characters.

At the same time, just as filmmakers tried to turn technical innovation into a viable business, they knew that they had to understand what moving pictures did best. Pioneer moviemakers, not many years after Edison, first hit upon what would be the terminal inspiration for home movies and then home videos: film could be used to record. Early viewers at city moving picture houses witnessed naval battles of the Spanish-American War. When they did not record history (Annie Oakley and Buffalo Bill also won immortality on celluloid), early movies recorded art. Before directors comprehended that they had their hands on a new art, they produced what amounted to filmed theater. The camera, like a polite spectator, "watched" from one controlled and fixed angle, while its distance from the players stayed constant. Gradually, innovators such as Edwin S. Porter, an unrecognized artistic genius, invented a technique that would become known as editing, achieved through a unit called the shot. Porter grasped that an image away from the scene could be used to advance a story. As early as 1903 he made films sophisticated enough to convey a dream within a story.

An industry was cutting its teeth on solving what would have been an artistic problem before that time—how to use sequences of pictures to make meaning in a way that print and words did not. Filmmakers had to imagine how viewers would interpret pictures. They had to guess and risk that a meaning had been conveyed clearly enough to keep a story going. While working on films that were all in some way experimental, directors relied on stories that were well known or depicted historical events such as the execution of Mary Queen of Scots (1895). Not until the visionary director D. W. Griffith popularized a new view, a "close-up" of an actor's face or even of an object, did the style of storytelling break ground by adding a new element, a degree of intimacy with an actor that theater goers had never experienced. The power of seeing an enlarged and moving human face projecting some strong emotion surpassed any viewing experience possible up to that time.

Because early movies were silent, they could be shown to an international public with captions written in the language of the country where they played. The film industry transcended national boundaries immediately. In the years after Edison and up to roughly 1914, American films were being exported and, for the same linguistic reason, foreign filmmakers could offer serious competition for American audiences, and they did. Movies from Italy allowed that relatively newly organized country to insist on the legitimacy of its culture as its directors made historical epics that Americans enjoyed; French directors, wanting to seem modern, marketed their serials full of drama and thrills. That cosmopolitan character would be lost only a few years later for reasons of politics, not art.

From the beginning of the American film industry, producers understood that in order to draw a large audience to pictures, they needed to promote stars, a system they borrowed from opera and the theater. But the stars of such a new medium had no references, in a sense, because they lacked long or illustrious careers, the capital of publicists. So the more enterprising publicity people invented pasts for their stars that were impressive and sometimes deliberately dubious sounding.

Theda Bara, the best-known American actress from 1914 until the mid-twenties, proved that publicists could create a star. The siren of silent movies, Bara endures in a form more lasting than film. Only one of her thirty-nine films still exists today, yet our language has preserved a memory of her first starring role in the word "vamp," the term she taught everyone to use to refer to a woman who entices and then destroys men. Her beauty drew huge audiences, but some observers thought she appealed more to women than to men, a fact she accepted and explained. "The vampire I play is the vengeance of my sex upon its exploiters. I have the face of a vampire but the heart of a feminist." (If "vampire" has a more monstrous sense today, that original meaning was popularized by a later film starring Bela Lugosi.)

Fittingly, it all started with a picture, of the nonmoving kind. A painting by the famous English artist, Sir Philip Burne-Jones, displayed in London in 1897, shocked museum-goers with its image of a beautiful young woman in profile, her long dark hair hanging loosely, poised in a vaguely ambiguous push-up position over the body of a man who was either dead or dead tired because of something the woman has just finished doing. That painting inspired Rudyard Kipling, one of the museum-goers, to write a poem entitled "The Vampire" which ultimately became the basis for Bara's first film, *A Fool There Was*, in which she first showed Americans her evil ways. One of the most famous lines of early movies, repeated by generations of would-be sultry females, came from that film. "Kiss Me, My Fool," also became an ironic cliché, as women (and maybe even men) uttered a command they had read, not heard at the movies. The huge success of that wicked role confirmed what would become one of the guiding principles of moviemaking: virtue is not much fun to watch.

Like so many wicked women, Theda Bara was made, not born. The publicists who created her understood that any woman associated with devilment could not resemble American women in the audience. She would have to be, or at least seem to be, exotic. The public accepted that concept so wholeheartedly that it also went along with the outrageous story behind the name of this creature of illusion. *Bara,* which is *Arab* spelled backward, and *Theda,* an anagram of "death," suited perfectly the woman who had been born on an oasis, "in the shadow of the Sphinx," according to her handlers. The particulars of her past varied a little in variant forms

The Bettmann Archive

Theda Bara, here playing Carmen, embodied the dangerous seductive powers of female film stars of her era, earning her steady criticism from the nation's pulpits.

of the legend. Her mother had been an Arabian princess who either raised her daughter in an unsheltered way or who died shortly after giving birth. Her father, an Italian artist, a sculptor, had taught his daughter languages. Her knowledge of many languages made her clever name somehow more plausible.

Bara's vague association with the Sahara, a region familiar to Americans from the pages of *National Geographic,* made her an object of great curiosity. Her objectionably loose morals, according to her roles, incited a strong reaction in a country witnessing every kind of reform guided by the moralistic President Woodrow Wilson. It was impossible to be indifferent to "The Vamp."

Theda Bara made her unverified theatrical debut in London after being associated with several theatrical companies in Paris, the publicity staff asserted. Once the stories circulated more widely, her employers worked to keep the facade from showing any cracks. For one thing, Miss Bara signed a contractual agreement not to be seen in public. She spent her time in a West End Avenue apartment in New York City. Even walks in Central Park were out of the question because people started to recognize her.

When directed to help out, the star took pains to make the story of her origins stick. On a trip to the West Coast, for example, for her first film made outside New York, Miss Bara stopped in Chicago where she agreed to grant a press conference. On a sweltering day—before air conditioning—when journalists were finally allowed into her hotel suite, they found the actress covered from head to toe in extravagant furs. Her publicists, of course, reminded the newsmen that Miss Bara came from a very hot region and that she had never adapted to northern climates.

Stories of that interview also say that as soon as the newsmen left, Bara burst out laughing, as she often did when she and her sister read the latest publicity yarn. But in keeping her contract and her mystique intact, Bara cooperated with the mythmakers from Fox. While she never talked about her passport, she did claim to have been an Egyptian in a previous life: "I remember crossing the Nile in barges to Karnak and Luxor as plainly as I recall crossing the Hudson Ferry today to come to the studio at Fort Lee." Other stories, not from her publicists, gradually began to challenge the official version, but they were resisted.

In September 1915, *Photoplay* magazine wrote that it would "disbelieve those stupid people who insist that Theda Bara's right name is Theodosia Goodman and that she is by, of, and from Cincinnati." The magazine no doubt spoke for the many fans who would have been insulted at being disillusioned. But this unthinkable truth, so dreary, had made publicity necessary. No serious studio would dare to tell America that "the vamp" grew up in Cincinnati and moved east with her parents, brother, and sister to help her acting career. Her family, who always stayed close by, happily relocated to the center of the film world, somewhere between Manhattan and Jersey City. The entire family—parents, brother, and sister—changed their names to Bara.

Unlike other early stars, Theda Bara, who really was called Theodosia Goodman, went to college. After she graduated from Walnut Hills High School in Cincinnati in 1903, she attended the University of Cincinnati for two years. The record of her being in that high school class, incidentally, helped settle the difficult question of when she was born. Bara would never, on principle, reveal her age because of her conviction that a woman who would tell her age would tell anything. Later in her career, she let it be known that she was born in 1890, but census records, compiled without her approval, make it 1885.

Part of the power of movies came from their taking illusion, the whole basis of theater, and magnifying it in every sense. Audiences new to this powerful illusion experienced the moral hazards of Miss Bara's character so profoundly that they forgot they were seeing an actress in a role. In movie theater lobbies, women defaced Bara's picture on movie posters; in New York, a mother called the police when her little boy spoke to Miss Bara. She was denounced in churches. When the Chicago censor refused a permit to a new film in 1915, she filed a lawsuit for $100,000 and won.

Bara's offense, in the eyes of moviegoers, amounted to breaking all the rules. She stole husbands, took men's money, and somehow, in the space between captions and pictures, took away their strength, or even made them die. As she went on, she got worse, and audiences welcomed the pleasure of feeling indignant and even outraged. As the stakes got higher, to destroy one man was not always enough.

After her first film, Bara made eight more that year. In *Kreutzer Sonata,* she portrays a wicked adulteress who betrays her sister before being murdered by that sister. In the next film, *The Clemenceau Case,* her husband murders her because she has betrayed him. Then she appeared as *The Devil's Daughter,* before being the main character in *Lady Audley's Secret,* a film about a concealed murder in the lady's past. Finally, because Bara refused to be the villain again, the studio let her play Henriette in *The Two Orphans,* a character who looks out for her blind sister in Old France. However, Fox feared that audiences would abandon a reformed Bara, and called the next film *Sin,* intended to compensate for her lapse from wickedness. In the promotional material for that picture, Bara was billed as "Destiny's Dark Angel."

In the years that followed, people saw more of the same. The 1916 film *Destruction* showed how much Bara raised audiences' threshold of gullibility. The evil engine of that film, she tried to destroy both a father and a son, and then came close to wiping out a town by starting a strike. Advance announcements told people what they would see: "The most famous vampire in her most daring role bring ruin and disaster to thousands."

Audiences did not go to Bara's movies to see moral lessons. As she worked her magic, Theda's necklines plunged to new lows. When she played Cleopatra in 1917, she showed people what an exotic queen wore "in the shadow of the Sphinx." That film, the first one made in California rather than Jersey City or Fort Lee, New Jersey, made one million dollars.

Not all audiences reacted with scorn and outrage. The actress also received letters from women asking her advice in how to deal with their boyfriends and husbands. Her appearance on the screen found its imitators, not so much in scanty costumes, as in a subtler element in her charm. Women noticed, then recreated, her heavy, dark eye makeup, something moviemakers relied on to accent her pale skin in black and white movies. In those same movies, she often appeared wearing black, again to make her look pale. Before long, young American women, especially collegians known as "baby vamps," wore a lot of black. Because her movies were silent, something between fashion posing and pantomime, women could not imitate her voice or manner of speaking. But they could imitate her languid poses and exaggerated, slinky way of walking. Young women evoked exotic appeal in ways that shocked their conventional parents, not far removed from Victorian propriety, when they made sure to have incense burning in the house as a hint to make visitors aware of their secretly smoldering wishes. Glamour attached itself to any gesture toward the exotic as Americans began to think about Africa and Morocco as real places as they avidly followed the safaris of Theodore Roosevelt.

Fans had no inkling that simple physical caution explained some measure of Bara's slinking gait. The actress was so near-sighted that she could not quite make out chalk marks that showed the camera's range. To compensate, she rehearsed conscientiously by learning the position of objects on the set, then she navigated.

As Theda Bara's career thrived, the American film industry jumped into worldwide prominence, then domination for reasons that can be called accident, luck, or politics. In Europe, World War I had broken out. Continental filmmakers instantly lost their ability to stay in the international market as European states commandeered all supplies for the war effort. Movies could not be easily made. At that moment, American filmmakers moved faster than ever not only to turn out more movies but to show things that far outdistanced the budgets of strained economies elsewhere. Screen glamour became their capital, a commodity they could generate in lavish costumes and settings. The need to have variety in settings had made another shift in the industry. Filmmakers began to favor southern California for their work, where the weather and light let them shoot outdoors in any season and where they could find great variety in background, going from coast to hills, and from lavish gardens to desert. Climate made Hollywood.

World War I encouraged Americans to see themselves as isolated from other countries, an outlook that hurt Theda Bara's career first because of a role and ultimately in a more general way. In 1919, when Fox was trying to satisfy the vamp's continuing demands to play something besides a home-wrecking man-eater, Theda Bara got the lead in a film called *Kathleen Mavourneen*, the story of an Irish heroine. But the same lack of sophistication that made women send her hate mail now enraged audiences for a less fanciful reason. The Hibernia Society, as many proud Irish immigrants called themselves, organized demonstrators to throw stones at theaters where *Kathleen Mavourneen* was playing and lob stink bombs inside. They objected, they explained, to seeing the heroine of their nation portrayed by a Jewish actress. The family origins of Theodosia Goodman, whose father was indeed a prosperous Jewish tailor from Poland and whose mother a refined French-speaking Swiss woman, mattered a great deal during the isolationist years of World War I. The Russian Revolution of 1917 was so close, and fear of Bolsheviks, whom many Americans thought of as Jewish, still threatened a country awaiting the outcome of a European war. Theda Bara had starred in *The Rose of Blood,* a film on the Russian Revolution that was produced near the end of 1917, another complication in the confusion of art and life.

By 1919 Theda Bara's contract at Fox expired. She had made thirty-nine films and a personal fortune. She could have withdrawn from public life but wanted to continue to act, away from California, in theaters. Her part in a play called *The Blue Flame* brought her praise and success as long as she remained with a touring company. The shock came when she played the same role in New York. Now, the woman who had once been considered the incarnation of female desire and what she called "the revenge of a woman on men" by way of explaining her mass appeal, now made audiences laugh. Not by design. The reviews of her New York performance tell the story. According to Heywood Broun in the *Herald Tribune*:

> At the end of the third act Miss Bara said that God had been very kind to her. Probably she referred to the fact that at no time during the evening did the earth open and swallow up the authors, the star, and all the company.

The flame burned for a total of forty-eight performances.

One partial explanation for that failure must come from the difference between the demands of a live audience and those of a movie camera. Bara had developed a style of gestures, even facial expressions, for a camera shot to be shown before the printed captions that gave either a brief and obvious line of dialogue or an explanation or comment on the preceding image. A theater audience, on the other hand, not watching a close-up, needed actors to use the classical resources, voice, tone, and more emphasis on dialogue than décor. The success of films had changed theater in a way that must have seemed unfair. Because film could show settings in motion, for example, the art of theater sets had to change. Sets suddenly had to be more spectacular since theatergoers would be comparing them to backgrounds in movies where real palm trees moved and real waves broke on real beaches. No more cardboard water. Theater had to rely more than ever on language and on voices so well trained that a nuance in tone could make a line screamingly funny or scathing in its sarcasm, shades that silent movies could not attempt in the same way.

In fairness, the appeal of Theda Bara could not have endured in a world of men returning from World War I. The idea of exotic women had been exciting in 1914 because the chances of American men meeting any remained safely remote. In Europe, soldiers did not meet vamps, but they did meet prostitutes. Of the 3.6 million men who went off to war, 48,000 were killed in combat, and meanwhile the number of American deaths caused by venereal disease doubled.

When the government of the United States recognized the proportions of this developing problem, it relied on the effective new medium of film to educate men and women. First, training films were shown to soldiers. In what can only be called propaganda movies, men were warned about the dangers they faced if they did not exercise self-control. In one of the most shocking uses of film up to that point, men were shown what they could expect if they contracted venereal disease. Unforgettable pictures of diseased body parts made an impression more disgusting than any sermon had ever managed. In the same spirit of public health, films were made for women who lived near army bases warning them of the dangers of casual sex with soldiers. Audiences who had seen diseased genitals up close on the screen could not experience the old pleasure of feeling indignant about a woman who laid men low with smoldering looks. America's innocence was gone.

In the same years that Theda Bara had grown famous, women had grown independent. By 1920, American women could vote. As part of their coming of age politically, they had created enough political pressure to bring about the Volstead Act of 1919 which began the era of Prohibition. That feeling of political muscle meant that women did not need to get their revenge on men by watching an exotic charmer who could make the likes of Mark Anthony weak in the knees. Closer to home, American women knew that they could punish their own husbands and fathers by withholding what they really wanted—a legal drink.

For their part, men who had fought in World War I, who had seen combat or had been gassed, could no longer suspend disbelief in the old way. They knew that they had nothing to fear from a screen vamp. A woman who had lost her virtue was to be censured at best or even enjoyed perhaps, according to the hardened young Americans, but she was not to be feared. The fact of women voting at home and beginning to work outside the home had finished off the distance between the separate spheres of men and women that Victorian propriety had valiantly tried to uphold. Moral rectitude shifted from being primarily a quality that men valued in their women, whom they worked to shelter from the corrupt world. In the new order, women saw moral rectitude as one more thing that they could demand of men.

As for the vamp herself, she held to her earlier plan. In 1921 Theda Bara married Charles Brabin, a film director who had worked first as an actor, playing Abraham Lincoln in an early Edison film, and then had been trained by D. W. Griffith. The couple met when he directed her in *Kathleen Mavourneen* (1919). They bought a home in Beverly Hills where they had a married life that gave no hint of either partner's misbehaving. The vamp liked nothing better than to cook for her friends, sometimes preparing gourmet meals or just as likely serving them sauerkraut and sausages.

The facts of Theda Bara's life matter far less than her legend. Many of the parts she played would inspire later directors and actresses in remakes of her early famous efforts: *Carmen, East Lynne, Under Two Flags, Romeo and Juliet, The Darling of Paris, Camille, Cleopatra, Madame DuBarry.* Her significance had been created and remained in the imaginations of her fans.

Even after she stopped appearing in films Bara continued to exist as a presence among American icons. When a drawing of her appeared in the February 1923 issue of *Classic*, its caption read:

THEDA BARA

Endless lure of pomegranate lips . . . red enemy of man . . . the somber brooding beauty of a thousand Egyptian nights . . . black-browed and starry-eyed . . . infinite mystery in their smoldering depths, never to be revealed . . . Mona Lisa . . . Cleopatra . . . child of the Russian countryside . . . daughter of the new world . . . peasant . . . goddess . . . eternal woman.

Theda Bara demonstrated one of the early miracles of how movies transformed our culture. Through her, Hollywood proved it could manufacture models for American fantasies.

QUESTIONS FOR THOUGHT AND DISCUSSION

1. Why were audiences in American so beguiled by motion pictures? Does the incredible popularity of many of Theda Bara's films challenge your notions about turn-of-the-century America?

2. What do the successful roles played by Theda Bara suggest about filmmakers and filmgoers in the early twentieth century? What do these roles suggest about attitudes toward women in this era? How was Bara affected when tastes in female movie roles changed after World War I?

3. How was Bara's life story "manufactured" by publicists? Why was it so important to make sure Bara's background was starkly different from those women who would go to see her movies?

4. What does the hubbub about Bara's appearance in the film *Kathleen Mavourneen* reveal about attitudes in post-World War I America?

SUGGESTED READINGS

Bara, Pauline. "The Real Theda Bara." *Motion Picture Classic*, December, 1920.

Bara, Theda. "How I Became a Film Vampire," *Forum*, June and July 1919.

Bodeen, Dwight. *From Hollywood: The Careers of 15 Great American Stars*. New York: A. S. Barnes, 1976, pp. 13–28.

_____. "Theda Bara," *Films in Review*. May 1968.

Card, James. *Seductive Cinema: The Art of Silent Film*. 1966. NY: Knopf, 1994.

Gessner, Robert. "The Moving Image." *American Heritage*, Vol. XI, Number 3, April 1960.

Mullett, Mary B. "Theda Bara, Queen of Vampires." *American Magazine*. September 1920.

Sinclair, Upton. *Upton Sinclair Presents William Fox*. 1933.

Walker, Alexander. *The Celluloid Sacrifice: Aspects of Sex in the Movies*. 1966.

11

Margaret Sanger

*I*n the period of growth and prosperity that began after the Civil War, America changed rapidly because Americans were changing, particularly in their national origins. In the forty years leading up to 1900, fourteen million immigrants came, but where they came from shifted. Until 1880, seventy-five percent of immigrants came from Northern Europe, most of them Irish and German. Before long, these new Americans were considered the "old immigrants," compared to more recently arrived people from farther south and east, mostly Italian Catholics and Eastern European Jews. The greatest number of the new immigrants stayed in the Northeast, but many went to large cities in other parts of the country, except for the South. In many of those cities the new people outnumbered the native-born Americans who were becoming conscious of themselves as a group.

When the immigrant-turned-reformer Jacob Riis published How the Other Half Lives in 1890, Americans saw photographs of the squalor and misery that surrounded so many other Americans in New York City. Some readers saw a need for legislation and sanctions against slumlords and the owners of sweatshops. Margaret Higgins Sanger, daughter of Irish immigrants, saw the numbers of the poor as the essence of the problem. In her analysis, the solution lay not with absent rich men, but with present poor women. By helping themselves, they would improve America. Her intention from the outset concerned a "new race" in America, as she worked to supplant sentimental Victorian notions of motherhood with a radical version of a woman's relation to her family.

Risking her own safety and tranquillity to bring about a change that would touch all women, Margaret Sanger spelled out the details of when she believed "birth control" (a phrase she coined) should be practiced: when either spouse has a transmittable disease; when the wife suffers a temporary infection of lungs, heart, or kidneys, the cure of which might be retarded in pregnancy; when a mother is physically unfit; when parents have subnormal children; if the parents are adolescents; if their income is inadequate; and during the first year of marriage. For such publication, she risked forty-five years in prison.

MARGARET HIGGINS SANGER was born into the Victorian world and came of age in the twentieth century, turning twenty-one in 1900. The strong contrast between what people think of as prudish and restrained Victorian morality and the new robust and vigorous way of thinking that would characterize twentieth-century America could not be more apparent than in the life of Margaret Sanger, so full of contrast and even conflict.

The sixth child in a family that would have eleven children, Margaret Higgins saw in her parents an emblem of the problem she would make it her business to correct. Michael Hennessy Higgins, her father, worked as a skilled artisan, a carver of stone monuments, and had a large family, a profile that let him qualify as a Victorian patriarch—but nothing else about him could be called conventional. Charming and a storyteller—traits he would pass on to Margaret—Higgins spent more time talking radical politics and dreaming of social equality than seeing to his business or watching out for his often suffering and frequently needy family. Margaret Higgins herself would refer to her father as a rebel, an artist, and even a philosopher throughout her life. His romantic side would apparently influence her idea of how men were supposed to behave, and her fondness for her father may explain her life-long attraction to a series of men who were in various ways rebellious and dreamers.

While her father lived past eighty, her mother, Anne Purcell Higgins, fell ill at forty-eight, so ill that Margaret Higgins had to interrupt her schooling to return home to help her sisters nurse her. After so much illness no one could save the weakened, tubercular woman who had given birth eleven times. Higgins believed that having so many babies shortened her mother's life. That conviction eventually expressed itself in a long and energetic career. While nursing her ill mother, Margaret contracted a case of tubercular gland as well. Since tuberculosis was thought of as terminal, her own tubercular condition made her reluctant to make strong bonds with the children she would eventually have, exposing her to strong criticism as an indifferent mother. Over the years, the demanding work of motherhood claimed little of her time. A combination of impulsiveness and a dogged patience in staying with her beliefs became a pattern for the bright, delicate-looking young woman. It could be that her own serious illness gave her fearlessness after she looked mortality in the face at a young age.

After a teacher's comments embarrassed her, Margaret Higgins refused to stay at the school near her family's home in Corning, New York. With the financial help of her two older sisters and her own contribution of working in the school kitchen to earn room and board, she was able to attend the socially exclusive Claverack College (a preparatory school) in the Catskills. For the first time, she met girls her own age from families who had given them advantages subtler than material comfort. Some of her classmates at the originally Dutch Protestant school came from New York City and brought with them a sophistication that fascinated the stone-cutter's daughter. At Claverack, she saw and learned things she had never even heard described while she was growing up. She learned that people with financial ease had opportunities for satisfaction and fulfillment in life, goals that even her father's dreams had not been able to include. That revelation changed her as much as any strictly intellectual element in her education.

It was just as Higgins was about to finish her three years at Claverack that she was called home to help her sisters with her mother, an interruption that kept her from graduating. With the training she already had, even without a diploma, she did find—probably through Claverack connections—a teaching position. Actually far more demanding than a first job had to be, the appointment put her in charge of a group of immigrant children in Little Falls, New Jersey. Before she could teach them lessons, she had to teach them English, a monumental assignment that overwhelmed the ailing girl, age nineteen, who was now called home again to help during the last stages of her mother's illness.

The other career choice possible for a young woman without money did not even come close to the respectability of teaching. By taking a big step down, Margaret Higgins considered going into training to be a nurse, a realistic goal for a young woman living not far from the hospital at White Plains, New York. A well-off family would have directed a daughter to study medicine and to become a physician, a choice that was then easier for a woman than it would soon become as the self-conscious professionalization of the practice of medicine began to take hold and put up obstacles to women. Because of its nurturing, healing side, medicine seemed a suitably feminine choice. But at that early date, the servant-like tasks that nurses were allowed to do meant that they received little respect. The drudgery and inhumanly long hours, not to mention the moral dangers, kept proper young ladies away. In the context of Victorian prudery, the idea that women might look upon the naked bodies of strangers automatically removed nursing from the domain of decent work.

Even within nursing there existed a hierarchy, a ranking of kinds of nursing in terms of how close they came to respectability, that primary social value which was lost at a woman's peril. At the top were "trained nurses," women who had been schooled in preparation for their work, as distinct from "practical nurses," who had merely done disagreeable tasks as practice for doing more of the same, usually thought of in terms of emptying bed pans. Yet that work suited Margaret Higgins better than teaching, even though nursing returned her to the same social milieu she had served as a teacher. For her training, Margaret Higgins went to New York City where she worked among the poor on the Lower East Side. In her autobiography, not always a trustworthy source of fact, she wrote what must be a truthful description: "These submerged, untouched classes were beyond the scope of organized charity or religion. No labor union, no church, not even the Salvation Army reached them."

In the summer before her last year of training she also met a young architect, William Sanger, whose passionate and idealistic nature changed both their lives. From all reports, the first time Sanger saw Margaret Higgins he fell hopelessly in love with her, knew he would have to marry her, and would not leave her alone until it happened. Even a young man of high political idealism saw no injustice in expecting a woman to drop out of school and abandon her plans in order to marry him. He was offering her security and marriage, after all. For reasons she later claimed she did not entirely understand herself, Margaret Higgins became Margaret Sanger on August 18, 1902.

As part of their early endeavors the young couple worked together in local radical politics. In another collaboration they had their first child, Stuart, in November

1903, a birth that proved so difficult that Sanger's physician expected her to be an invalid for life. Rejecting the idea of anything less than full normal activity, she worked hard with her husband after her release from a sanitarium where she had been sent to recover from childbirth. Considering the treatment that patients endured at the sanitarium, the fact that Sanger survived says that she must have had a strong constitution even after illness. A diet with the accent on dairy products (a dozen eggs and four quarts of milk per day) followed by a daily dose of creosote would have done in the feeble woman her physician thought he had in his charge.

The Sangers lived in Manhattan, continued their political work, joined the Socialist Party and became friends with such radical notables as Emma Goldman, all while having two more children, a son in 1908 and a daughter less than two years later. From these years, which Sanger would later downplay in her version of her early work, she learned the importance of organizing people, public speaking (something at which she did not gain confidence even with great experience), and publishing. She also saw that immigrants lived in a different country from the America of her uptown friends.

To think of herself as better off than immigrants did not make Margaret Sanger a snob nor a racist, at least not compared to other Americans of her time. She did have a sense of herself as "native-born," a term and a concept that was becoming more commonplace in the speech and the thinking of Americans as more and more Europeans continued to arrive. Political leaders and moral leaders noticed significant differences between the two classes, as they were perceived to be. Immigrants not only came in great numbers, but worse, in native-born eyes, they continued to "breed like rabbits" after they arrived. Some of what native-born leaders noticed could not be mentioned in polite company. Victorian ladies had discovered, and not talked about, ways of limiting the size of their families. Some of these ways included abstinence from sexual relations within their marriages, a way of life which led to frustration and, according to some speculation, a thriving trade in pornography. In other words, native-born families in general were smaller than those of immigrants who came to America full of enthusiasm for everything, including producing babies they counted as new little Americans. In a change that could be seen overall but not uniformly, American families began to shrink. In 1800, the average family size was seven children but grew smaller with each generation so that by 1900 the average family had four children. The immigrants remained outside this silent trend.

The imbalance, eventually blamed on the selfishness of native-born American women, meant a growing inequality in numbers of the two classes, a social disadvantage that leaders would not accept. Native-born American women were patently encouraged to have more children to avoid what was identified as "race suicide." Theodore Roosevelt, among others, identified himself with pronatalism, as this belief in the importance of large American families was called.

In the view of the pronatalists, the problem had to do with too few babies, but at the same time Margaret Sanger worked among the poorest of the poor immigrants where she observed the opposite. Margaret believed the problem came from too many births, too many poor women sacrificing their health—as her mother, not an immigrant and not so desperately poor, had also done—in having too

UPI/Bettmann

Margaret Sanger liked to appear conventional, particularly when she spoke radically about "birth control," a phrase she coined.

many children. The women she worked with, she claimed, would have their "weary misshapen bodies . . . thrown on the scrap heap before they are thirty-five."

The booming belief in progress and in plenty, so much a part of America's outlook at the time, could not have been more at odds with the idea of a limit as a solution. But for Margaret Sanger, the misery and poverty she saw in her work could have been checked if only the women themselves were allowed to have some say in how many babies they would be made to produce, if only they could learn what better-off women were doing.

In her early work among the immigrants, Sanger met a woman who almost ended up passing into myth as she became famous in a story that Margaret Sanger would repeat to many audiences. The story no doubt found its basis in Sanger's experience, but if she combined in it several events or several people to help the story, she never bothered to say so. In the story, the woman is called Sadie Sachs, wife of a truck driver and the mother of more children than she wanted. Like other desperate women unable to care for the children she already had, Sadie tried to end a pregnancy on her own, a dangerous act which led to her meeting the young nurse, Margaret Sanger. When Sadie had asked her doctor if he knew of anything she could do to avoid more pregnancies, the story goes that the physician gave advice that was not exactly medical: "Tell Jake to sleep on the roof."

That story may appear to point out a callous attitude of a physician, bordering on cynical, the sort of thing that would be called at best unprofessional today. In fact, the training of physicians early in the century did not include information on contraception. The medical curriculum had nothing to say about the prevention of conception, a subject that people did not discuss anywhere. Silence on the subject kept women ignorant, to be sure, but also allowed a confusion of contraception with other bodily subjects not talked about in polite company. In the vagueness that goes with silence or innuendo, facts about how to avoid pregnancy—especially in written form—had become associated with indecent printed matter, in other words, pornography. That blurring of titillation with simple facts of biology would seem an amusing parenthesis in American Victorian culture if it had not taken on legal importance for Margaret Sanger, for her husband, and for women in America. Maybe middle class women would have guarded their intimate secrets if the Sangers had not refused to cooperate in the successful charade of respectable hypocrisy that excluded the likes of Sadie Sachs.

Before either Margaret or William Sanger were born, a zealous dry goods sales-man named Andrew Comstock had dealt himself the job of purifying America, New York in particular. While he dabbled in cleaning up gambling, he applied his full strength—five foot ten, two hundred ten pounds, and built like a bull—to stamping out smut. Comstock seemed happy working by himself—his eighty-two pound wife, ten years his senior, reportedly seldom said a word in public—in finding porno-graphic publications, looking them over carefully, and then taking them to the New York police, who also looked them over carefully. He progressed from arresting dealers to going after publishers when he allied himself with the New York Young Men's Christian Association and influenced them to form the Committee for the Suppression of Vice. In time, Comstock became such an embarrassment to the YMCA that it cut off all its ties to the Committee, which then became the Society for the Suppression of Vice with Comstock as its president and main worker.

The reason that anyone still talks about Comstock comes from his stunning success when he went to Washington to persuade Congress to make a law—it became known as the Comstock Act of 1873—that declared it a federal offense to send through the United States mail any material that was "lewd" or "indecent" and "obscene." It was enacted virtually without debate. The pure motive of this law did not help in its enforcement, since it did not anywhere define exactly what was meant by "lewd" or "indecent" and "obscene." Yet it did list particular kinds of material that were subsumed in that definition, such as contraceptives and advertisements for them.

Much later, when Margaret Sanger would hear of the Comstock Act of 1873, she had stopped her work as a nurse among immigrants to give her efforts on their behalf a new direction. (Again, her impatience and her tenacity both showed.) After 1912, she began to concentrate on spreading information about contraception, the knowledge she was convinced poor women and other women lacked. That effort made sense because of her conviction that the solution lay in finding a method within the control of women for limiting family size. She did not bother trying to promote a method that required the cooperation, or even the knowledge, of men.

From her association with radical political thinkers and activists, Margaret Sanger saw the force of writing and publishing as ways of distributing information. In March 1914, she began publishing her militant journal, *The Woman Rebel,* which carried on its masthead the slogan, "No Gods; No Masters." In that magazine, people also read for the first time the words "birth control," a phrase which Americans associated with Margaret Sanger's name for the next five decades. Her commitment to promoting a new version of freedom for women went beyond the political position of what she published. To the great unhappiness of her continually more distant husband, she began to act upon her sense of personal independence in having intimate liaisons with his radical political friends. In Margaret Sanger's view, if radicals were going to reject middle class thinking, they had no reason to respect conventional moral barriers such as the notion of fidelity within marriage.

The riskiest act so far for Margaret Sanger came in the publication of *Family Limitation,* the most explicit, practical advice available in English on contraception. At that point, in August 1914, Sanger was indicted on nine counts of sending contraceptive information through the mail. These charges made her liable to a term of forty-five years in prison. In the face of that future, Sanger found herself alone. The friends she had met working on their own political causes, including woman suffrage, continued to concentrate on their goals but ignored her need for assistance.

Rather than wait around to be called into court, Margaret Sanger showed her impatience in an act that may be counted as reckless or a fitting reaction to an unjust charge. On the eve of her trial, without the permission of the court, she fled to Europe and stayed almost a year. While in Europe she worked to advance her cause by attending a clinic in the Netherlands on the use of a new contraceptive device, the diaphragm. During that same time of exile she became romantically linked to Havelock Ellis, the British sexologist whose unconventional ideas and behavior let Margaret Sanger believe that she had transcended conventional sexual mores. While she pursued the ideas of Havelock Ellis, Andrew Comstock pursued William Sanger.

Using a technique that had worked for him before, Andrew Comstock disguised himself and went after the lion in its den. Posing as a destitute father who wanted to help his wife to avoid more pregnancies, Comstock went to the Sanger apartment in New York City in his quest for one of the offending pamphlets. It worked. Sanger sold Comstock a copy of *Family Limitation* and Comstock had

Sanger arrested. For his sins, William Sanger spent one month in The Tombs, the infamous prison in New York City.

Charges against another Sanger made the papers and had people talking about Andrew Comstock and his methods. In fact, for much of the time that Margaret Sanger was abroad, the press discussed her ideas, her offense, her fate, and her husband. The result of all the publicity went head-on against Comstock's notion of an offense to decency. One of the reasons for Margaret Sanger's indictment had been the spread of information on a subject considered taboo. But as more outrage found its way into the press and into public debate, paradoxically, newspapers had to break the taboo in order to report the news. Americans had to talk about an unspeakable subject because it was in the air. By the time Margaret Sanger returned to the United States, her offense seemed far less serious, and the charges were dropped.

While in Europe, Margaret Sanger had been given the benefit of the practical advice of Havelock Ellis. According to her new advisor, the tactics of her radical friends, the plan of mobilizing the masses, was not the way to go. What she needed, to be truly effective, was the support of prominent American socialites whose money and connections would promote her cause and guarantee its acceptance in ways that rallies could never achieve. Margaret Sanger probably would have started following a new tack on her return even if she had not been driven to activity by personal tragedy and grief.

In 1915, after she returned from Europe and before she was sure that the government would not press its charges, Margaret Sanger lost her daughter Margaret, age five, a victim of pneumonia. Not long afterwards, she began what can only be called a campaign, a nationwide tour, bringing to women not only technical advice but changing profoundly their ideas of what they could discuss. Her writing in that period makes its appeal to well-off women, arguing in effect that immigrants must not be allowed to reproduce excessively. Sanger wrote about the notion of a new kind of American in her first book called *Women and the New Race*. She encouraged women to think about what the "new Americans" were going to be like if present trends continued, pointing out that four-fifths of the populations of Chicago and New York were made up of "white foreign stock." In other words, not native-born. (This, from a woman whose grandfather had left Ireland around the time of the great potato famine of 1848.) Yet in her speeches, Sanger always adjusted her message to suit her particular audience, repeating the story of Sadie Sachs with a different spin for working class audiences.

As interest in birth control grew, it attracted women who thought that Margaret Sanger could not deliver permanent, legitimate change. When she and her sister, Ethel Byrne, opened the first birth control clinic in the United States in Brooklyn, New York, in 1916, it was closed down after ten days. It had served 488 women. This time, Sanger spent thirty days in jail. Some advocates of birth control may have admired her courage, but others, including Mary Ware Dennett, a veteran of the suffrage movement, believed that if lawmakers could be made to see the need for birth control, then a change in the law would be inevitable. Dennett saw in Sanger's actions and record more of a belief in breaking the law than in trying to change it. In Margaret Sanger's view, a woman from Mary Ware Dennett's privileged background could not comprehend that lawmakers were the last people to be counted on to take risks, to rock the boat, or to work for change. As a result of this disagreement at the top, the National Birth Control League did not get far. Margaret Sanger had a rich rival.

As worries about being outnumbered by immigrants faded among national concerns, so did interest in birth control. The advice of Havelock Ellis had a lasting effect, however, as Margaret Sanger continued to seek the help of "angels," or wealthy supporters, an effort in which her persuasive arguments and estimable charm served the cause well. After divorcing William Sanger in 1920, a change that he had long resisted, she moved farther away from her radical past and married J. Noah Slee, a millionaire whose fortune came from the manufacture of Three-in-One Oil. Meanwhile, Sanger had become president of the American Birth Control League, a national organization that would change its name to the Planned Parenthood Federation of America in 1942.

Resistance from lawmakers and political leaders had weakened somewhat as women won the vote and gradually made inroads into more professions and careers, all in the direction of female independence. In 1937, for example, the Comstock Act was reinterpreted in a way that allowed information on contraception to be distributed. The thinking of physicians also changed, as the American Medical Association allowed birth control a place in medical practice. But in the years of World War II, Americans had little interest in Sanger's cause. After the war, the great national optimism and feeling of victory resulted in a spontaneous "boom" of babies. By the time the postwar babies were coming of age, medical research had made great progress in the area of hormones, a subject that had been studied during the war because of the interest in understanding the role of hormones in relation to combat fatigue. Margaret Sanger remained instrumental in putting together researchers and the philanthropists who backed them.

Before marketing their most important product, a synthetic hormone to be used as an oral contraceptive immediately known as "The Pill," American pharmaceutical companies tested their product outside the United States. Scientists who worked on that project still recall how many reservations and doubts they had about testing a product with risks that were still so poorly understood. But when they saw the poverty and suffering in Puerto Rico, and saw the many women whose greatest fear was to be judged not healthy enough to be given The Pill in the field tests, they understood the need for population control differently. Later, when The Pill reached the United States and became available to the huge numbers of American women who had been born as "baby boomers," social attitudes had to adapt to a new reality. Mothers could no longer tell their daughters that "a moment of weakness may lead to a lifetime of regret," as the coded warnings of their mothers had maintained. The liberation of women's bodies had been achieved in one sense, as their thinking about sexuality had become suddenly more complex.

Margaret Sanger continued to work throughout her life for the promotion of birth control, especially in poor countries. Her ideas about racial betterment and eugenics had been discredited by the fanatical goals of the Third Reich. Her accomplishments, by the time she died in 1966 at age eighty-two, could not have been imagined in the Victorian world she did so much to embarrass.

QUESTIONS FOR THOUGHT AND DISCUSSION

1. What led Sanger to her strong advocacy of birth control in the early 1900s? Did she have primarily a feminist motive?

2. Did it take a political radical like Sanger to champion the birth control movement in its formative years, or did her early radicalism impede the acceptance of the movement?

3. Do Sanger's eugenicist statements, warning about too many births by undesirable elements in society, discredit her crusade in your eyes? Was she, despite her political radicalism on other issues, merely following the conventional opinion of the times on racial superiority?

4. Would Sanger, who died in 1966, approve of the sexual freedom that her promotion of birth control devices and "the pill" helped to make less costly? Was she a modern heroine?

SUGGESTED READINGS

Andrist, Ralph K. "Paladin of Purity." *American Heritage*. Vol. XXIV, Number 6, October 1973, pp. 4–7, 84–89.

Broun, Heywood and Margaret Leech. *Anthony Comstock, Roundsman of the Lord*. New York: Literary Guild, 1927.

Chesler, Ellen. *Woman of Valor: Margaret Sanger and the Birth Control Movement in America*. New York: Simon, 1992.

Davis, Kenneth S. "The Story of the Pill." *American Heritage*. Volume XXIX, Number 5, Aug/Sept 1978, pp. 80–91.

Gray, Madeline. *Margaret Sanger: A Biography of the Champion of Birth Control*. New York: Marek, 1979.

Kennedy, David M. *Birth Control in America. The Career of Margaret Sanger*. New Haven: Yale UP, 1970.

Sanger, Margaret. *Woman and the New Race*. (Preface by Havelock Ellis). New York: Brentano's, 1920.

12

Huey Long

In the freewheeling 1920s, as many Americans bought automobiles, radios, refrigerators, and other consumer goods, few noticed that a growing segment of the population was less and less able to keep pace with the general prosperity. Throughout the South and Southwest, where cotton was still the staple crop upon which the rural majority depended for its livelihood, cotton prices were steadily falling until, by the early 1930s, they reached twenty percent of the 1920 price to farmers. Thousands of helpless farmers could not keep up with their property taxes or borrow money for seeds from local banks, much less participate in the national good times.

Once before, in the financially-depressed 1890s, a populist movement had gathered strength, only to wane after the 1896 presidential elections. But as the worst Depression since the beginning of the Industrial Age deepened in the 1930s and wholesale foreclosures of farm mortgages forced families off their hard-won land, resentment grew against the wealthy, the bankers, and the "big-money" interests.

One politically ambitious Louisiana "hilly billy," as Huey Long liked to call himself, became the impassioned champion of rednecked men in suspenders and grim-faced women in bonnets. This flamboyant Robin Hood figure promised a better way of life to millions of rural Americans at the expense of the rich, who called him a dictator.

FRANKLIN DELANO ROOSEVELT was afraid of very little. He wasn't afraid of Hitler or the Japanese Imperial Army, or even polio: he fought and overcame all of them. "We have nothing to fear but fear itself," he liked to say. But there was one man who frightened him, who almost ruined his chances for reelection as president, and who forced him to alienate his own class by swinging far to the left and greatly increasing taxation of the rich and the corporation and creating the Social Security system. That man was Huey Pierce Long and, for a short time in 1935, at the nadir of the Depression, he seemed destined to become the first populist president.

Huey Long liked to say, when he was on the stump, that he had been born poor, in a log cabin in Winnfield, the parish seat of Winn Parish (county) in northern Louisiana. Like so much of what he said, it was more calculated for effect than for accuracy. It was true that, when he was born August 30, 1893, the eighth of nine children of Huey and Caledonia Tison Long, the family lived in a four-room log house, but it was larger than many Louisianans in the piney woods lived in and, within a year, the Longs moved to a large house surrounded by more than three thousand acres of land. His father, a landowner prosperous enough to send six of his children to college, had accumulated the land by hard work, shrewd investment, and frugal, unadorned living. It must also have helped that an uncle owned the town's leading bank.

His mother, a Bible-quoting, no-nonsense Southern Baptist, taught Huey a strong sense of communal responsibility and sharing: he liked to recall carrying baskets of food and clothing prepared by her to needy families. He early developed a second sense: that the outside world was encroaching on his community and must be challenged and resisted. When he was a boy, the first railroad line was run into Winn Parish, bringing in its wake lumber mills to process and exploit its pine forests. Soon there were more people and more businesses owned by outsiders. When he was eight, Huey watched in horror a farm foreclosure, a crowd standing sullenly as the sheriff auctioned off a property for a debt owed a store as the evicted owner pleaded with his neighbors not to bid. Huey never forgot his sense of anger mixed with shame as his own cousin bought the land; it was "the meanest thing I ever saw in my life," he told an interviewer. It seemed "criminal" to Huey.

There was little very promising about Huey Long's boyhood except his arrogance. He liked to play baseball, but would only play if he could be the pitcher. He would later claim that he worked hard in his father's fields, but his siblings later disputed this. In fact, they said, he displayed a keen dislike for hard farmwork. If he did any, it had become a legend by the time he wrote his famous autobiography, *Every Man a King:* "the rows were long; the sun was hot; there was little companionship. Rising before the sun, we toiled until dark, after which we did nothing except eat supper, listen to the whippoorwills, and go to bed." His "every sympathy" went out "to those who toil." If Huey Long the presidential aspirant was trying to make his own Abe Lincoln style log cabin myth (he also mentioned log-splitting), the truth was a country mile or two away. Biographers have assembled a portrait of, as Alan Brinkley puts it, a boy who was "bright, outspoken, opinionated, restless . . . and intensely, consumedly self-centered." All of which may explain why he ran away from home at least three times, the first time making it fifty miles at age ten before his father hauled him back.

Just why he couldn't admit that, despite his aversion to studying, he was a good student and champion debater at Winnfield High School is impossible to fathom— except that the whole subject of his schooling was a sore one in the years after he won a partial scholarship from debating to Louisiana State University, which he couldn't afford to accept because a slump in cotton prices put his expenses temporarily beyond his father's reach. It must have galled young Huey, whose six elder siblings had gone through LSU and one its law school, that he had to go to work after high school, which he left in 1910 without a diploma.

For five years, Huey Long wandered the South and Midwest selling products door-to-door, especially Cottolene, a cottonseed oil substitute for cooking lard. He was an aggressive salesman, capable of walking past a surprised housewife into her kitchen where, tying on an apron, he would bake a cake while waving a Bible and citing the Old Testament Jewish ban on using the products of swine with food. More persuasive than frugal, he saved nothing over the years, and when he met Rose McConnell at a Cottolene baking contest and decided two years later to marry her, he had to borrow the ten dollars for the preacher from her.

At age twenty, Huey the newlywed decided to get serious about his future and become a lawyer. He borrowed money from a brother and moved with Rose to a tiny apartment in New Orleans, where he crammed law studies day and night, completing a three-year curriculum in eight months. Requesting a special bar examination from the state Supreme Court, he breezed through it. He had accomplished what no law student, before or since, has matched. In 1915, at twenty-one, he hung out his shingle in his home town of Winnfield, where he shared an office with his brother, Julius. But Huey's arrogance made the partnership impossible, especially after he described one of his brother's law briefs as worthless and tore it up.

Setting up his own one-room office over his uncle's bank, Huey over the next year slowly built a practice in a new field, workmen's compensation law, winning small settlements for workers injured on the job. Some months he had to resume selling products door-to-door to pay the four dollar office rent, but he was emerging "on the side of the small man—the underdog," he later wrote, and he was proud that he never took a suit "against a poor man." He was successful enough to move to Shreveport, a much bigger city, where he not only won bigger cases but began to get involved in politics.

Louisiana state politics on the eve of the United States entrance into World War I followed a familiar, Southern, post-Civil War pattern: blacks had been disenfranchised and poor whites were almost equally powerless because the Southern gentlemen who ruled them paid little heed to their wishes. The politics of Louisiana were unusually complicated, however, because of several splits: Delta French Cajuns in the south versus Protestant Anglo-Saxons in the north, and rural farmers versus machine-dominated New Orleans. The average Louisiana voter, however, was inept, and the state ranked near the bottom in all state services. There was no electricity, and only pumped or carried water, few schools and no hospitals for the poor, who could rarely travel because there were few paved roads and no bridges over major rivers.

When war came, Huey stayed home, exempt as a husband, father, and notary, and began agitating against a new law that limited the amount of money a worker injured on the job could receive—and Huey's cut of it. He drew up a series of amendments and persuaded a state senator to introduce them to the legislature and then testified in their behalf. His debut before a legislature, he later wrote, disgusted him—all the "formalities, mannerisms, kowtowing, and easily discernible insincerities"—but his amendments, sponsored by State Senator S. J. Harper, were adopted. His mentor was a Socialist who published a book denouncing U.S. involvement in World War I. When he was inevitably indicted by a federal grand jury, Huey Long took on his defense—and won.

Suddenly prominent, Long, now twenty-three, wanted to run for state office, but Louisiana's constitution barred most state offices until age thirty. Impatient, Long found that one office had been overlooked by lawmakers: he ran for the state Railroad Commission. Brushing up his salesman's knowledge of door-to-door canvassing and advertising, he drove all over northern Louisiana in a flashy new car, using mailing lists, handing out hundreds of posters, and circularizing every town as he attacked the opposition bitterly. Winning barely, he assumed state office at age twenty-five. Not only had his political career begun but he had pioneered a new kind of political campaigning.

The Railroad Commission, later renamed the Public Utilities Commission, was usually a political dead-end. Long saw it differently. He worked hard to limit the utilities' power, to cut rates, and improve service. He became chairman in 1922, turning his energies for the first time to challenging the stranglehold of the Standard Oil Company on the state's politics and economy. While he made little headway, he made many headlines. By 1923, at age thirty, he decided to run for governor: denouncing Standard Oil corruption, he campaigned as a Jeffersonian outsider opposing the oligarchy of Southern gentlemen enriched by special interests. He ran third in the 1924 Democratic primary, but he polled thirty-one percent of the vote, carrying twenty-eight parishes, more than any of his opponents. Sweeping the north, he made inroads in the south.

Defeated narrowly, he began at once campaigning for the 1928 election. He had already settled on a populist strategy, campaigning first against charging tolls to cross a new bridge over Lake Pontchartrain. Whenever and wherever he spoke, there were large crowds: over them waved his campaign banner: "Every Man a King, But No One Wears a Crown." Long's savage campaign attacks startled opponents. They called in outside help: U.S. Commerce Secretary Herbert Hoover came to Louisiana and made the mistake of pooh-poohing the Evangeline myth so sacred to Catholic Cajuns. Long gave a torchlight speech under the fabled Evangeline oak:

> And it is here under this oak where Evangeline waited for her lover, Gabriel, who never came. This oak is an immortal spot, made so by Longfellow's poem, but Evangeline is not the only one who has waited here in disappointment. Where are the schools that you have waited for your children to have, that have never come? Where are the roads and the highways that you send your money to build, that are no nearer than ever before? Where are the institutions to care for the sick and disabled? Evangeline wept bitter tears in her disappointment, but it lasted through only one lifetime. Your tears in this country, around this oak, have lasted for generations. Give me the chance to dry the eyes of those who still weep here.

Fusing Catholic and Protestant rural voters, Anglo-Saxon and Creole, north and south, the populist Huey Long won the largest total vote and the largest victory in Louisiana history. Moreover, he had won along economic class lines, attracting national attention: the 1890s politics of economic protest was reborn in Louisiana as, at age thirty-five, Huey Long was elected governor.

The crowd that gathered at Huey Long's inauguration horrified Baton Rouge's genteel middle class. They saw tobacco-juice-spitting and sunburned farmers in

AP/Wide World

Leading the Louisiana State University band into a football game was typical of the flamboyant populist style that made Huey "Kingfish" Long a contender for the presidency in the 1930s.

red suspenders with their gingham-dressed, sunbonneted wives pouring in on mules, in buggies, in jalopies, and on foot. Around the ornate state capitol building, Long had ordered construction of a dance pavilion for country music and jazz bands. Not since Andrew Jackson's presidential inauguration in 1829 had there been such an outpouring of the poor or a more startled reaction. In three years, Long built 2,500 miles of paved roads (previously there had only been 300), 6,000 miles of new gravel roads, twelve bridges, and a thirty-four story new Capitol building. His public works program employed thousands of poor whites and blacks. The white aristocrats who had run Louisiana for decades shuddered at the popularity of Huey Long. A few noted that he had become one of them. He had built a lucrative law practice and a fancy house in Shreveport, wore expensive tailored suits, or silk pajamas, and always had a big new car.

The wealthy had every reason to shudder, and the poor to celebrate: few governors, if any, ever carried out the sweeping reforms or fulfilled more campaign promises than Huey Long in his one term (the state constitutional limit). The legislature, under his direct daily goading, abolished poll taxes, enacted new taxes on businesses, declared a statewide moratorium on debt, reduced property assessments twenty percent, exempted the poor completely from property taxes, gave away all textbooks free, opened night schools, and provided free school buses so that 175,000 illiterate adults learned to read and write. He treated blacks and whites equally, prompting angry threats against him from the Ku Klux Klan. When the Klan's head personally threatened to come into Louisiana and wage a campaign of terror against him, Long told reporters:

> Quote me as saying that that Imperial bastard will never set foot in Louisiana, and that when I call him a son of a bitch I am not using profanity but am referring to the circumstances of his birth.

The Klan stayed quiet and other critics, including newspaper editors, were silenced, too, some of them beaten or jailed. At first Long was above criticism: he was the Kingfish, taking his nickname from a flamboyant character on the popular radio show, *Amos 'n' Andy*.

What finally brought a strong reaction from his opponents was his call for an "occupational license tax" of five cents on every barrel of petroleum refined in the oil-rich Gulf state. No other oil state taxed Standard Oil, which saw a dangerous precedent. Oil lobbyists and their money poured into Baton Rouge, fueling conservatives in the legislature who managed to defeat the license tax, handing Long his first major setback. When his opponents tried to press their advantage and called for his impeachment, Long's Speaker of the House tried too late to adjourn the session. There was a wild melee in the legislative chamber: harsh words, fists, and inkwells flew. After a mass meeting where a Standard Oil Company band played, the House of Representatives voted to impeach Long on eight charges. Long held his own rally; an enormous crowd turned out to hear him denounce the impeachment as a Standard Oil-subsidized plot to end his populist program. By the time his trial began, Long's machine had reached many supporters who, in turn, protested to their state senators that Long was able to survive the first impeachment vote. Then a "Round Robin" petition appeared, signed by fifteen senators who said they could not convict him on any of the other charges despite the evidence because the special session of the legislature had expired. There are still rumors that the fifteen senators, (one more than the necessary number of votes) received political-plum jobs from Long, but there is no proof.

The impeachment movement collapsed, but it left Huey Long bitter. "I used to try to get things done by saying 'please,'" he said with some exaggeration. "That didn't work and now I'm a dynamiter. I dynamite 'em out of my path." Surrounding himself now with armed bodyguards, Long assembled a ruthless political machine based on patronage. Every government job in the state was brought under his direct control—no opposition or disloyalty was tolerated. He had a bridge attendant fired when he learned the man was friendly to a Long political foe. Political workers were expected to contribute cash to a huge slushfund—the "deduct box"—that paid for Huey Long's wardrobe, Cadillac limousine, bodyguards, radio broadcast time, and newspaper advertisements. When U. S. Treasury Department agents made a cursory investigation in 1932, they reported back, "Long and his gang are stealing everything."

But as the Depression hit Louisiana, Long's support only grew. No one dared oppose "the Dictator," as his opponents now called him matter-of-factly. An attempt was made to block his plan to demolish the Governor's Mansion: Long personally led a work crew of convict laborers who tore it down. He wanted a new Capitol building, too, and when the legislature did not immediately agree, he had a hole drilled in the roof of the old capitol during the rainy season right above the head of a leading opponent. When rumors flew that he had taken as his mistress his divorced secretary, he appointed her Secretary of State.

Under Louisiana law, Long could not succeed himself as governor. He announced that he would run for the U.S. Senate, and won the seat. Long arranged for a compliant lieutenant, aptly named O. K. Allen, to serve him as governor. Allen's servility became legendary. "A leaf once blew in the window of Allen's office and fell on his desk," a Long relative recounted. "Allen signed it." Rarely appearing in Washington, D.C., during his first Senate term, Senator Long strutted back and forth on the floor of the Louisiana legislature, ramrodding through his legislative program. In one two-hour session, the state Senate passed forty-four bills introduced only the night before.

Between 1930 and 1934, Long ruled Louisiana by an alliance with the Old Regulars, the New Orleans Democratic organization. He refused to resign as governor when he ran for the Senate to prevent a hostile lieutenant governor succeeding him. His public improvement program presaged Roosevelt's national public works efforts: he taxed business heavily to build thirty million dollars in new roads, a five million dollar Capitol, and a massive expansion of Louisiana State University. He created a national sensation when he received the commander of a German Navy cruiser in his pajamas and, again, when he pushed through a law barring a cotton crop in 1932 in an effort to create a shortage and drive up prices.

Outside his home state, Long seemed a buffoon at first. In the U.S. Senate, he devoted his efforts to trying to get "potlikker," the broth of pork and greens at the bottom of a kettle, added to the Capitol Hill cafeteria menu. He began preaching the redistribution of wealth as the cure-all to the Depression. Editorial cartoons portrayed him as a Communist. When the Senate rejected his proposals, he broke with tradition by resigning his committee assignments. But his constant currying of publicity was helping him to build at first a regional and then a national following. He barnstormed through Arkansas to help the reelection of Mrs. Hattie Carraway, a widow serving her late husband's unexpired term: Long was largely responsible for her becoming the first woman elected to a full term in the U.S. Senate. Similar efforts for populist candidates in Texas and Mississippi made him the Southerner to reckon with at the 1932 Democratic National Convention, where he championed Franklin D. Roosevelt—and bullied Southern delegates to do likewise.

When President Roosevelt ignored Long's wealth redistribution ideas and failed to make him one of his close advisors, however, Long turned against him. Using an obscure rule that allowed members of Congress access to the federally-licensed airwaves, he went on national radio only five days after FDR's first "fireside chat" to add his own commentary on the economic health of the nation, a practice he continued for the next three years. As Long became Roosevelt's most frequent Democratic critic in the Senate, FDR, at first only annoyed, grew steadily more concerned and retaliated by cutting off federal patronage jobs in Louisiana.

With FDR's tacit support, resistance to Long grew in Louisiana. The Old Regulars broke with him, in 1934 defeating his candidate in the New Orleans mayoral election. By now Long, increasingly despotic at home, sent in National Guard troops and placed the city under martial law. When the former husband of his reputed mistress threatened to file alienation of affection charges against him, he had the man kidnapped and flown around until the polls closed, then released. He avoided further political defeats by manipulating the state legislature as it reorganized the government's structure, making it the most complete absolutism that ever existed in the U.S. During 1934–35, in eight sessions the legislature passed into law without debate a code of laws that abolished local government, leaving Long control over the hiring and firing of every policeman, fireman, and schoolteacher in Louisiana. He assumed control of the militia and set up his own private police for the Criminal Investigation Bureau. Every judge, tax assessor, and election official also came under his control.

Yet his popularity among the nation's poor, the elderly, and many middle-class whites made him, by late 1933, a national spokesman against wealth and privilege. He paid to publish 100,000 copies of his autobiography, *Every Man a King,* and when 80,000 copies went unsold, distributed them free. Denouncing FDR as "a liar and a faker," he conducted a series of dramatic filibusters against FDR New Deal legislation in the Senate. In January 1934, he organized a Share-Our-Wealth Society, promising a homestead allowance of $6,000 and a minimum annual income of about $2,500 for every American family, at the time a livable amount. The revenue supposedly would have come from limiting fortunes and taxing wealth heavily. Based on the fallacy of taxing physical and monetary wealth equally, the proposal drew seven million members to Long's society by 1935. It was a major factor in driving a reluctant FDR, whose New Deal was by then stalled, to declare a second New Deal in 1935 that included higher, progressive personal income taxes, corporate income taxes, and a Social Security pension system for all Americans. Long had driven FDR farther to the left on the eve of his bid for reelection.

By March 1935, when Long announced he would bolt the Democratic Party if Roosevelt was renominated and run as a third party candidate, he was the second most popular American politician. He went so far as to write a second book, *My First Days in the White House,* in which he laid out his populist agenda—and said he would make FDR his Secretary of the Navy.

Returning to Louisiana in September 1935, to ride heard on a special session of the Legislature, he was hurrying from one legislative chamber to the other at the end of the busy legislative day, walking out far ahead of his gun-toting bodyguards, when a tall, young ear-nose-and-throat specialist, Dr. Carl A. Weiss, stepped into his path. Weiss, who had studied political systems in Europe and whose father-in-law and two other family members had lost their jobs because of Long's ironfisted policies, took a small 32-caliber automatic pistol from his jacket pocket and fired a single shot before he was himself gunned down in a fusillade by Long's bodyguards: fifty-nine holes were found in his body.

Long, hit in the stomach, staggered away, and mumbled, "I wonder why he shot me" as he was helped into a police car and taken to the hospital where he died of peritonitis two days later. More than 250,000 people filed past the open coffin where, laid out in white tuxedo with tails, lay the body of the man who had come to embody long-smoldering agrarian discontent in America. Then they buried the man who almost stopped Roosevelt's reelection on the Capitol lawn. He was forty-two years old. His son, Russell, would be elected in 1948 to his Senate seat, for nearly thirty years quietly carrying out much of his father's agenda.

QUESTIONS FOR THOUGHT AND DISCUSSION

1. How would you account for Huey Long's decision to enter politics? Was he motivated by conviction, greed, or something else? How do his motives compare to those of other politicians?

2. How and why did Long avoid the racist rhetoric that characterized many similarly popular Southern politicians of his day? Does he deserve credit for this, or did it simply not fit into his general scheme to attain power?

3. What was Long able to accomplish as governor of the state of Louisiana? Were the tactics he used a necessary means to a noble end? How do you account for the one-man rule he was able to establish in Louisiana by 1934?

4. Why were millions of Americans so sympathetic to Long's message in the 1930s? Was he a dangerous demagogue, or a true champion of the downtrodden?

SUGGESTED READINGS

Brinkley, Alan. *Voices of Protest: Huey Long, Father Coughlin and the Great Depression.* New York: Knopf, 1982.

Hair, William Ivy. *The Kingfish and His Realm: The Life and Times of Huey P. Long.* Baton Rouge: Louisiana State UP, 1991.

Long, Huey P. *Every Man a King.* Intro. by T. Harry Williams. New York: Quadrangle, 1993.

Opotowsky, Stan. *The Longs of Louisiana.* New York: Dutton, 1960.

Williams, T. Harry. *Huey Long.* New York: Knopf, 1978.

13

Eleanor Roosevelt

In the first two years of the Great Depression, a kind of gloom never seen before engulfed America. By late 1931, the gross national product had fallen by twenty-five percent. The unemployment rate had skyrocketed from a 3.2 percent average in 1929 to a record 16.3 percent. Already drooping in the 1920s, farm prices were falling steadily as panic and anger grew among farm families.

As the economy worsened and middle-class Americans, the majority now living in cities and suburbs, began to lose their jobs, they had to rely on their savings to pay the rent, make the car payment, and buy food and clothing. As they withdrew their savings and the value of bank investments plunged and more and more people defaulted on their mortgages, more and more banks closed their doors. From mid-1929 to July 1930, approximately 640 banks failed; during the next twelve months, another 1,553 closed. In all, by March 1932, 5,500 banks had locked their doors to angry, milling crowds.

As the nation teetered on the edge of complete economic collapse, an unlikely couple offered words of reassurance—newly inaugurated President Franklin Delano Roosevelt used the powerful new medium of radio to rally the nation with a series of "fireside chats"; more frequently, over the next thirteen years as First Lady, Eleanor Roosevelt, in speeches, a daily newspaper column, and magazine articles, brought hope to millions of people, especially women, blacks, and the poor her husband's political problems put beyond reach.

FEW WOMEN HAVE personified the changing lives of American women in the twentieth century more than Eleanor Roosevelt. A New York aristocrat brought up with all the privileges and handicaps of a woman of her class, she was raised under the watchful tutelage of her domineering uncle, President Theodore Roosevelt, until he personally "gave her away" to a cousin, Franklin Delano Roosevelt, who was himself bent on occupying the White House.

Never very far from wealth and power, she never had to support herself—nor would have been allowed to try. Surrounded by servants and tutors, she never went to school until she was fifteen and did not learn to drive, swim, ride a horse, shoot a gun, or type until she was forty—when she learned them all with a vengeance. Her long, slow evolution from a sheltered Victorian debutante to the world's most conspicuous advocate of human rights after World War II closely paralleled the painful emancipation of American women during her nearly eighty years of life.

Born Anna Eleanor Roosevelt, on October 11, 1884, her father, Elliott, was Teddy Roosevelt's younger brother. Her mother, Anna Ludlow Hall, was a famous beauty descended from the Livingstons, land barons who had settled thousands of acres along the upper Hudson River in the eighteenth century. Her father's family had arrived in America even earlier: they were among the original Dutch settlers of New Amsterdam and were wealthy merchants, importers, and mine owners, connected by marriage to many of New York's leading families. Both sides of her family had long considered themselves members of America's ruling class.

Always serious, often sad, Eleanor, as she called herself (Granny, as her mother mockingly called her) was not beautiful like her mother or so many of the socially elite girls around her. Her mother considered her an ugly child who would hide when guests came and suck her fingers until her mother called to her, "Come in, Granny," explaining "She's such a funny child, so old-fashioned that we call her Granny" which only made Eleanor want to die.

One reason she was sad was that her father, a sensitive man whom Eleanor adored, was increasingly addicted to alcohol and drugs and spent much of her early childhood away from home playing polo, riding to hounds, competing in horse shows, drinking, recovering in sanitariums, and taking long voyages with his male hunting and gaming friends. When she was two, Eleanor's father stopped working; on her fourth birthday, the Roosevelt clan gathered for a lavish party. Eleanor threw her arms around her father's neck and told him that she loved everybody and knew everybody loved her. Shortly after that, her father shattered his ankle while rehearsing somersaults for a society circus. The ankle healed improperly and was broken again. He treated the pain with liberal doses of alcohol, morphine, and opium.

When Eleanor was five, her brother, Elliott, Jr., was born. Her father only drank more, rode more recklessly, and partied more. When her Uncle Teddy received legal papers accusing her father of impregnating a former family servant, her father fled the Austrian sanitarium where he had taken refuge, moved his family to Paris, and took a mistress. Uncle Teddy urged her mother to leave him. Instead, she had another of his children. Eleanor's brother, Hall, was born while seven-year-old Eleanor was sent off to a convent outside Paris. That year of 1891, Uncle Teddy filed suit to have his younger brother, Eleanor's father, declared insane. The suit failed, but the scandal hit the New York papers. Uncle Teddy did manage to have the family send Eleanor's father into exile in Abingdon, in southwestern Virginia, ostensibly to oversee family coal mines, but actually to dry out. Once again, Eleanor was heartbroken by their separation.

There was little affection between the child and her mother, who kept up a busy social round and turned her over to servants and tutors all day, only meeting her child after afternoon tea to read aloud to all her children and, after the boys were put to bed, giving her one solitary hour in the evenings she was home. She did not go to school: her mother arranged classes for a small group of the daughters of her rich friends and hired a socially-acceptable tutor. By age seven, Eleanor could neither read nor write. Her new routine was soon interrupted when her mother went to the hospital for surgery, and, while recovering, contracted diphtheria and died suddenly. In a scene she would never forget, she sat in a dark room in her grandmother's house as her father, allowed home briefly from Virginia, told his children of his grief. In her autobiography, she wrote nearly a half-century later how she had promised that:

> Someday I would make a home for him again, we would travel together and do many things . . . . to be looked forward to in the future . . . that he and I were very close and someday would have a life of our own together.

But her father had to return to Virginia, where he wrote long letters to his "dear little Nell." She saw him again the next year, when she was nine and her little brother, Elliott, also died of diphtheria.

When he did move back to New York City, her father took another mistress, drank heavily, and rarely visited Eleanor. In August 1894, after a bout of delirium tremens, he died. Eleanor Roosevelt, age ten, lapsed into "my dream world," where she was to remain closer to her father than she had ever been "when he was alive."

As a ward of an autocratic grandmother, Eleanor lived in a Thirty-seventh Street mansion through her adolescent years, studying French and history, but never playing. When invitations came from classmates, the answer was "no." Only rare family reunions broke the gloom, most often at Uncle Teddy's home, Sagamore Hill, at Oyster Bay, Long Island. She was, he insisted, his favorite niece. To prove it, he tried to teach her to swim in Long Island Sound, nearly drowning—and completely terrifying—her. At one family Christmas Party, when she was fourteen, she danced for the first time with her sixth cousin, Franklin. Her grandmother kept her in short little-girl dresses and she had more than one reason to blush, yet she refused the loan of a more stylish gown from another cousin.

It was probably her Uncle Teddy's idea to send her away to a finishing school shortly after she turned fifteen. She dreaded separation from her family, but she set her mind to succeeding when she arrived in England and found her way to Allenswood, outside London, where her beautiful Aunt Bamie had once been a student. It was her good fortune to find there a remarkable headmistress, Marie Souvestre who, for the next three years, lavished time and affection on Eleanor, refining so many of her instincts. An atheist, a free-thinker, and a brilliant woman unafraid of all sorts of Victorian conventions and censure, Souvestre was the intimate of many writers, politicians, and artists in England and France. She made the sensitive American girl her protegé and, in the summers, her companion as they traveled through Europe. At Allenswood, Eleanor emerged as a leader of the student body. Her school years, she later wrote, were the happiest of her long life. She especially loved traveling:

> Traveling with Mademoiselle Souvestre was a revelation. She did all the things that in a vague way you had always felt you wanted to do. As I think back over my trips, I real-

ize she taught me how to enjoy travelling . . . to be comfortable . . . to go where you would see the people of the country you were visiting, not your own compatriots.

Traveling to learn about people all over the world would become central to Eleanor's way of life, but she always regretted that she had little formal education, learning how to become an accomplished Victorian lady but never even approaching a college level of studies.

Returning at age eighteen to New York City a graceful, very tall young lady now fashionably dressed by her mother's sisters, she stood out among that year's debutantes not for her appearance—she had big, protruding teeth—but for her intelligent conversation. Her debut at the Assembly Ball meant she could join the newly formed Junior League and teach as an unpaid volunteer at the Rivington Street Settlement House in the Lower East Side of Manhattan. With her friend, Jean Reid, she taught classes in calisthenics and dancing to young girls taking a respite from the harsh life of the tenement and the sweatshop. She quickly learned to love her newfound role as an albeit-untrained social worker. She soon enrolled in another group, the New York Consumers' League, where she came face-to-face for the first time with terrible living and working conditions as she helped to investigate the daily life of young women working in garment factories and department stores. League inspections led to "white lists" of businesses which provided adequate safety and sanitary conditions and paid fairly. Stores not listed were boycotted by other upper-crust shoppers.

In the fall of 1903, Eleanor was also spending more and more time with her cousin, Franklin, a handsome, debonair, young man who had earned, at private school at Groton and college at Harvard, a reputation as a good-natured fellow noted for his charm and mindless chatter. Franklin seemed uncharacteristically drawn to this serious, thoughtful, young kinswoman, even if she did not ride, swim, or sail, his favorite activities. When twenty-one-year-old Franklin informed his mother, the formidable Sara Delano, that he intended to marry nineteen-year-old Eleanor, she objected that they were too young and persuaded Franklin to wait to announce their engagement for one year. Without asking Eleanor, he agreed. In the meantime, he was to go back to Harvard (where his mother took an apartment nearby) and Eleanor remained in New York. The strange relationship foreshadowed decades of intrusion and manipulation by Sara Delano; in the end, all she succeeded in doing was delaying the marriage.

On March 17, 1905, Eleanor and Franklin were married. It was St. Patrick's Day and President Theodore Roosevelt had to be in New York City anyway. Two hundred guests gathered in the drawing rooms of two adjoining family mansions on East Sixty-Sixth Street as President Roosevelt charged into the festivities and escorted Eleanor, "giving her away" while "keeping the name in the family," as he put it. The bride and groom were all but forgotten in the swirl around the President. They were summoned to Sara Delano's estate at Hyde Park on the Hudson for a week before leaving on their honeymoon. Once again, Eleanor did not object, even when Sara sent along Franklin's lawbooks for him to study while they sailed to England.

For the next ten years, she would put aside her settlement house work and devote herself to pleasing her husband and her mother-in-law while giving birth to six children. "Their tastes and interests dominate me," she wrote of her husband and his mother. After the birth of James, their first son, mother-in-law Sara built twin townhouses with connecting drawing and dining rooms and upstairs hallways that joined; for summer vacations, she built them a cottage on Campobello Island off the coast of Maine—next door to her own.

When he was asked to run for the New York State Senate, for the first time, Franklin, encouraged by Eleanor, disagreed with his mother in 1910. His speeches were slow and painfully halting, but to everyone's surprise, he won. The young family moved to Albany, for the first time away from Sara's iron grip. Eleanor, still unsure that she could have any political role—"It never occurred to me"—dutifully raised the children, ran the household, and watched her husband from the Senate gallery.

After Franklin supported Woodrow Wilson in the 1912 election against Cousin Teddy's candidacy on the Bull Moose ticket, he was offered the post of Assistant Secretary of the Navy, a post Teddy Roosevelt himself had once held. Once again they moved, this time to Washington, D.C., in 1913; to help her with her busy social calendar, Eleanor hired a beautiful young secretary, Lucy Mercer. Eleanor and the children joined Sara at Campobello each summer as Franklin spent most of the summer in Washington. By 1916, Franklin was spending more and more time with Lucy Mercer. Eleanor's cousin, Alice Longworth Roosevelt, with a disloyalty Eleanor never forgave, helped to arrange their meetings.

In July 1918, Franklin was sent on an inspection tour of American forces in Europe. He arrived home two months later suffering from acute pneumonia. As Eleanor nursed him back to health, she discovered love letters from Lucy Mercer. Franklin confessed their love affair. Eleanor offered to divorce him. Only Sara's threat to cut off her son's inheritance and allowance if he left his wife and children dissuaded him from marrying Lucy Mercer. Devastated, Eleanor was never again physically intimate with her husband, but she decided not to destroy his political career by leaving him.

After the United States entered World War I, Eleanor helped organize Red Cross canteens in Washington to offer hot food, kind words, and postcards to thousands of troops being shipped through the Capital en route to Europe. In 1919, when Franklin was assigned to go to Europe to oversee the decommissioning of Navy forces, he urged Eleanor to come along. Together, they toured frontline trenches, cemeteries, and hospitals. Eleanor became one of a small number of American women to see the horror of the "war to end all wars," gaining knowledge that proved invaluable. They were in Paris while President Wilson negotiated the Versailles Treaty and advocated the League of Nations to prevent future wars. In June 1920, Franklin was nominated to run for Vice President on the Democratic ticket. Eleanor traveled with him, the only woman among the entourage of politicians and journalists, as he made his campaign tour by train. By now, Franklin was becoming an avid public speaker; Eleanor yanked his coattails when she thought he'd gone on too long.

Women voted for the first time in 1920. At first, Eleanor was opposed to women's suffrage. She mostly didn't vote for the Democrats who based their campaign on United States ratification of the Versailles Treaty. Spending more time away from her husband and his mother, Eleanor became active in the League of

Women Voters. In 1921, she traveled as a New York state delegate to the organization's second national convention. That summer, after Roosevelt went for a swim at Campobello, he was suddenly stricken with polio and was left permanently crippled from the waist down. When Sara urged her son to retire to Hyde Park, he resisted her. Eleanor became his proxy. She began attending meetings and speaking for him.

She also became more politically active in her own rite, joining the Women's Trade Union League. While her husband worked ceaselessly to regain some use of his limbs, spending winters first in Florida, then in Warm Springs, Georgia, Eleanor converted a separate cottage at Hyde Park, where she lived with two close friends, Nancy Cook and Marion Dickerman, helping them to build a furniture factory at Val-Kill, New York, that later also produced pewter and weaving. Franklin gave the three women lifetime rights to the land. Now, Eleanor only drove over to dinner at Sara's and stayed in her mother-in-law's house during Franklin's visits. Although she was wealthy, she insisted on earning her own money. She began to teach three days a week at a private school in New York City. As she began to emancipate herself, she learned how to cook, drive, and type. Her reeducation began when her husband ran for governor of New York and won in 1928. She maintained her Val-Kill-New York City schedule half the week, played First Lady in Albany the other half, with the help of a secretary answering every letter addressed to the Governor. She also became her crippled husband's surrogate on countless inspections of state facilities, driven around the state by a handsome state trooper, Corporal Earl Miller, who taught her to use a handgun, to ride and swim. As her biographer, Joseph Lash, puts it, "she in turn mothered his romances."

After two terms in Albany, Eleanor and Franklin emerged as a team which operated smoothly as FDR ran for and won the Presidency in 1932. She was the idealist; he was the pragmatist. When he was elected President, Eleanor attempted to maintain their intimate working routine, but FDR refused to let her go on answering his mail after he moved into the White House. She, in turn, refused to be limited to the traditional role of First Lady as social hostess. She began to see herself as an instigator and agitator of social changes that FDR might have taken longer to initiate. Through a daily column, "My Day," eventually syndicated to 350 newspapers and through a monthly column in *Woman's Home Companion*, she proselytized reforms that were *theirs* as much as *his*. Sometimes, they were hers, first. Taking a voice coach, she overcame her fear of speaking and became a polished, passionate speaker, never reading a speech or looking at a note after preparing thoroughly. She hired a lecture agent and toured widely, rebuffing criticisms that she was using her position to make money. She was making a lot of it, she said, but she gave much of it away and she paid taxes.

As time went on, she frequently was more radical than FDR. She openly favored the Loyalists in the Spanish Civil War, but did not push her husband. When Madrid fell to the fascist Franco forces, she told a militant New Deal ally, "We should have pushed him [FDR] harder." When the House Un-American Activities Committee began to grill youth leaders in 1939 for Communist ties, she invited them back to the White House for dinner after they testified before the committee. Because she believed young people had been especially hard hit by the

AP/Wide World

Always careful to keep her husband in the limelight, Eleanor Roosevelt brought idealism to Franklin Delano Roosevelt's pragmatic New Deal policies.

Depression, she became personal friends with several leaders of the pro-Communist American Youth Congress, helping them before government agencies and fundraising for them. When World War II broke out, she felt especially betrayed to learn that the AYC was Communist-backed and controlled by Moscow.

As she traveled the country during the Depression, she became convinced that government had to encourage and protect human welfare and social justice. "We have come to recognize that government has a responsibility to defend the weak." In the impoverished hollows of West Virginia, she donated substantially to create a coal miners' community called Arthurdale, where she helped finance prefabricated workers' housing and an experimental school and paid teachers' salaries. She visited frequently, joined in the square dancing, and bounced miners' children on her knees while she listened sympathetically to their mothers.

While FDR's New Deal did little specifically to help blacks, it prevented the worsening of economic conditions among blacks as well as whites. The perception that FDR helped the black community was largely the result of Eleanor's efforts as she pressed FDR, who was wary of loosing the support of white Southern Democratic leaders and voters. She pushed FDR to appoint black educator Mary McLeod Bethune to the National Youth Administration. She toured black schools, churches, and relief programs, spoke at conventions of black organizations, and invited black leaders to White House receptions. In May 1936, after she inspected a black reformatory for girls in Washington, D.C., she described terrible conditions there at her next press conference to the all female press corps she founded to cover First Ladies. Then she invited the young women prisoners to a garden party on the White House lawn. "It seems to me," she said, "as every young person enjoys an occasional good time, these youngsters should have an occasional good time." When black opera star Marion Anderson was refused permission by the Daughters of the American Revolution (DAR) to sing at Constitution Hall, Eleanor quite publicly canceled her membership in the organization.

So respected had she become among Democrats by 1940 that, when FDR decided to seek an unprecedented third term, breaking with the two-term tradition set by Washington and Jefferson, she personally confronted a revolt at the Democratic National Convention in Chicago by insisting that the delegates accept the Progressive, Henry Wallace, as FDR's running mate even as they accepted FDR. "You cannot treat [this nomination] as you would treat an ordinary nomination in an ordinary time," she admonished them. Wallace was nominated and FDR's candidacy was safe—without FDR ever leaving the White House.

As she became more influential, Eleanor began to encounter more resentment from Congressional leaders. FDR asked her to become co-chairman of the Office of Civilian Defense (OCD) just before Pearl Harbor. Politicians who dared not attack FDR in wartime made OCD a scapegoat, slashing funds for social programs she intended for women and blacks. In February 1942, she resigned. Instead, she began making fact-finding trips for FDR, visiting England in 1942 and the South Pacific in 1943, touring field hospitals and front lines, encouraging thousands of troops and trouble-shooting for her husband.

Yet she knew her constant pressuring of her husband for better conditions at home and abroad was a delicate matter. To her "My Day" readers, she wrote:

> When we are dealing with busy people, no matter how interested we ourselves may be in a subject, we must put what we have to say in the briefest possible form. This is even more important if the person to whom we are talking is listening because of our interest and not because of his own. We may be able to impart some of our enthusiasm to him if we do not first bore him to death and make him impatient because he is being asked to listen to too many words.

That she often failed to follow her own advice can be deduced from the film FDR requested to be shown at an intimate after-dinner gathering in the White House on Eleanor and Franklin's fortieth wedding anniversary: it was *The Suspect,* an English murder mystery about a man driven to kill his nagging wife. The vivacious FDR always preferred lighthearted chatter and banter to serious talk and confrontation. He spent many hours in the company of a beautiful Norwegian princess-in-exile who lived in the White House all through the war. "Nothing is more pleasing to the eye than a good-looking lady," he once remarked, "nothing more refreshing to the spirit than the company of one, nothing more flattering to the ego than the affection of one."

If FDR could still wound Eleanor, he managed to, even when he died in Warm Springs, Georgia, in April 1945, while Eleanor remained at work in Washington. At FDR's side when he suffered a fatal cerebral hemorrhage was Lucy Mercer, his old flame from World War I, now a widow but still beautiful. Eleanor's final humiliation at the hands of FDR was to learn that Lucy had visited FDR many times at the White House and had gone for long drives with him while Eleanor globetrotted as his unofficial ambassador. Eleanor later wrote:

> He might have been happier with a wife who was completely uncritical. That I was never able to be, and he had to find it in some other people. Nevertheless, I think I sometimes acted as a spur, even though the spurring was not always wanted or welcome. I was one of those who served his purposes.

At the 1944 Democratic convention, Eleanor had opposed the nomination of Harry S Truman as Vice President. Now succeeding FDR, Truman appointed her one of five delegates to the first United Nations General Assembly in London. A hard-driving delegate, she was assigned to Committee III, charged with humanitarian, social and cultural affairs. President Truman also appointed her to the United Nation Human Rights Commission, given the task of drafting an international bill of rights. At the second General Assembly she chaired the eighteen-member commission. She was the driving force behind the United Nation's adoption of the Human Rights Charter, adopted by every member nation except eight Soviet-bloc members who abstained.

Eleanor remained a United Nation's delegate for eight years until the Eisenhower Administration replaced her in 1953. She had publicly criticized Dwight Eisenhower during his election campaign for not disavowing the scare tactics of McCarthy Era Red-baiters. She had made other enemies as well. Because of her writings in her column in favor of birth control, and because of her outspoken opposition to federal aid to parochial schools, Francis Cardinal Spelman, Roman Catholic archbishop of New York City, denounced her as anti-Catholic and accused her "of discrimination unworthy of an American mother." The mother of six defended herself stoutly in print in a "My Day" column: "The final judgment, my dear Cardinal Spelman, of the worthiness of all human beings is in the hands of God."

Working vigorously as an unpaid, unofficial ambassador-at-large for the American Association for the United Nations, she visited the Middle East, Asia, and Europe, working tirelessly through her seventies for the establishment of a Jewish state. Although she had opposed his nomination, President John F. Kennedy named her to the U.S. delegation of the United Nations where she worked unsuccessfully until her death to see the Human Rights Charter given the force of international law. Longtime honorary chairman (and a co-founder) of Americans for Democratic Action, she gave up forty years of opposition to an equal rights amendment to the Constitution for women and, in her last public service, served as chair of the Commission on the Status of Women appointed by Kennedy. She died at age seventy-eight on November 7, 1962. She took a dim view of her own importance and certainly would not agree to the title of First Lady of the World conferred on her by *Time* magazine. As a girl, she had imbibed her Uncle Teddy's optimistic advice: "Do the best you can with what you have where you are." A lifetime of disappointments and sadness as well as achievements tempered her own advice in an Edward R. Murrow interview in 1953: "You have to accept whatever comes and the only important thing is that you meet it with courage and with the best that you have to give."

QUESTIONS FOR THOUGHT AND DISCUSSION

1. Do you think Eleanor Roosevelt should have remained married to her husband after she learned of his affair? Was their marriage a good one?

2. What affect did Franklin's struggle with polio have on Eleanor? In what ways did it liberate her, even as it limited movement for her husband?

3. How did Eleanor Roosevelt deviate from the traditional role of first ladies? How did her agenda differ from that of her husband?

4. Why did Eleanor come so late to support an equal rights amendment for women? Had society changed, or had she?

SUGGESTED READINGS

Cook, Blanche Wiesen. *Eleanor Roosevelt*. Volume I: 1884–1933. New York: Viking, 1992.

Goodwin, Doris Kearns. *No Ordinary Time*. New York: Simon, 1994.

Lash, Joseph P. *Eleanor and Franklin: The Story of Their Relationship*. New York: Norton, 1971.

_____. *Eleanor: The Years Alone*. New York: Norton, 1972.

Roosevelt, Eleanor. *This Is My Story*. New York: Harper, 1937.

Scharf, Lois. *Eleanor Roosevelt: First Lady of American Liberalism*. Boston: Twayne, 1987.

_____. *My Days*. New York: Dodge, 1938.

14

George Patton

The twentieth century brought a new era of warfare that put into the hands of governments an array of new weapons produced by technologies developed since the Industrial Revolution. New tools for mass killing proliferated until this century became the deadliest of all times, by one estimate claiming the lives of 160 million soldiers and civilians. World War I commanders used mass conscription and the new technologies: railroads, dirigibles, airplanes, machine guns, poison gas, tanks, automobiles, trucks, submarines, and cannon that fired fifty miles. The new weaponry would be further refined for use in World War II, which broke out only twenty-one years later.

The introduction of the latest weapons speedily by all combatants led to a long, bloody stalemate only broken by the entrance of the Americans, who brought five million fresh, if all but totally inexperienced men in on the side of the exhausted French and English. The few seasoned fighters in the United States were experts mainly in cavalry tactics, but horses had already been rendered useless by entrenchments, barbed wire, and machine guns. Ironically, it was a cavalry officer who became the most distinguished practitioner of armored and mechanized cavalry warfare in World War II. He was George S. Patton, Jr., the first American "tanker" and possibly the most controversial American in either war.

GEORGE SMITH PATTON, JR. had few doubts about things (except himself). From his boyhood, he never doubted for a moment that he wanted to be a soldier, like so many of his ancestors, and that he would someday be a general because the public would regard him as a hero and insist that he be made one. He never doubted that he would have the opportunities he would need to accomplish whatever he wanted and have enough money or know the right people who would, of course, want to advance his interests and reward him. The only doubts he ever had were mostly about his own physical courage, which he confided only to a few family members and his wife. Certainly, no one else ever doubted his courage, which from early childhood he was sure he should always demonstrate as ostentatiously as possible.

Patton's confidence as well as his carefully concealed self-doubts came from a family he was only half proud of—his father's half. His father, a lawyer when George was born on November 11, 1885, was the elected district attorney of Los Angeles County. He later became the wealthy owner of thousands of acres of Southern California vineyards and farmlands. With Henry E. Huntington, he was the principal developer of Pasadena and San Gabriel and was the first mayor of San Marino. More important to young George was his father's Virginia ancestry. His first American forefather, Robert Patton, emigrated from Scotland on the eve of the American Revolution and married the daughter of General Hugh Mercer, bayoneted to death at the Battle of Princeton in 1776. Mercer, a close friend of George Washington, was George Patton's first hero. Robert Patton's son Robert, Jr., and his wife Margaret had twelve children, including seven sons, all of whom fought as officers in the Confederate Army in the Civil War: three studied warfare under Professor Thomas J. "Stonewall" Jackson at Virginia Military Institute (VMI). One of George's grand-uncles died at Gettysburg in Pickett's charge. Seven Patton first cousins were also Confederate officers. George's favorite family hero was his grandfather, who practiced law until John Brown's raid, then organized the Kanawha Rifles. These West Virginians became Company H, 22d Virginia Infantry, under Colonel Patton raiding Washington, D.C., with Jubal Early's corps and nearly capturing President Abraham Lincoln. At Cedar Creek in September 1864, Patton was killed leading his troops.

Any chance of being born a Virginian was lost to George, Jr., when his grandmother left the wartorn Old Dominion forever and traveled to Los Angeles, where her brother was a lawyer. She taught school and scraped by until she married her husband's cousin, also a VMI graduate and Confederate colonel in the war. Little Georgie Patton loved to hear his grandfather's Civil War stories. "Men of my blood," he later wrote, "have ever inspired me. Should I falter, I will have disgraced my blood." His father, too, had briefly followed family tradition returning to Virginia long enough to attend VMI and, as the first captain of cadets, led VMI's gray-uniformed students on parade in Philadelphia during the nation's Centennial in 1876—the first Southern military formation on Northern soil since the Civil War.

Oddly, George's pride of heritage did not extend to his mother's family, remarkable for its toughness in the face of physical hardship, charm, drive, and willpower. George's father, a French instructor at VMI briefly, returned to Los Angeles and married Ruth Wilson, whose family was as colorful as the Pattons. George's maternal grandfather, B. D. Wilson, was a major in the American Revolution who became a pioneer in Tennessee, a member of the Territorial Assembly and Speaker of the House. His fifteen-year-old son went West to New Mexico: there, he was a fur trapper, Indian trader, and storekeeper before settling in San Gabriel, California, in 1841 and purchasing 2,200 acres to make up a cattle ranch which covered present-day San Bernardino and Riverside. He married Ramona Yorba, the Mexican girl next door, whose family's ranch included most of today's Orange County.

Accepting a U.S. Army captain's commission in the Bear Flag Revolt, B. D. Wilson moved to downtown Los Angeles, bought a vineyard, started a general merchandising business, bought a hotel, bought town lots at auction, grew rich, and became the first mayor of Los Angeles. His 4,000 downtown acres include the University of California, Los Angeles campus. Gradually, he also amassed 14,000 rural acres including present-day Pasadena, San Marino, and San Gabriel. George Patton's parents owned so much land and were so wealthy that he didn't know how well off he was until his own future father-in-law asked his father for a financial statement.

Like Woodrow Wilson, whom he detested, George Patton suffered from dyslexia. He did not go to school until he was nearly twelve. His father read aloud to him and trained his memory. The books he loved to hear included Sir Walter Scott's romantic tales, chivalric epics of Scottish lore, Homer's *Iliad* and *Odyssey*, Xenophon's adventures, Shakespeare's tragedies, with a light dash of Rudyard Kipling. His father was a mystic who believed in prophecies as well as in a self-righteous Old Testament God. Dyslexia forced young Patton to struggle, honed his drive and lifelong yearning to read and master history.

One month before his twelfth birthday, George enrolled in Cutter Clark's School for Boys in Pasadena, where he loved to study the lives of the military heroes of ancient Greece and Rome, as well as Joan of Arc and Napoleon. At home, he revelled in visits from a neighbor, Colonel John Singleton Mosby, the famous Confederate raider who had become a lawyer for the Southern Pacific Railroad. Other former Confederates came to call and he was thrilled whenever the talk turned to Robert E. Lee. Outdoors much of the time, he became an expert rider, hunter, sailor, and fisherman, in the summers catching enormous sea bass and marlin off Catalina Island, where his parents had a cottage. After six years at Clark's school (where he never learned to spell), he followed family tradition and enrolled at VMI, at the same time applying to the U.S. Military Academy at West Point. That summer, he also met Beatrice Ayer, two years younger but already a fearless sailor.

Handsome and six feet-tall, Patton was a model cadet at VMI, although his dyslexia caused serious trouble. He had to struggle to decipher every word. Accepted to West Point in 1904 after a year at VMI, he again ran into difficulties, this time flunking mathematics and posting poor marks in French. He had to repeat plebe year. He was only a little more successful in sports. He played so recklessly in football practices that he injured his arm and failed to make the team. He tried out for track and earned a letter in high hurdles. In his second year, as a cadet officer he gave out so many demerits to incoming plebes that he became unpopular and was demoted from second to sixth corporal. Obsessed with the idea that he was a coward, he joined the fencing team and became an impressive broadswordsman. He also earned a reputation as a daring horseman. In his final year, after climbing back up through the ranks of class officers, he became adjutant of the corps of cadets, the leader of his class.

Through his years at West Point, Patton was Bea Ayer's constant escort. When she asked him why he wanted a soldier's hard life, he explained he felt the pull of heredity, love of excitement, and a reputation: "If you take away these three things, what is left in life?" It had taken Patton five years to complete West Point. Graduating in 1909, he stood forty-sixth in a class of 103. He chose to be commissioned a second lieutenant of cavalry. One year later, he married Bea, daughter of a wealthy Boston textile manufacturer. They would have three children.

Posted first to Fort Sheridan, near Chicago, he used his ample leisure time to ride to hounds, lay out a polo field, coach a football team, and start a self-study course in military reading. His commanding officer rated him "the most enthusiastic soldier of my acquaintance [who] misses no chance to improve." One other thing he practiced was a more fearsome facial expression, standing for hours in front of a mirror to alter his boyish appearance into the sullen glower of a man of war. He developed a lifelong reputation for spit-and-polish. Even when he and his bride settled into a tiny house on the base, he insisted that they dress for dinner. "The poorer the surroundings," he said, "the more important it is to keep up your standards."

He also learned at Fort Sheridan the art of wire-pulling. His commander, his father, and his father-in-law all used their connections to find him a post at Fort Myers, Virginia, where the Army Chief of Staff was stationed and where a gentleman could attract attention by his horsemanship in polo matches and military funeral processions. Arriving in 1911 at Fort Myers, within a year he won a place on the U.S. Olympic team. In the Stockholm Olympics, where a Native American, Jim Thorpe, won three gold medals, Patton scored fifth in modern pentathlon, missing the target twice as he fired his pistol on horseback. But he was the only fencer who beat the French champion and he obtained permission to stay on in France to take private sword and saber lessons from him. Back in Washington, D.C., he continued to make a name for himself in steeplechase races, explaining to his father-in-law:

> What I am doing looks like play to you but in my business it is the best sort of advertising. It makes people talk and that is a sign they are noticing . . . . The notice of others has been the start of many successful men.

It was as a swordsman that Patton attracted early attention that led to rapid advancement. Within a few years, automatic weapons and armor-plated tanks would permanently alter the nature of cavalry warfare, but in the last few years before World War I, no one could foresee this. George Patton designed a new straight saber for the use of cavalry and managed to have it adopted by the Army after he besieged the Army Chief of Staff with journal articles on the subject. Early in 1913, the Secretary of War ordered the manufacture of 20,000 of the new Patton sabers. After a summer in France where he learned the fine points of saber instructorship, Patton was transferred to the Mounted Service School at Fort Riley, Kansas, where he was given the title "Master of the Sword" and wrote regulations for the new sword. Once again, he had used connections to avoid being sent to the jungles of the Philippines with his unit.

When American troops were sent to Vera Cruz, Mexico, in April 1914, to protect American business interests during a civil war, Patton began a personal campaign to get himself posted to Fort Bliss at El Paso, Texas, on the Mexican border. There, he attracted the attention of the new American commander, Brigadier General John J. Pershing, with a dazzling demonstration of marksmanship. While out hunting one day, he shot a running jackrabbit at fifteen yards while riding at a trot. On March 9, 1916, Pancho Villa raided Columbus, New Mexico, killing seventeen Americans. President Wilson ordered Pershing to lead a Punitive Expeditionary Force to hunt down Villa. The year-long, 400-mile incursion into northern Mexico's rugged mountain terrain was a failure—except for Patton. Lying to Pershing that he was experienced in dealing with war correspondents, he was taken along as Pershing's temporary aide-de-camp. Pershing, whose wife and children had recently perished in a fire, was also attracted to Patton's sister, who visited him several times. The high point of Patton's Mexican adventure came when Patton decided to search for a Villa captain, Julio Carderas, who lived on a ranch near Rubio. Using three staff cars crammed with cavalry troopers, Pershing flushed out the Villistas, who tried to ride him down and escape. Blazing away with a pistol, Patton got off five shots that killed one man, then fired his rifle at three men trying to escape. In all, Patton killed three men. Then he strapped their bodies on the hoods of the cars and sped away as forty mounted Villistas charged on horseback after him. Patton's picture appeared for the first time on the front page of the *New York Times* and in papers across America. Pershing praised him in official reports. Patton had made military history, using a motorized unit in battle for the first time.

In April 1917, Patton, promoted to captain and still on Pershing's staff, sailed to France when the U.S. entered World War I. Appointed post adjutant of U.S. headquarters east of Paris, he was in charge of 250 men and ninety vehicles. He became interested in a new weapon, the tank, invented early in the war by the English and French. Promoted to major, he was assigned by Pershing to direct the first U.S. tank school, using borrowed light French two-man tanks. In this first command, he built a reputation as a popular leader. When his first 200-man contingent arrived by train, he had a hot meal ready, latrines already dug, and sleeping quarters arranged on neighboring farms.

Late in April 1917, he organized the 1st Light Tank Battalion; two months later, the 1st Light Tank Brigade. Attending the Army General Staff College as a student, he also taught on tank tactics. By August 1918, he commanded fifty officers, 900 men, and twenty-five tanks. On September 12, he led the first American tank corps of 174 tanks into battle in the great St. Mihiel offensive, riding into action atop a tank to encourage his men as machine gun bullets spattered around him. Only three tanks were lost in the American victory. Less than two weeks later, Patton's tankers were ordered to attack again. Advancing five miles, they captured Varennes. Whenever German artillery opened fire, Patton took cover in a ditch. Four out of six of his staff were shot before Patton himself was shot through the thigh. Hospitalized briefly, he was promoted to colonel at age thirty-two and awarded the Distinguished Service Medal and the Distinguished Service Cross for "conspicuous courage, coolness, energy and intelligence in directing the advance of his brigade . . . under heavy machine gun and artillery fire." His wife asked him whether his conscience hurt after killing. He said he felt the way he did when he landed his first swordfish.

In the interwar years, Patton commanded the 304th Tank Brigade at Camp Meade, Maryland. By 1922, chafing for action in peacetime, he rejoined the cavalry at his old rank of captain. Serving tours at Fort Riley, the Command College, in Boston and Hawaii (sailing there with his wife and children aboard their own sailboat), he was appointed to the office of the Chief of Cavalry in Washington in time to witness the rout of the "Bonus Marchers" by General Douglas MacArthur in 1932. He spent much of his free time writing articles on military procedure, history, weapons, and tactics.

UPI/Bettmann

Preferring daring attacks over long distances, America's first "tanker" general, George Patton, wore pearl-handled revolvers into combat in two world wars.

When German tanks overran Europe in the opening months of World War II, Patton was given a tank brigade at Fort Benning, Georgia. In April 1941, promoted to major general, he was made commander of a tank division. Within a month of the declaration of World War II by the United States, Patton was made a corps commander in charge of the Western Task Force. He set up the first large-scale tank training center in the desert where Arizona, Nevada, and California meet. With the training motto, "Kill or be killed," he introduced integrated combat tactics allowing tanks, artillery, and infantry to work together.

When the Allies launched Operation Torch in November 1942, to drive back the Germans in North Africa, Patton led the Americans landings on the Atlantic beaches west of Casablanca, Morocco, at the same time the Allies under Dwight D. Eisenhower were landing in Algeria. Patton coordinated three distinct landings over a 200-mile stretch of Atlantic beach. His forces moved inland quickly and seized the only modern airport in Morocco. Meeting stiff Vichy French resistance, he threatened to attack the crowded capitol of Casablanca itself unless the French surrendered. On Patton's fifty-seventh birthday, Casablanca surrendered. He allowed the French to keep their arms and merely confined them to their barracks, thus freeing American troops to streak west after the Germans. To an ovation from American soldiers and sailors and to the delight of the press at home, Patton emerged from Casablanca the hero of North Africa.

When Allied leaders arrived in Casablanca for their first summit meeting in January 1943, Patton, the new Allied commander in North Africa, served as the unofficial host. He met with President Roosevelt, with his old friend, Army Chief of Staff George C. Marshall. The Allies decided to attack Sicily, close to the Italian mainland, next in a joint Anglo-American operation. In March, the Germans under Field Marshal Erwin Rommel counterattacked fiercely in Tunisia. Patton had been busy building American morale. He had visited every division, prodded officers, insisted on official uniforms, salutes and courtesy, and fined officers and men for violations. He harangued his troops on the need to kill rather than die for freedom: "We must utterly defeat the enemy." When the massive German counterattack came at El Guettar, Patton's divisions held, drawing off German divisions from the main British force. Once again, he took great personal risks in a jeep, leading his tanks through mine fields. When General Marshall praised his latest victory, Patton commented, "War is very simple, direct, and ruthless. It takes a simple, direct, and ruthless man to wage war."

Promoted to lieutenant general, Patton, in command of the U.S. Seventh Army, joined the equally flamboyant Bernard L. Montgomery, heading the British Eighth Army, in the invasion of Sicily. Patton's three amphibious divisions were to sweep across western Sicily and take Palermo. This he quickly accomplished, even as Montgomery took over the road to Messina assigned to Patton's forces. Infuriated, Patton ignored the Allied plan and raced into Messina ahead of the British, who had bogged down. Credit for the Allied conquest of Sicily in only thirty-eight days of heavy fighting largely fell to Patton, further fueling British resentment of his grandstanding tactics.

Increasingly, Patton's high-handedness offset his enormous popularity. On August 10, 1943, as he toured military hospitals in Sicily, he slapped and cursed at two soldiers suffering from combat exhaustion, denouncing them as cowards. Actually, one of the men was also suffering from malaria and dysentery. Patton's immediate superior hushed up the matter, reluctant to lose such a good officer. To strike an enlisted man was a serious offense. But medical staff at the hospital reported the incident to Allied commander-in-chief Dwight D. Eisenhower, who demanded Patton apologize to his troops. When the story broke in the American press, Patton's career was almost ruined.

In March 1944, Eisenhower transferred Patton to England to train the U.S. Third Army not for the initial D-Day landings in France, but for second-stage operations in Normandy. He tried to keep Patton's whereabouts secret: the Germans, considering him the American Rommel, feared Patton more than other Allied leaders and tied down their entire Fifteenth Army at Pas de Calais, thinking Patton would land there. On August 1, 1944, nearly two months after D-Day and after the Allies broke through German defenses at St. Ló, Patton landed and led his Third Army in a brilliant breakout. Rolling in high gear, Patton sent his main force west toward the walled port city of St. Malo, as some 20,000 French resistance fighters rose up in Brittany. The Germans barricaded themselves inside the port cities of St. Malo, Lorient, Brest, Nantes, and St. Nazaire, depriving the Allies of badly-needed ports. Patton sent one of his four corps after them and besieged each city until only rubble remained. At St. Malo, German anti-aircraft guns on fortified offshore islands were turned against the medieval walls; inside, Patton's tanks and 155 millimeter guns dueled with German 88's for thirty days until nothing was left of the city. Brest also was pounded into burned-out ruins before the Germans finally surrendered in mid-December. Lorient's German garrison held out until the war ended.

Earning the nickname "Old Blood and Guts," Patton drove his main fighting force relentlessly east, determined to cross the Rhine River and reach Germany before the British commander, Montgomery. He learned from a German message intercepted by Ultra, the secret intelligence decoder in England, that Hitler had ordered a massive counterattack for August 8. Patton rushed north to cut off the Germans from the rear. Only Omar Bradley's direct order to stop until the Canadians, who had slowed down, could overtake him prevented Patton from enveloping and annihilating a crack 150,000-man German army. Instead, Patton's armored divisions raced eastward, liberating Chartres and Orleans. Coming to the outskirts of Paris, he allowed the city to be liberated by a French division under his command. Patton was moving so fast that he had to be supplied by air in what he termed "the fastest and biggest pursuit in history." On August 15, as the Allies rolled into Paris, Eisenhower released Patton's name to the press for the first time since the Sicilian slapping incident. Once again, Patton was the hero of the war. To his wife, Bea, in Boston, whom he had not seen in nearly two years, he wrote, "Well, I am delighted and know that your long and loyal confidence in me is justified."

With his army racing eastward toward familiar World War I battlefields and his advance units travelling seventy miles in a single day, Patton outran his supply lines, his historic onslaught sputtering out as his tanks ran out of gas. The dogged German defense of the Channel ports had created tremendous fuel shortages. Patton pleaded for 400,000 gallons of gas so that he could pursue the enemy into Germany and smash the retreating Germans before they could reorganize. But Eisenhower decided first to supply the British attack through Belgium toward German launching sites for the V–1 and V–2 rockets that were killing thousands of civilians in London. In a single month, Patton had liberated almost all of France north of the Loire even as his armies attacked on three different fronts, but now he was reined in. To reporters, he railed indirectly at Eisenhower: "Whenever you slow anything down, you waste human lives."

All Patton could do was wait for resupply. He tried to keep morale high, making sure that the men whenever possible got hot food, clean socks every day, hot showers, mail from home, and visits to rear-area towns. By the time gasoline arrived with orders to attack again on November 8, rain was falling every day, four inches of mud covered everything, the tanks bogged down, and the Germans were ready and waiting, contesting every inch of soil in savage fighting.

A creature of intuition, Patton was sure the Germans were going to counterattack. Throughout the war, he maintained a high regard for their fighting abilities. While other American officers thought the Germans had been beaten, Patton prepared his men. On December 16, the Germans, reinforced by 250,000 fresh troops and fast new Tiger tanks, began a massive assault through the Ardennes forests of Belgium, driving back the Americans and encircling the 101st Airborne Division. The Battle of the Bulge caught Eisenhower unprepared: not so Patton. He told an incredulous Eisenhower he could swing his army north and begin to hit the Germans in three days. With 250,000 men slithering on icy winter roads and with thousands of tanks and trucks, he charged north and broke the German siege. In the bloodiest fighting of the American war effort, there were 77,000 American casualties: thousands of highly-trained sixteen-year-old Hitler youth died in the last great battle in Europe.

To his wife, Patton wrote, "Destiny sent for me in a hurry when things got tight." Publicly, Patton gave most of the credit for his greatest victory to his men:

> The people who actually did it were the young officers and soldiers . . . . Marching all night in the cold, over roads they had never seen, and nobody got lost, and everybody getting to the place in time—it is a very marvelous feat: I know of no equal to it in military history . . . . I take off my hat to them.

It was Patton's final victory. He was a warrior, he was not suited to peace. The Third Army crossed the Rhine in March 1945—he sneaked over at night on the eve of the scheduled British assault—and allowed himself to be photographed urinating in the Rhine. Encircling the Ruhr, he crushed sporadic German resistance and took 500,000 German prisoners as his forces hurtled toward Czechoslovakia and Austria. He saw the Russians as a greater threat than the Germans; he wanted to beat them to Berlin and to Prague, but Eisenhower constantly put on the brakes. Discovering concentration camps en route, Patton made local officials and citizens visit them: the mayor of one town and his wife went home and hanged themselves. Patton vomited when he toured Dachau.

Promoted to four-star general in April 1945, he was ordered to halt his eastward advance in Bavaria; he wanted to go on to Moscow. He was obsessed by Russian expansion into Central Europe. He called the Russians "the Mongols" and predicted a Communist takeover of all of Europe. He longed to continue east and smash the Red Army while U.S. forces were within reach, but no other American leader agreed with him. After the Germans surrendered in early May, his best units were peeled away and shipped to the Pacific Theater to finish the war with Japan. Patton was left behind as military governor of the American zone of occupied

Germany. In a final well-publicized controversy, he defended the employment of former members of the Nazi Party in administrative and skilled jobs. He refused to purge former Nazis. At a press conference in September 1945, he agreed with a reporter's suggestion that most Nazis had joined the party "in about the same way that Americans become Republicans or Democrats." This time, Eisenhower stripped him of his Third Army command. To the end, Patton believed Germany must be rebuilt to fight at the side of the Americans against the U.S.S.R.

His death amid this controversy created unfounded Cold War rumors of a plot that were never substantiated. On a hunting trip in December 1945, his staff car was rammed by an Army truck. Patton's neck was broken. He died twelve days later of a blood clot. He was buried in a military cemetery in Luxembourg with his troops.

QUESTIONS FOR THOUGHT AND DISCUSSION

1. Early in life, George Patton set his sights on a heroic military career. Why? Does such a fixed determination to achieve such success and acclaim appeal to you?

2. How much credit does Patton deserve for the success of US and Allied operations in the European Theater during World War II?

3. Does the military need such daring, disciplined bulldogs as "Old Blood and Guts" in order to win wars? Would you want to serve under the command of an officer like Patton?

4. If Patton had his way, the Allies would not have stopped at Germany in World War II, but would have pressed on eastward to attack the Soviet Red Army. Why did other Allied leaders, including Dwight Eisenhower, reject such an idea? Who do you agree with and why?

SUGGESTED READINGS

Blumenson, Martin. *Patton: The Man Behind the Legend, 1885–1945*. New York: Morrow, 1985.

_____. *The Patton Papers, 1885–1940*. Boston: Houghton, 1972.

_____. *The Patton Papers, 1940–1945*. Boston: Houghton, 1974.

Essame, Hubert. *Patton: A Study in Command*. New York: Scribner, 1974.

Farago, Ladislas. *Patton: Ordeal and Triumph*. New York: Astor-Honor, 1963.

Mellor, William Bancroft. *Patton, Fighting Man*. New York: Putnam, 1946.

15

Iva
Toguri

In a nation of immigrants, American involvement in wars against the homelands of immigrant groups caused special problems. In World War I, German Americans were targets of American hostility. German bakers found themselves without American customers and their businesses collapsed. Germans in America not yet qualified for naturalization found themselves declared enemy aliens by act of Congress, their mills, candy factories, breweries, lumberyards, and machine shops were seized by the Alien Property Custodian, their incomes taken and converted into Liberty Bonds. In cities with concentrations of German immigrants, German Americans were required to line up at police stations to be fingerprinted as if they were common criminals.

The outbreak of World War II brought renewed hysteria, especially after Japanese aircraft carriers steamed within bomber range of Pearl Harbor and launched a massive surprise attack that all but wiped out the U.S. Pacific Fleet. Rumors of imminent Japanese invasion helped to fan long-smoldering animosity toward hard-working, prosperous Japanese Americans in California, Oregon, and Washington. Japanese victories early in 1942 stirred a yearning for vengeance that was promoted by men who would later be celebrated as liberals—Earl Warren, Abe Fortas, Milton Eisenhower, and Hugo Black.

In Hawaii, where the Japanese attack had begun, there was a high proportion of Japanese aliens, but the Army moved quickly to cooperate with Japanese American leaders and after a few suspects were questioned, no charges were brought and there was no systematic persecution. In California, however, where only one percent of the population were Issei (first generation Japanese Americans) or Nisei (the children of Issei), reprisals against Japanese Americans began the day after Pearl Harbor. Governor Culbert Olson and the state Attorney General Earl Warren orchestrated the immediate dismissal of Japanese Americans from civil service jobs. Checking and savings accounts were seized, licenses to practice law and medicine were revoked, and commercial fishermen were barred from their boats.

Newspaper columnists led a chorus of intolerance. "I hate the Japanese and that goes for all of them," wrote one, suggesting that they be expelled to the interior. "I don't mean a nice part of the interior, either. Herd 'em up, pack 'em off and give 'em the inside room in the bad lands." On March 30, 1942, Executive Order 9066, signed by President Roosevelt, triggered the mass "relocation" of approximately 120,000 Japanese Americans. Notices tacked to doors gave forty-eight hours to sell homes and businesses. Then, soldiers with fixed bayonets, shouting, "Out, Japs!" escorted families with only bundles of clothing into Army trucks that carried them to the Rose Bowl, to Santa Anita racetrack, and to a brewery—in all, to fifteen crowded, filthy assembly areas until they could be shipped on to eleven barbed-wire-enclosed internment camps. For the Toguri family, taken to the Arizona desert, there was a special nightmare: daughter Iva, visiting relatives in Japan, was trapped along with 10,000 other Nisei behind enemy lines.

IVA TOGURI WAS born on the Fourth of July 1916, the first American citizen in her family. She was the eldest daughter of Jun and Fumi Toguri. Her parents and her older brother, Fred, had been born in Japan and were Japanese citizens. Iva had dual citizenship until she was six. When the Japanese invaded Manchuria, Jun struck his daughter's name from the family register in Japan: from then on, she was 100 percent American.

Her father had come to the U.S. in 1899 at age seventeen after completing high school in his native Yamanashi prefecture. Granted permanent residence in the U.S., he worked for awhile in Seattle. As anti-Oriental feeling mounted on the West Coast, he found he could not get U.S. citizenship. Returning to Japan, he married Fumi Iimuro, who remained in Japan for six years with her family. Jun returned to America, worked several jobs, and returned several times to Japan on visits: there the Toguris' first child was born.

In 1913, the Toguris arrived in San Francisco and, when Iva was three, her parents moved to Calexico, on the Mexican border, where Toguri tried to raise cotton. They moved on to San Diego, where two more children were born, then on to Los Angeles, when Iva was twelve. Jun Toguri finally prospered, expanding an import business into a retail grocery and variety store selling goods from Japan. Iva, like all of the children, worked in the store after school and also helped to take care of her mother, who suffered from diabetes and high blood pressure.

While the Toguri store sold Japanese products, Iva's father had no intention of bringing up his children in the traditional Japanese culture. Iva later testified that:

> Our family home was located in a typical American community. I went to the neighborhood grammar school and attended church in the neighborhood. I took part in normal activities at school and at [Methodist] church . . . . There was some Japanese spoken in our family until we started to attend public school, thereafter English dominated. We followed both Japanese and American cooking in the home. My par-

ents tried to raise us according to American customs. We celebrated all the national holidays, all Christian holidays.

Jun Toguri wanted his children to be Americans and he limited their contacts with other Japanese Americans. He bought a house in a largely American neighborhood: Iva's playmates were nearly all Americans.

As a consequence, Iva grew robust on American food, and became competitive like American teenagers. In addition to joining the Girl Scouts and playing field hockey in high school, she made the tennis team. An average student, she wanted to be a doctor. Only about one in twenty *Nisei* women went on to college, but Iva enrolled in Compton Junior College, after one semester transferring to the University of California, Los Angeles, to prepare for medicine. Remembered by professors as lively and lighthearted, she majored in zoology and on weekends and vacations took camping trips. She especially enjoyed paleontology field trips into the Mojave desert, looking for fossilized specimens. One professor recalled Iva's good sense of humor, her kidding, and joking—"she seemed 100 percent Yankee." She liked to attend UCLA football games and to help her father with the driving on long business trips around the United States.

Registering Republican in 1940, she was, she later said, totally unaware of social prejudice:

> I never felt racial prejudice while in school. I never felt there was prejudice among teachers or schoolmates. Racial prejudice was never discussed at home and [I] never was aware of the existence of it.

This was a remarkable statement for a Japanese American looking back on California in 1940, where there was a long history of anti-Japanese sentiment. Especially during the Depression era of the 1930s, bitter resentment of Asian Americans had grown as they competed for jobs with white workers. As early as 1913, the resentment of the white majority had found voice in politics: under the Alien Land Law, *Issei* were barred from owning or leasing land. The teaching of Japanese was forbidden in the schools. Japanese immigration, thriving since the 1850s, was limited in 1907, then prohibited in 1924: Japanese could only get resident-alien status. As industrious Japanese like Jun Toguri prospered in the 1930s, hostility towards them only grew. Part of Jun Toguri's insistence on integration into the American way of life was to blind Iva to the racial prejudice around her.

After graduating from UCLA with a B.A. in zoology in 1940, Iva decided to go to graduate school, taking premedical studies the following year. Then, in June 1941, her mother received a letter from an in-law in Japan. Fumi's only living sister was ill and wanted to see her for the first time in thirty years. But Iva's mother was too sick for such a long journey. The family decided it was Iva's duty to go before she continued her studies. Iva was not looking forward to this trip—she spoke no Japanese and detested Japanese food—but she acceded to her parents' request.

There could not have been a worse time for such a trip. When her father wrote to the State Department in Washington, D.C., to apply for her passport, no reply came. Diplomatic relations between Japan and the U.S. were at their lowest point in the twentieth century. The Toguris seemed completely oblivious to what many Americans knew. Only last minute talks underway in Washington, D.C., could avert war now that Japan had become an Axis ally of Nazi Germany and fascist Italy, and was continuing its territorial expansion. Still, Iva and her father went ahead with their plans. Iva raced around gathering bags of food, clothing, medicines, and other gifts for her Japanese relatives. Scheduled to sail on the *Arabia Maru* on July 5, when she had not received a passport by July 1 she went to the immigration office, where she was told to take along a sworn certificate of identification: that would do. Once in Tokyo, she could go to the U.S. embassy and apply for a passport to come home.

Iva turned twenty-five the day before she sailed. There was a big celebration, combining her twenty-fifth birthday, the Fourth of July, and her farewell, at a Chinese restaurant. That Fourth of July 1941, Iva had a last supper with her family. It was the last evening they ever had together. The next day, the family went to see Iva off at San Pedro. Her father helped her lug the baggage, made heavier by all the American food he was thoughtfully sending along, enough to last through her stay. In all, Iva took thirty pieces of luggage. With an eighteen-year-old girlfriend, Cheiko Ito, who also was going to Japan to visit relatives, she stood at the railing and waved until they could see their families no more.

Iva's troubles in Japan began immediately. Japanese officials refused at first to give them entry visas since they had no passports. She was finally allowed ashore the next day. Her aunt and uncle were kind to her, but she found the sounds, the smells, and everything "strange." "People were stiff and formal to me. I felt like a perfect stranger, and the Japanese considered me very queer." She looked Japanese, but she spoke no Japanese. She had trouble adjusting to being treated like a child again, how to sit on the floor, and how to eat without utensils. She particularly resented not being allowed to leave the house without a chaperone, her cousin, a woman her age. Her one time of relaxation seemed to be at morning classes at a Japanese language school.

As communications with the U.S. grew worse (none of her letters reached her family), she managed to get a letter to her parents by entrusting it to a returning *Nisei*. She was anxious to go home. The day she arrived in Japan, the Japanese Army occupied French Indochina. The next day, President Roosevelt declared economic sanctions against Japan, freezing all Japanese assets in U.S. banks, bringing Japanese-American trade to a virtual halt. In retaliation, Japan ordered the freezing of all U.S. funds. The Japanese ambassador to the U.S. was informed by President Roosevelt that if the Japanese tried to extend further their military conquests in Asia, the U.S. would take steps to oppose them. By the time Iva heard from her parents on October 9, 1941, the Japanese government had already decided in secret to attack the Hawaiian Islands and declare war on the U.S. unless the U.S. abandoned China, lifted the freeze on Japanese assets, and restored trade relations. By this time, Iva and Cheiko were anxious to go home, even if they could not read a Japanese newspaper to glean any hint of the rising tensions.

On November 25, 1941, the day the U.S. Secretary of State and the Japanese Foreign Minister broke off talks in Washington, Iva and Cheiko called their parents long-distance and told them they still were unable to get passports at the U.S. Embassy, but that they wanted to come home right away. One week later, Iva received a telegram from her father telling her to book passage home on a ship

playing off the name of Japan's most-feared fighter plane and the time of an attack, was intended to make GIs homesick by broadcasting discouraging news from home. In fact, because of the good music it provided and the light, breezy patter of the *Nisei* women announcers reading scripts written with mocking irony by the Australian and American writers, the show, broadcast early in the evening, became enormously popular with the GIs, anything but demoralizing them, they later testified. In mid-November 1943, Major Cousens requested that Iva Toguri be released from her typing duties to become one of six women reading *The Zero Hour* scripts.

When Iva protested that she had only agreed to become a typist, she was informed by her Japanese supervisor that she must follow Japanese Army orders. Major Cousens tried to reassure her:

> I have written it and I know what I'm doing. All you have to do is look on yourself as a soldier under my orders. Do exactly what you are told. . . . You will do nothing against your own people. I will guarantee that personally because I have read the script.

Two and a half years after leaving California, Iva made her first broadcast with more misgivings about her voice than her patriotism. "Major Cousens said my voice is not what you call a gentle and sweet voice," she later testified, "but he wanted a Yankee voice." Her job was to sound cheerful. The major urged her to talk as if she were in a group of GIs. He suggested that she take the name "Orphan Ann."

After a Boston Pops recording of "Strike Up the Band," Iva opened her fifteen-to twenty-minute segment by saying, "Here comes your music," then, after reading a greeting written by Cousens, played three or four 78 rpm records, mainly classical or dance records, selected by Cousens, ad libbing a few introductory comments. The fast-paced scripts were full of double meanings, slang words, and jokes beyond the English language capabilities of the Japanese staff.

So popular was the show, according to American news stories the Japanese monitored, that the Japanese decided to expand the use of prisoners-of-war, assembling them at a special secret facility in Tokyo. Twenty-six more POWs arrived in December 1943. There was intense psychological pressure and occasional beatings by guards. Major Cousens urged the others to "fight" the Japanese by helping covertly to boost GI morale with the broadcasts. Gradually, the health of the POWs grew worse as they were fed only radish soup and grain usually used only to feed chickens. Iva, buying black-market food with pay from a third job typing for the Danish consulate, smuggled food and medicines to Major Cousens, who distributed it among his men. She even smuggled in a precious woolen blanket wrapped around her under her clothing for an ailing POW suffering from a fever and chills.

In the spring of 1944, Iva, who had become close friends with a part-Japanese, part-Portuguese staff member at Domei, Filipe J. d'Aquino, moved in with his family; in late January 1945, they decided to get married. She began to take more and more time off from her broadcasting job. Iva used intensifying Allied air raids on Tokyo as an excuse for missing work. Filipe urged her to quit her job and stay home, but a visit by State Security Police persuaded her to continue playing records on *The Zero Hour*.

UPI/Bettmann

At the 1949 trial in San Francisco for her allegedly treasonous "Tokyo Rose" broadcasts, Iva Toguri listens to tapes as the jury hears them for the first time.

On August 15, 1945, Felipe and Iva held hands and cried when they heard a broadcast that no Japanese had ever expected to hear: the voice of Emperor Hirohito, going on the air for the first time after the atomic bombings of Hiroshima and Nagasaki, announcing his decision to "endure the unendurable" and surrender. But for Iva Toguri, an even longer private war was only beginning. American journalists arriving in Tokyo competed for "scoops." They searched for the elusive "Tokyo Rose," the name GIs had invented for a mythical seductive-voiced Japanese woman announcer. One rumor had it that "Tokyo Rose" was really the missing American aviator Amelia Earhart! The best rumor was that there were six women, including Iva Toguri, who had broadcast to GIs. Two notoriously sensational journalists, Clark Lee of the Hearst-owned International News Service and Harry Brundidge of *Cosmopolitan,* teamed up to find "Tokyo Rose" and beat out other journalists with an exclusive interview. Bursting into Radio Tokyo, they asked the manager to identify the real "Tokyo Rose." At first, he insisted there was no such single person, but his own wife was one of the six announcers. Evidently to protect her, he named only Iva Toguri.

With the help of a Hawaii-born *Nisei* who had worked with American journalists in Tokyo before the war, they tracked down Iva and Felipe d'Aquino through the bombed-out streets of the city, inviting them to meet them at a posh hotel the next day. There, dangling a $2,000 payment—a fortune in war-torn Japan—they interviewed Iva and asked her to sign an exclusive contract in which she was identified as "the one and only Tokyo Rose." (She never received the $2,000 payment.) Amid more interviews and a press conference during the next few days, Iva was asked if she would mind talking to U.S. Eighth Army intelligence officers.

Press stories filed in Tokyo may have been lighthearted, but back home in the United States they produced a storm of outrage. Iva Toguri was dubbed a "traitor" in news stories before there were any official charges against her, but as a result of news stories, the Army decided to arrest her. For one full year, she was held without bail in solitary confinement in Sugamo Prison, which housed such war criminals as Marshal Tojo. Denied permission to hire a lawyer or to see her husband, she was repeatedly interrogated by an FBI agent sent to prepare a case against her. Eventually, the Justice Department ordered her released for lack of evidence of any wrongdoing.

Ironically, now that she was free, Iva wanted more than anything to go home to America. When she became pregnant, she applied once more for a passport. Her request, received against a backdrop of treason charges flying thickly in the U.S. during the Red-hunting hysteria of 1948, led to her rearrest. American Legion and Native Son Lodge members in Los Angeles, active in the 1942 relocations, demanded her trial for treason. Syndicated radio and newspaper columnist Walter Winchell, frequently attacking government officials for being "soft on traitors," met with the U.S. attorney for Los Angeles and demanded that the Justice Department reopen the case. In his broadcasts, which reached twenty million Americans, he crusaded against Iva Toguri. Yielding to pressure, the Justice Department ordered her rearrested shortly after her baby died and taken on shipboard to San Francisco. Iva Toguri became the first American woman ever tried for treason. She was convicted after a three-month, million dollar trial in which the government produced fifty witnesses—many of them brought at government expense from Japan—that her broadcasts had demoralized U.S. troops and that she had not been coerced into making them. Her defense attorneys were not paid to bring witnesses from Japan to corroborate her story. The trial judge refused to allow a mistrial when the jury deadlocked for four days, repeatedly sending the jury back to deliberate until it reached a guilty verdict.

In the end, Iva Toguri was sentenced to ten years in prison and fined $10,000. Immigration officials refused to allow her husband to stay in the U.S. after the trial and somehow persuaded him to sign an agreement never to return to the U.S. They stayed married but never saw each other again. Iva served seven years in federal prison before she was released in 1956. She remained stripped of her citizenship, and for nearly thirty years was a stateless person, unable even to obtain a passport to leave the United States.

In the early 1970s, as Japanese Americans, who had at first considered Iva's case as a disgrace to all *Nisei,* began to speak out against the scapegoating of Iva Toguri. U.S. Senator S. I. Hayakawa, himself a *Nisei,* took up her case in his *San Francisco Chronicle* column. He personally went twice to the White House to plead her case. On his last day as President, Gerald Ford issued a full presidential pardon to Iva Toguri, restoring her U. S. citizenship. She has lived quietly in Chicago since her release, first working in, and then finally managing, her father's department store.

QUESTIONS FOR THOUGHT AND DISCUSSION

1. Were Iva Toguri and her family more American or more Japanese? Aside from physically living in the U.S., how does an immigrant become an American?

2. Should Toguri's family have known better than to allow her to travel to Japan during a time of growing conflict between that country and the U.S.?

3. Do you consider Toguri's "Tokyo Rose" broadcasts treasonous? Should she have refused to make these, whatever the consequences?

4. If you were Iva Toguri, would you have wanted to remain in the U.S. after what she and her family experienced during and immediately after World War II?

SUGGESTED READINGS

Daniels, Roger. *Prisoners Without Trial*. New York: Hill, 1993.

Daniels, Roger, Sandra C. Taylor and Harry L. L. Kitano. *Japanese Americans: From Relocation to Redress*. Salt Lake City: U of Utah P, 1986.

Duus, Masayo. *Tokyo Rose: Orphan of the Pacific*. Intro. by Edwin O. Reischaucer. New York: Kodansha International/Harper, 1979.

Hatamiya, Leslie T. *Righting a Wrong: Japanese Americans and the Passage of the Civil Liberties Act of 1988*. Stanford: Stanford UP, 1993.

Irons, Peter H. *Justice at War*. New York: Oxford UP, 1983.

Meo, L. D. *Japan's Radio War with Australia*. Melbourne: Melbourne UP, 1968.

Smith, Page. *Democracy on Trial: The Japanese American Evacuation*. New York: Simon, 1995.

16

Harry S Truman

The end of World War II left many Americans expecting prosperity, new peacetime opportunities, and the chance to build on social reforms made on the home front during the epic conflict. With Germany, Japan, England, and France devastated, the U.S. stood as the world's leading economic and military power. It was, proclaimed Life *magazine publisher Henry Luce, "The American Century." Women, African Americans, and an unprecedented fifteen million labor union members joined ten million returning servicemen who looked forward optimistically to the future. Yet only five years later, the optimism had dissipated and, in retrospect, seemed naive. While as many women remained employed as at war's end, they mostly held inferior jobs at far lower pay. African Americans, who had contributed so much to the war effort, were disenchanted by unabated racism and segregation. Union members had nearly brought the nation to a standstill on several occasions after bruising confrontations with President Harry S Truman, the man labor had backed in his rise to power. For those still seeking equality of opportunity, the Truman years brought only a reduced vision.*

In the wake of the first nuclear explosions that Truman had personally authorized to end the war with Japan, a Cold War atmosphere of fear and suspicion pervaded the country, leading to witch hunts for Communist spies at home and the bloody Korean War in Asia. For many Americans, the postwar years indeed brought unparalleled prosperity. War plants were converted to producing consumer goods. Suburban subdivisions sprawled. Hundreds of thousands of new houses began to fill up with the latest labor-saving appliances. New networks of highways smoothed the way for shiny new cars. Stepping out of the giant shadow of Franklin Delano Roosevelt and his New Deal, Truman announced he would campaign for a "Fair Deal" for all Americans. Systematically attacking big business, big labor and the military, Truman became the champion of the ordinary people. For a time, this plain-spoken, decisive Missourian, the poorest President since Lincoln, was the most popular of the twentieth century.

ALTHOUGH HARRY TRUMAN wanted to be a soldier from the time he was a little boy, he was so nearsighted that, from the time he had to start wearing eyeglasses at age six, he not only had to face the fact that he could never pass the physical for West Point, but he could not engage in sports or play like other children. "I was so carefully cautioned by the eye doctor about breaking my glasses and injuring my eyes," he later wrote, "that I was afraid to join in the rough-and-tumble games in the schoolyard and back lot." Instead, Harry turned to the more introverted world of books and music. "My time was spent in reading, and by the time I was thirteen or fourteen years old I had read all the books in the Independence (Missouri) Public Library and our old Bible three times through." He also learned to play the piano well enough to dream of a concert career. When the great pianist Ignaz Jan Paderewski came through nearby Kansas City, Missouri, Harry was given a private lesson and learned from him how to play his Minuet in G. But all his plans seemed to be dashed by his father's repeated business failures.

The families of Truman's parents had migrated from Kentucky to Missouri by steamboat in the 1840s. The Truman side was English, its name derived from the Saxon, "Tru man." His mother's family, the Youngs, were prosperous Scots-Irish farmers, their Grandview, Missouri, farm earning the modern equivalent of over $200,000 a year by the early 1900s. Both sides of the family had been slaveowners when they helped settle the Independence region. Truman's grandfather, Solomon Young, led wagon trains along the California Trail through Salt Lake City to San Francisco. In addition to owning 5,000 acres of Jackson County, Missouri, at one time he owned much of what became Sacramento, California. He was away during the Civil War when Union raiders attacked the farm, slaughtered all the hogs, and stole the family silver and a favorite quilt. Truman's grandmother never forgave the Yankees and never got used to seeing Harry in a U.S. Army uniform.

On the Truman side, the family's luck ran out before it got to Harry's father, who worked at different times as a farmer, a cattle and horse trader, a grain speculator, and a night watchman. Passionately Democrat, his loyalty to the party earned his son Harry an early introduction to politics—which he badly needed after a series of youthful failures.

Born on May 8, 1884, in a rickety little farmhouse in Lamar, Missouri, Harry got a middle name that stood for nothing. Neither parent wanted to give offense to the other's relatives who had "S" names so they made it simply "S." Fascinated by military history, he worshipped Andrew Jackson. His favorite President, George Washington, was also a general. As a Jackson County official, Harry Truman built two equestrian statues of Andrew Jackson. As President, Truman appointed more military men to high office than any other President.

Living on a farm in the rural South until he was six, Harry then moved to Independence, which remained home for most of his long life. For the next twelve years, the family prospered as his father speculated in grain harvests. In the summers, Harry and his younger brother, Vivian, returned to the Youngs' farm in Grandview, where Harry learned how to handle horses and raise livestock and crops. Then his father had a disastrous year. They had to sell everything. As the family fled to the obscurity of rented rooms in Kansas City, Harry had to give up any idea of ever attending college. He was the last American president not to go to college.

After graduating high school, Harry uncomplainingly worked for the summer as a timekeeper for construction workers extending the Atchison, Topeka, and Santa Fe railroad tracks. Saving enough money for a brief stint at a business school, he got the first of two jobs as a bank clerk in Kansas City, working his way up from a $35 a month job to $100. He lived in a boarding house, carried sandwiches to work, and became a Baptist. He loved to go to concerts, even though his father's business failures had ended his piano lessons. When the Metropolitan Opera came to town, when there were vaudeville shows or Shakespeare plays, young Harry often went free, ushering at one of the theaters.

When he was twenty-two, his father took a job managing his mother's family farm and they all moved back to Grandview. For eleven years, Harry was a farmer, essentially running the vast farm. Working morning to night, he used the latest technique of rotating crops to rest the soil as he produced wheat, corn, oats, and clover, much of it to feed his herd of sleek Black Angus cattle. For the first and only time he had plenty of money, which he invested with little luck. He invested in a zinc and lead mine in Oklahoma that failed, losing him $2,000. He bought oil leases in Texas, Oklahoma, and Kansas but stopped drilling only 100 feet short of striking the rich Teter Pool that would have made him a millionaire.

But some things began to go well for the ever-resilient young Truman. He joined the Missouri National Guard, attending drills and going on maneuvers for many years. In April 1917, Congress voted a U.S. declaration of war that provided, during the little more than a year of American participation, the turning point of Harry Truman's life. Working hard to find recruits to expand his National Guard artillery battery into a full regiment, Truman was surprised to be appointed first lieutenant. At training camp near Fort Sill, Oklahoma, Truman and a friend from his bank teller days, Sergeant Eddie Jacobson, set up a regimental canteen, collecting two dollars from each of 1,100 men to buy supplies not provided by the Army. As men from surrounding units lined up, Truman and Jacobson made a modest profit for his men, which may explain his popularity as a junior officer. On March 18, 1918, Truman's 129th Field Artillery Regiment sailed for France.

He had said "goodbye" to the young woman he had admired since first grade, Bess Wallace. Her parents considered themselves vastly superior to the Trumans. For years, he had hesitated even to talk to her; she was the prettiest girl in his class and the best student. Blue-eyed, blond-haired Bess played basketball, tennis, played third base on the baseball diamond, fenced well, and even put the shot. Harry, who was allowed to do none of these things because of his eyeglasses, was in awe of her. "I only had one sweetheart from the time I was six." After her father's suicide, Bess went away to Barstow's Finishing School in Kansas City. They did not begin dating seriously until 1913, when she was twenty-eight and he was nearly thirty. But one day he got up his nerve and returned a cake plate from his aunt's to Bess's fourteen-room, Victorian mansion on Delaware Avenue. For many years, he didn't think he could ever support her. By the time he went off to war in 1917, they were engaged.

Promoted to captain, he was made commander of Battery D, a difficult collection of 180 Irishmen, mostly Kansas City railroad workers who had made short work of several former commanders. In what was one of the most important transitions of his life, he proved a tough disciplinarian, informing the corporals and sergeants of his unruly unit that they would have to please him, as he was not going to try to please them. He warned anyone who didn't obey his orders that he would "bust them back right now." He later admitted that he was frightened when he faced "the boys" of his battery, but he didn't show it. Truman later summed up his relations thenceforward with his men: "We got along."

Commanding his artillery unit in almost every American engagement of the 1918 campaign, Truman dueled with German artillery. Battery D distinguished itself at St. Mihiel and in the Meuse-Argonne offensive. Under their first barrage, Truman's men panicked and started to flee, deserting the 75 millimeter guns and horses. Captain Truman refused to run. Rallying them by swearing at them profusely until they returned to help him hitch up the horses to the guns, he led them in an orderly retreat from the deadly German barrage. Truman fired one of the last barrages—hundreds of rounds of deadly poison gas—of the war.

Truman returned to the U.S. a seasoned man with a strong sense of accomplishment. Marrying Bess Wallace, on June 28, 1919, the day the Versailles Peace Treaty was signed, Truman moved into her mother's house. He never would own his own house, and his often disapproving mother-in-law lived with the couple much of the next forty years.

Trying to build on his wartime success as a merchant, Truman entered a partnership with Sergeant Eddie Jacobson. They took a long lease on a large store on Twelfth Street in downtown Kansas City and opened a men's luxury clothing store. It flourished for three years, as long as the grain market put extra cash in men's pockets, but as the postwar recession deepened, the value of merchandise on the shelves plummeted and the flow of customers dried up. In 1922, Truman and Jacobson's failed, leaving young Truman $28,000 in debt. Jacobson eventually filed for bankruptcy, but Truman worked off the debt, paying monthly installments and sacrificing any luxuries for the next fifteen years until his debts were paid.

Truman's forays into business may have been disastrous, but there had been a dividend: his clientele had included hundreds of veterans and he had become known to Kansas City politicians. Truman loved veterans: "My whole political career is based on my war service and war associates," he later said. Among his army acquaintances was Lieutenant James M. Pendergast, nephew of Thomas J. Pendergast, political boss of Kansas City. Pendergast's brother, Mike, arranged Truman's nomination as the elected assistant administrator of the rural eastern district of Jackson County (the area around Independence). His local reputation for honest hard work and his popularity among veterans compensated for his poor speeches. When his speeches broke down, his following of veterans bellowed, "Three cheers for Captain Harry." Truman won by a scant majority of 288 out of a vote of 11,000. For the next two years, he could look forward to a comfortable $6,000 salary. But he had made enemies. He had refused membership in the Ku Klux Klan, which had revived after World War I and claimed five million members nationwide in the 1920s. Truman refused a Klan demand that, in return for its support, he would promise never to give jobs to Catholics, the majority of his veteran constituency. When he sought reelection in 1924, the Klan opposed him, and he was defeated in the only election he ever lost.

Supporting himself by selling memberships in the Kansas City Automobile Club, he asked political boss Pendergast for the $25,000-a-year post of County Collector. Pendergast turned him down but nominated him for Presiding Judge of all Jackson County, his post for the next eight years. Restructuring the county's debt and winning popular support for a series of bond issues, he built 224 miles of roads, making Jackson County's highway system the second best in all America (second only to Westchester County, New York). He laid the foundation for a unique, fiscally-conservative, Democratic, social welfare agenda during those early years, building a county hospital for the elderly, cutting deadwood from the county payroll, and attacking expense account abuse. He built a twenty-story county courthouse, insisting on competitive bidding and on-site personal inspections. At a 1928 meeting in Pendergast's office, he refused to give contracts to three kingpins of the Kansas City machine, insisting on awarding a contract to the low, out-of-state bidder. "Didn't I tell you," Pendergast told his minions, "he's the contrariest cuss in Missouri?" Creating thousands of construction jobs, he became the friend of labor and the foe of fat-cat contractors and suppliers. He learned first-hand how taxpayers' money was wasted. He built the courthouse under the estimate with enough left over for a huge Andrew Jackson equestrian statue to honor his reform-minded hero.

Despite his longtime association with the corrupt Pendergast machine, Truman won a reputation as scrupulously honest. "Pendergast never asked me to do a dishonest deed," Truman insisted. "He knew I wouldn't do it if he asked it." By 1929, he had become leader of the Democratic Party for the Eastern District of Jackson County. In 1930, he became president of the Greater Kansas City Planning Association and a director of the National Conference on City Planning. When the Depression hit Missouri, Truman accepted President Roosevelt's dollar-a-year appointment as reemployment director for the Federal Emergency Relief Administration (FERA).

In 1934, with Pendergast's support, Truman was elected to the U.S. Senate. He was handicapped at first by the label "the Senator from Pendergast." Assigned to the Appropriations and Interstate Commerce Committees, he loyally supported FDR's New Deal programs. He helped draft the Civil Aeronautics Act of 1938 to regulate the new airline industry and the Transportation Act of 1940 to strengthen the regulatory powers of the ICC. He consistently voted pro-labor. He won support among African Americans by voting for a federal anti-lynching bill, an end to poll taxes, and creation of the Fair Employment Practices Committee. Born a Southerner, he slowly shucked his rural Missouri turn-of-the-century racial prejudices. At age twenty-seven, he had written to Bess:

> I think one man is just as good as another so long as he's honest and decent and not a nigger or a Chinaman. Uncle Will says that the Lord made a white man from dust, a nigger from mud, then threw up what was left and it came down a Chinaman. He does hate Chinese and Japs. So do I. It is race prejudice I guess. But I am strongly of the opinion that negroes ought to be in Africa, yellow men in Asia and white men in Europe and America.

By his 1940 senatorial reelection campaign, Truman, already the sworn enemy of the Ku Klux Klan, showed how far his thinking had changed. He publicly put aside his traditional Missouri prejudices and made his first strong civil rights pronouncement in a speech at Sedalia. There were a quarter of a million black voters in Missouri by this time, mostly in St. Louis. It was here, with strong support from blacks and labor, that Truman barely won reelection in one of the most bitterly-contested elections of the year. It was his first famous come-from-behind victory and he had displayed characteristic resilience and determination.

He returned to his tiny apartment in Washington (as he often did without Bess and their daughter, Margaret, who stayed with Mrs. Wallace in the big house on Delaware Avenue) to a hero's welcome. He wrote to Bess virtually every day; on August 9, 1940, he recounted his surprise to learn how closely watched his campaign had been. One senator told him "that no race in his stay here had created such universal interest in the Senate . . . he's having lunch for me today. I guess it will be a dandy. It almost gives me a swell head." Outside the Senate, Truman had led a lonely existence on Capitol Hill during his first term, often too strapped for money to travel home. At this moment of triumph, he still could not raise the money to save the family farm. It galled him that the foreclosure had been politically motivated. The Jackson County tax office moved quickly to foreclose on the $35,000 mortgage when Truman got behind on his interest payments. The whole farm was gavelled under at a sheriff's sale. His brother lost his livelihood, and his eighty-eight-year-old mother and his sister were evicted. Truman tried to take stoically the public humiliation caused by his helplessness, saying that lots of people in Missouri had suffered the same fate. To help ease his money troubles, Truman quite publicly put Bess on his Senate office payroll, paying her $4,500 a year when she was in Washington, D.C., to sort mail and act as his paid political advisor.

With the onset of World War II, the nation's defense spending skyrocketed. Truman, who remembered all the waste and corruption he had seen in Missouri construction projects and the post World War I investigation of military overspending, pushed in the Senate to set up a powerful oversight committee to watch defense spending as it occurred. Convinced that wasteful contracts were being given too fast and freely to defense suppliers, Truman got into his Dodge coupe and made a month-long, one-man tour of inspection. He returned to Washington, D.C., to report shocking waste. Early in 1941, Truman was named chairman of the new Committee to Investigate the National Defense Program. The Truman Committee, as it became known, saved taxpayers about fifteen billion in 1940's dollars and made Truman a household word for the first time, emerging as the public enemy of "bigness." Gradually, his committee grew to a staff of twelve investigators. Truman traveled constantly by train and Army plane when he was not conducting widely publicized hearings. By 1943, he was appearing on the covers of *Time* and *Look* magazines.

In 1944, Democratic leaders generally believed that, while President Roosevelt would seek and win an unprecedented fourth term, he would not live through it. Whoever they chose for the vice presidency would succeed to the presidency. The ensuing power struggle split the Democratic Party, with many liberals supporting the reelection of the left-leaning vice president, Henry A. Wallace, and others favoring Supreme Court Justice William O. Douglas or former Justice James F. Byrnes, a Southerner. Roosevelt refused to state a preference. He did not even attend the

UPI/Bettmann

President Harry Truman tells the nation in a 1952 radio and television address that additional Marshall Plan aid "may make the difference between the life and death of the free world."

Democratic National Convention in Chicago. In this impasse, national party chairman Robert E. Hannegan of St. Louis, whose support of Truman in 1940 had been decisive, now advanced Truman as a compromise candidate. FDR's sole reason for acquiescing in the choice seems to have been that he wanted to avoid a reoccurrence of the debacle when the League of Nations charter had been defeated in the Senate after World War I. With Truman presiding over the Senate, FDR believed the United Nations charter, his last great concern, would be ratified.

But Truman himself remained unconvinced. It took a telephone call between Roosevelt and Hannegan with Truman in the room to persuade him:

Hannegan: "He's the contrariest Missouri mule I've ever dealt with . . ."
Roosevelt: "Tell him that if he wants to break up the Democratic Party in the middle of the war, that is his responsibility."

According to Truman's daughter, Margaret, after Roosevelt hung up, her father said, "Well, if that's the situation, I'll have to say yes. But why the hell didn't he tell me in the first place?" After one perfunctory luncheon meeting in shirt sleeves with FDR for the benefit of photographers, Truman went off to campaign, forbidden from traveling by air. "One of us has to stay alive," said FDR.

After Roosevelt's reelection, they met only once more before FDR left for Yalta for nearly three months. Shortly after FDR returned, he left Washington, D.C., again, this time for his retreat at Warm Springs, Georgia. Truman was left to preside over a Senate that had little to do. On April 12, 1945, Truman was visiting Speaker of the House Sam Rayburn's office for an after-hours bourbon when a telephone call summoned him to the White House. Eleanor Roosevelt informed him that FDR was dead.

Sworn in as the thirty-third president three hours later, Truman tried the next day to explain to the White House press corps how he felt:

I don't know whether you fellows ever had a load of hay or a tree fall on you. But last night the house, the stars, and all the planets fell on me. If you fellows ever pray, pray for me.

Completely ill-prepared by FDR, he began a seven-year embattled presidency. He had never even been told by FDR of the existence of the Manhattan Project to manufacture the first atomic bomb. The new president could not have been more different from FDR. With a flat, staccato speaking voice and plain speech, he became famous for his fast, two-mile morning walks (called "constitutionals") that left reporters and photographers breathless. He did not believe in finessing decisions or delaying them. Instead, he would often hot-temperedly rush into them. On his desk, he summed up his view of presidential decision-making with a sign, "The buck stops here." Truman was fortunate to have General George C. Marshall, FDR's logistical genius, as his Secretary of State and principal advisor. Truman was not a diplomat himself. His blunt manner, admirable in confronting a corrupt Kansas City machine, proved dangerous in the tense atmosphere of post-war relations with the Soviet Union. In his very first meeting with the Soviet foreign minister, V. M. Molotov, he accused the Russians of reneging on agreements over Poland. Molotov, second only to Premier Stalin, emerged angry and shaken. Truman was at first amazingly popular. As he set off for the last World War II summit conference at Potsdam, he had an eighty-seven percent Gallup poll rating, higher than FDR ever received.

During the conference, Truman received a secret message that the first A-bomb had been successfully exploded at Alamogordo, New Mexico. He now had to decide how to use the other three. In the aftermath of bloody fighting in the Pacific, as the U.S. high command prepared to invade the Japanese home islands, Truman received an estimate from General Marshall that there would be at least 500,000 Americans killed in the attack (no estimate of Japanese military or civilian casualties was ever given). In his diary for July 25, 1945, Truman wrote:

> It is certainly a good thing for the world that Hitler's crowd or Stalin's did not discover the atomic bomb. It seems to me the most terrible thing ever discovered, but it can be made the most useful.

In his diary, he also noted that he had instructed the Pentagon to use the new weapon only against "soldiers and sailors" and "not women and children." Tokyo and Kyoto were to be spared, but he approved targeting Hiroshima and Nagasaki, two cities crowded with civilians as well as factories and military units. According to notes Truman wrote at Potsdam at the time of his fateful decision and not made public until after his death in 1980 by historian Robert Ferrell, the president feared its use could lead to the end of the world, but he believed he must try to save American lives by ending the war without an all-out battle on Japanese soil. Later, he was to say that he felt he had no political alternative: had hundreds of thousands more Americans been killed and then it became known that he could have averted further bloodshed by using the terrible new weapon, he would have faced just as certain an outcry as his decision ultimately brought him.

When Truman informed Soviet Premier Josef Stalin what he already knew, that the U.S. had completed the atomic bomb tests, Stalin said he hoped Truman would use it against Japan. The decision of a former artilleryman who had fired thousands of shells filled with poison gas at an unseen enemy had little immediate effect on his popularity or effectiveness as a postwar president. Truman desired to carry on many of FDR's "New Deal" policies. His postwar reconstruction program, presented to Congress in September 1945, included extensive control over the economy in the conversion back to peacetime production; a national health insurance program; and permanent fair employment legislation to protect minority rights. The Republicans managed to block all of his major proposals. By the 1946 off-year Congressional elections, Truman's presidency had been hobbled by labor disputes and shortages of consumer goods that sent angry voters to the polls and brought about the first Republican-controlled Congress since the Depression. Even when he vetoed the anti-labor Taft-Hartley Act, which heavily restricted union activity, Congressional Republicans were able to override his veto.

By 1947, the Cold War developing between the Soviet Union and the U.S. and its former allies reached a crisis. The Soviet Union was installing Communist regimes in Eastern European nations occupied by the Red Army and in adjacent countries where pro-Moscow minorities could exploit the postwar confusion. Visiting Missouri with President Truman, Winston Churchill declared that an "Iron Curtain" had descended over Central Europe. Truman admired Churchill and eagerly imbibed his anticommunism without questioning whether he was adopting Churchill's imperialism and militarism as well. France and Italy seemed about to fall into the Communist camp. Truman decided that the U.S. would have to take the lead in opposing Communist expansion. Its wartime ally, England, was too enfeebled and impoverished, despite massive postwar loans from the U.S.

When the British government secretly notified Truman that it could no longer afford to support anticommunist forces in Greece and Turkey, Truman went before Congress for an emergency appropriation. In March 1947, Truman enunciated the Truman Doctrine: "I believe that it must be the policy of the United States to support free peoples who are resisting attempted subjugation by armed minorities or by outside pressures." With bipartisan support, Truman won $400 million in appropriations to support anticommunist regimes in Greece and Turkey. This policy of containment was to result in a buildup of U.S. bases and intelligence-gathering operations from Germany to South Korea that would eventually lead to the Korean and Vietnam Wars.

Even more alarming to Truman and Congress at the time was the apparently imminent economic and political collapse of Western Europe itself. Truman, collaborating with Secretary of State Marshall and a staff directed by former U.S. Ambassador to the Soviet Union George F. Kennan, drew up the so-called Marshall Plan that provided for German economic recovery as part of a general European recovery. Under its European Recovery Program, massive aid was offered to all European countries, East and West. Stalin rejected the Marshall Plan. He thought it would increase U.S. influence in Europe, threatening Soviet hegemony and security. Stalin's formal rejection of aid in July 1947, finally divided Europe into two hostile camps. Further, Stalin refused to accede to the requirement that participating countries reveal their financial needs to an all-European conference that would determine the amount required from the U.S.

The Soviet response to Marshall plan aid was to instruct Communist parties in the West to "bend every effort" to defeat the Marshall Plan. In February 1948, the Communists carried out a coup d'etat in Czechoslovakia. Truman declared that the Czech coup proved that the Soviet Union intended to expand Communism "to the remaining free nations of Europe." His firm stand persuaded Congress to appropriate some $17 billion to help rebuild Western Europe. He also introduced a bill in Congress calling for universal military training and the return of the draft.

When Truman and his Western counterparts decided to reform West Germany's currency as a first step to reconstructing the German economy, Stalin blocked all land traffic into and out of Berlin, in effect taking two million West Germans hostage. Truman responded by shuttling American B–29 bombers—the type that had dropped the atomic bombs—from bases in Japan and in the U.S., to British airfields, defying Stalin. His Berlin Airlift brought in food and supplies at the rate of one plane every two minutes, and took out refugees for 339 days before Stalin ended his Berlin Blockade.

As Cold War tensions mounted, it appeared that the Republicans might win the 1948 presidential elections. The Democratic Party was badly split. By the time of its convention, many liberal Democrats had left the party to form the Progressive Party, with former Vice President Henry Wallace as candidate. Truman's courageous response was to support a strong civil rights plank in the platform moved by Hubert Humphrey of Minnesota. Adamant segregationists, led by Governor Strom Thurmond of South Carolina, walked out of the convention and formed the State's Rights (or Dixiecrat) Party, weakening traditional Democratic support in the South.

The Republicans chose Thomas E. Dewey of New York, who had lost to FDR in the 1944 presidential election, but had given Roosevelt his closest race. Every poll predicted Dewey would defeat Truman in a landslide. But Truman never lost his fighting spirit: he traveled 31,000 miles by train in a "whistle-stop" campaign, hammering away at the Republican Party "of special privilege" and the Republican-controlled Congress, "the do-nothing, good-for-nothing, worst-ever 80th Congress." He lashed out in 350 staccato speeches from the rear platform of his special railroad car (with a second car for the press it was hooked onto conventional trains criss-crossing the continent). He drew ever-larger crowds, some days making as many as sixteen speeches. At the end of each whistle-stop, Truman would say, "And now I would like you to meet Mrs. Truman"—a blue velvet curtain behind him would part—"and now my daughter Margaret."

Truman's hard-working, plain-spoken, anti-bigness campaign appealed to labor, farmers, liberals, and minorities. He won the support of Jewish voters for his determination to push for an independent state of Israel. His campaign was in sharp contrast to the complacent Dewey's, whom he managed to characterize as a tool of big business interests. In one of the biggest upsets in political history, Truman won twenty-eight states and swept to victory.

The election had provided only a brief respite from the Cold War. In 1949, while the Berlin Blockade still dragged on, Truman sponsored formation of the ten-member (eventually sixteen) North Atlantic Treaty Organization (NATO) to augment U.S. forces in Europe and guarantee retaliation by NATO if any member nation was attacked. By this time, the Soviet Union had also detonated its first A-bomb. To strengthen U.S. ground forces in Europe, Truman pulled out most of the forces stationed in Korea since the end of World War II. The withdrawal triggered the next ratcheting-up of Cold War hostilities.

On June 25, 1950, Soviet-trained North Korean forces invaded South Korea. Truman, on a short visit home to Independence, thought World War III had begun, according to his daughter, who was there that day as his Air Force plane took off for Washington, D.C., without its navigator. Truman correctly assumed that North Korean leader Kim Il Sung had the approval and support of Stalin and Communist Chinese leader Mao Tse-tung. Actually, neither had foreseen Truman's decisive, strong reaction. U.S. failure to intervene in the titanic Chinese civil war, Truman felt, had led to the victory of Chinese Communist forces only nine months earlier. Truman saw Korea as a test of the United Nations. He felt the United Nations could now redeem the failure of the West to use the League of Nations in the 1930s to prevent the outbreak of World War II. To prevent World War III, he firmly married U.S. interests to the United Nations. He sent in massive U.S. reinforcements with the active aid of nineteen United Nations allies.

Truman's secondary goal over the last two years of his Presidency was to try to stop the spread of the Korean War. When General Douglas MacArthur led a daring amphibious landing at Inchon deep behind North Korean lines in late August 1950, he quickly recaptured all South Korean territory and hurtled north toward the Chinese border. MacArthur wanted to use nuclear weapons and pursue Chinese jets over the border. After the Chinese intervention, MacArthur began to speak out against Truman's policy of merely trying to return Korea to its prewar *status quo*.

MacArthur's refusal to cease making impolitic statements led Truman to fire him: "That is what he got fired for . . . I was ready to kick him into the North China Sea."

In the midst of the Korean crisis, Truman survived an assassination attempt. On November 1, 1950, two Puerto Rican nationalists tried to invade Blair House, temporary quarters for the First Family while the White House was being extensively renovated. They killed one Secret Service agent and wounded another: one assassin was killed and the other captured. Truman commented tersely, "A President has to expect these things."

What he did not expect was the outraged reaction of many Americans to his firing of MacArthur, who received ticker-tape parades in cities from San Francisco to New York City and bade a tearful farewell to an unprecedented joint session of Congress with the words, "Old soldiers never die, they just fade away."

Many conservative Americans considered Truman "soft on Communism" for limiting the war to Korea and refusing to seek a declaration of all-out war or to use nuclear weapons as Allied casualties in Korea mounted toward 500,000. The criticisms coincided with charges of Communist infiltration into the federal government by Senator Joseph R. McCarthy of Wisconsin. Truman strongly rejected McCarthy's charges and they were never proven, but he did set up a federal board to investigate the loyalty of government employees. Congress passed new antisubversion laws and the Truman Justice Department prosecuted leaders of the American Communist Party.

Against this Cold War backdrop, Truman also authorized a massive peacetime military buildup, including long-range bombers, thermonuclear bombs (H-bombs), and Polaris-class missile-firing nuclear submarines. The annual defense budget jumped to fifty billion dollars. Truman's Korean War-era policy of containment triggered a forty-year arms race that eventually bankrupted the Soviet Union and helped to leave the U.S. with a huge national debt.

His blunt, hard-hitting style made him one of the most popular American presidents at home and abroad. He was noted for his fierce devotion to his family. When his daughter Margaret, a coloratura soprano, performed at Constitution Hall at the end of her 1950 tour, Paul Hume, music critic for the *Washington Post,* panned her singing as "flat," adding, "she cannot sing with anything approaching professional finish." Enraged, President Truman wrote a longhand letter and personally mailed it:

> I have just read your lousy review buried in the back pages. You sound like a frustrated old man who never made a success, an eight-ulcer man on a four-ulcer job . . . . I never met you, but if I do you'll need a new nose and a supporter below.

On March 29, 1952, Truman announced he would not seek reelection that fall. In all, he served as president for seven years and nine months: "I have served my country long and I think efficiently and honestly. I do not feel it is my duty to spend another four years in the White House." Extremely unpopular by the time he left Washington, principally because of the ongoing Korean conflict, he was happy to return to Independence, where he lived nearly twenty years more. With no presidential pension, he supported himself in retirement with his writings, making occasional campaign trips and two long visits to Europe, where he had become the symbol of anticommunist resistance.

In 1952, Prime Minister Winston Churchill visited President Truman in Washington for the last time. After dinner one night on the presidential yacht, *Williamsburg,* Churchill told Truman how, at Potsdam, he had held Truman "in very low regard:"

> I misjudged you badly. Since that time, you, more than any other man, have saved Western civilization. When the British could no longer hold out in Greece, you, and you alone, sir, made the decision that saved that ancient land from the Communists. You acted in similar fashion . . . when the Soviets tried to take over Iran. Your Marshall Plan rescued Western Europe. . . . Then you established the North Atlantic Treaty Alliance and collective security for those nations against the military machinations of the Soviet Union. Then there was your audacious Berlin Airlift. And, of course, there was Korea.

Across the table, the two old Cold Warriors grinned.

Harry Truman devoted his retirement years mostly to building the Truman Library, where he met schoolchildren, tourists, and other presidents—Richard Nixon, Lyndon Johnson. It was here, when the Missourian was eighty-one years old, that President Johnson formally signed the Medicare bill into law in 1965, nearly twenty years after Truman had unsuccessfully campaigned for the first time for a national health plan. He died on December 26, 1972, at age eighty-eight. He was buried in Independence in the Truman Library courtyard.

QUESTIONS FOR THOUGHT AND DISCUSSION

1. Given Harry S Truman's background, did he seem destined from birth to become President? Does his success suggest something about the American political system?

2. Given FDR's ill health in 1944, were the Democrats wise to put Truman on the ballot as the vice presidential nominee? Did Truman have the "right stuff" to follow in FDR's footsteps?

3. Was Truman's decision to use the atomic bomb against Japan to end World War II the right one? Were there alternatives he might have explored that would have been preferable?

4. How would you rate Truman's policies in responding to the communists during the early years of the Cold War? Would a more conciliatory (or more confrontational) stance towards the Soviets have been a better policy for the U.S. and our allies?

SUGGESTED READINGS

Alperovitz, Gar. *The Decision to Use the Atomic Bomb.* New York: Knopf, 1995.

Ferrell, Robert H. *Harry S Truman and the Modern American Presidency.* Boston: Little, 1985.

_____. *Harry S Truman: A Life.* Columbia: U. of Missouri P, 1994.

Hamby, Alonzo. *Beyond the New Deal: Harry S Truman and American Liberalism*. New York: Columbia UP, 1973.

Jenkins, Roy. *Truman*. N.Y.: Harper, 1986.

_____, ed. *Dear Bess. The Letters from Harry to Bess Truman, 1910–1957*. New York: Norton, 1983.

McCulloch, David. *Truman*. New York: Simon, 1992.

Truman, Harry S. *Autobiography*. Ed. by Robert H. Ferrell. Boulder: Colorado Associated UP, 1980.

Truman, Margaret. *Harry S Truman*. New York: Morrow, 1973.

17

Jack Kerouac

𝒯he generation born immediately after World War II learned early that strength lay in numbers, their own huge numbers. Schools had to expand, or new schools built to accommodate the largest classes that many American communities had ever seen. When those young people came of age, they saw in their numbers a political weapon, or at least a weapon. The motto "Don't trust anyone over thirty" guided the Class of 1968, the Flower Children who opposed war and opposed their parents.

Their long hair and bell-bottom pants were new, but many of their attitudes came from an American "beat" writer of the age of their parents. These young idealists, when idealism was still possible, believed in opening themselves up to experience by trampling barriers of conformity that bounded the suburbs most of them came from. Their spiritual guide, Jack Kerouac, had little in common with these children of the middle class. Nothing about him came from a mass movement although he wrote a classic known to the young mass protesters of 1968. Kerouac's 1957 novel, On the Road, *inspired and sustained a generation that refused and mistrusted authority. He started and remained an outsider, a position that let him both criticize everything and risk everything, as his Catholic, French-Canadian outlook prepared him to do. A New Romantic, Kerouac rejected what his Ivy League professors preached—that poetry must be impersonal—and went back a century to Walt Whitman, to a belief that what is authentic comes through in a rush, in overpowering emotion that it is the writer's business to pursue through experience.*

> . . . the only people for me are the mad ones, the ones who are mad to live, mad to talk, mad to be saved, desirous of everything at the same time, the ones who never yawn or say a commonplace thing, but burn, burn, burn like fabulous yellow Roman candles exploding like spiders across the stars.
>
> Jack Kerouac, *On the Road*

IN 1944, AT AGE TWENTY-TWO, Jean-Louis Kerouac, known as Jack, had already quit college, given up a football scholarship at Columbia, been discharged from the Navy after spending time in a military mental hospital, gone to jail for failing to tell the police about a murder and helping the murderer dispose of the weapon, been released from jail long enough to marry the woman who promised to pay his $100 bail if he married her (his father refused), and it all fit his serious, well-thought-out career plan. Jack Kerouac wanted to be a writer.

For him to be able to imagine being a writer in the first place showed a powerful imagination. Such an impractical goal, demanding a long apprenticeship, just did not add up, not to the people he knew in his hometown mill town of Lowell, Massachusetts. Most of all it made no sense to his parents.

Leo Kerouac (born Joseph Alcide Léon Kirouack), Jack's father, had already achieved a modest success in having come to Lowell, Massachusetts, after his parents had migrated south with him from Quebec province in 1889. Leo left his parents in Nashua, New Hampshire, fourteen miles away, to work in Lowell as a reporter for a struggling paper, *L'Etoile*. In Lowell, most newcomers, drawn by the textile mills and shoe factories, were French Canadians and Greeks. The town's older inhabitants, heavily Irish, kept their distance. French Canadians, unlike newly arriving Europeans, had already gone through the trauma of leaving the mother continent and had found Canada lacking or no longer hospitable.

Their double migration, first from France and then from Canada, left the French Canadians ("Canucks" or "Frenchmen" in the racial slang of New England) with fewer stars in their eyes than other immigrants. Because they had already spent generations in America—North America, that is—they knew exactly what paved the streets. It was snow and ice more often than it was gold. Based on their own hard experience, they did not expect to have sons who would become president or even surgeons. The link of education to getting ahead, axiomatic to many new Americans, did not match their views or values. Because they brought with them the memory of being an outgroup in English Canada, they expected to remain a group, a strong and identifiable community. They did not urge their children to go away and diminish the community's strength. Most French Canadians hoped their children would grow up, get good jobs (maybe in the mills), stay close by, and raise large families. Most did.

Such hedged aspirations, so easy to criticize, produced a culture marked for its vitality and human warmth. Identity crises were not a problem for French Canadians, who had a strong sense of what it meant to belong to their group. The cheerful, almost wiseguy peppiness that New Englanders soon recognized as French gave a shot in the arm to many otherwise sleepy towns. Their dark hair and strong features made them stand out from the paler natives, but more than that, they spoke French. When they learned English it was with a strong, easily mocked accent that never mastered certain sounds. Their style of saying words like "three" or "thirteen" provided the punch line to many cruel jokes. No one ever called them lazy, but racial prejudice finds a way to belittle the defining qualities of an outgroup—even if it requires distortion. Instead of being praised for being energetic, the "Frenchmen" were laughed at for being "jumped up." Their pride in every form of neatness, both in personal appearance and in their scrubbed and tended houses, was criticized as being fanatical. All that excess energy, neighbors hinted, went with their being oversexed.

Being Catholic, French Canadians provided one more affront to Protestant New England in their religion. Worshipping in ornate churches that seemed gaudy compared to Congregational severity, they had services half in Latin with sermons in French. Not much in their way of life made assimilation easy.

Intelligent French Canadians, like the working class parents of Jack Kerouac, noticed all the time that barriers kept them in their part of town because they were "Frenchmen." They also knew that if they wanted to get along in Lowell, fighting the system would only waste their time. Jack Kerouac did not grow up hearing about prejudice against his family and people like them. But when his father explained unlucky breaks as being "politics," no one had to ask him to explain what he meant.

Unlike many of their neighbors, Leo and Gabrielle Kerouac had only three children. When Jack, the youngest, was born in 1922, Leo's business opportunities were beginning to look up. By putting in longer hours than he had to, Leo had managed to teach himself the printing trade and to buy and run his own printing business. He and Gabrielle, an orphan who had worked in a shoe shop since she was a girl, expected to do better gradually in providing for their three children. Besides the baby, there were Charlotte, age four when Jack was born, and the sickly Francis Gerard, age six at Jack's birth.

More than just French, the Kerouacs knew that they were Breton, coming from the westernmost part of France, the part settled by Celts. That seafaring population, never far from physical hardship and uncertainty, both facts of life near the sea, developed tenacity. Being a Breton meant being stubborn, they proudly taught their children. Being Breton had also given the Kerouacs their unusual name, which they proudly kept. When Jack would later leave the tight community of Lowell he would hear himself called "Keroach" by people too rigid to get the odd sound right.

The Kerouacs would need all their centuries of genetic tenacity to cope with the great sadness of their young family. Gerard, their elder son, turned out to be sickly, fatally so. From an early age he suffered from rheumatic fever, an ailment that destroyed young hearts. The much younger son watched sad visitors come to the gloomy house to see the suffering and saintly boy. In their devout household, Gabrielle compared her frail son with other child saints so prominently venerated in the early years of the twentieth century. The recently canonized Thérèse of Lisieux, the "Little Flower," had linked youth, sickness, and sainthood in the prayers and consciousness of pious Catholics. Gabrielle knew that her innocent son was being taken from her to sainthood. She made sure that visitors and neighbors knew, too.

Jack, who was only four when Gerard died, brought the news of the death to his father. Not sure exactly what he was reporting but knowing that people treated it as important, he thought he was telling his father something that would make him happy. For years his father's reaction of shock and scolding for his flippancy would haunt Jack. That death also meant that his family now more than ever expected a great deal from their one remaining son.

Crushed at his own loss, Leo could not keep a hold on his growing business. Within his own community, and in Lowell in general, people warmed to the lively, intelligent, likeable man who continued to get good accounts for his printing business. Because he did the printing for the movie theater, for example, his children were able to go to movies without paying, for years. But his family did not enjoy much of this prosperity because at the same time Leo was drawn more and more to gambling, to betting on horses, and to working out a system to make his money work for him.

Leo always managed to pay the rent and keep food on the table, but there was no question of spoiling Jack in a material way. In terms of affection and protectiveness, however, his mother coddled her son. Thinking that Jack had been punished enough by losing his sainted brother, Gabrielle usually took pains to keep him from rough treatment. She let him spend hours alone in his room playing imaginary games of baseball and always writing things down, keeping tiny notebooks, putting down the record of all these imaginary, solitary games. She could not bring herself to insist that he go outside and play with neighborhood children.

The Marist brothers who taught French children at Saint Louis de France school did not coddle their charges. Because of the double goal of maintaining their heritage and having an American education, they demanded two days of work every day at school. In the morning the children spoke French, studied French, and learned Canadian history and geography, all taught in French. In the afternoon they switched languages and subjects. At the end of fifth grade, the town informed the Kerouac family that because they had moved (Leo was losing money), they lived over the line for Saint Louis school. Jack would have to start the next year at the local public junior high school. His education up to that point had been so good that when he started in the new school he was able to go directly into seventh grade, skipping sixth. His teachers noted two qualities that had everything to do with his Catholic school training: they found him extremely polite and very neat.

When Jack Kerouac began to make a name for himself at Lowell High School it had nothing to do with brains. At baseball, track, and football he stood out for his physical talent. At five foot eight inches, he was so fast and strong that he could play running back because when he ran with the ball, he could not be stopped or brought down. He had been playing for years with his friends, even when they used a stocking stuffed with rags because no one owned or could afford to buy a football.

Praise for playing football did not turn Kerouac's head because he saw beyond its excitement to the brutality. The part of football he liked least was knowing that people could be hurt. Although his unusual talent and limited prospects might have encouraged a high school junior to think about a sports career, a future of playing ball did not attract Jack. In the fall of his junior year, when he was only fifteen, he knew that he wanted to become something he had never seen in Lowell, and he knew that no one in Lowell would know what he meant, or almost no one. Doing what any French-Canadian high school student would have done to investigate a bright ambition, Jack Kerouac went to talk to his parish priest to tell him that he wanted to be a writer. The startling reaction he got from Father Armand Morissette made a tremendous difference in the rest of his life. The priest did not laugh. He gave the best serious advice he could think of, starting with the hard fact that Kerouac would have to leave Lowell and somehow get himself to New York.

Up to that point Kerouac's high school studies had been in the commercial course, the curriculum that was standard for young people who knew they did not intend to try to go to college but expected to go directly from high school to jobs in business, as it was still possible to do. From this training Kerouac had become an excellent typist, a skill that would become a significant influence in his literary career. Now he would have to change course in high school and in life. As soon as he started the college course, the importance of sports changed as college coaches became interested in the young football star. The Boston College coach in particular put pressure on Jack to think of coming to the Catholic, New England school. What he offered went far beyond tuition, room, and board. He hinted that if Jack accepted a scholarship at Boston College, the coach could arrange a good job for Leo. The coach leaned hard.

Jack Kerouac had never been to New York when Columbia accepted him. The admissions officials understood what that meant and also wisely predicted that going from Lowell High School to an Ivy League university in New York City would be too brutal a transition for a young man of seventeen. They required him to spend a year getting ready at Horace Mann School, an excellent preparatory school also in New York City. During that year Kerouac lived with a relative, took the subway to school, and brought his own bread and butter or peanut butter sandwiches because he did not have enough money for cafeteria food. He also played football and maintained a .92 academic average.

The summer before starting Columbia he went back to Lowell and at the last minute considered not taking the scholarship. He knew that moving away meant less than it did to leave everything he had known, but according to his notion of being a writer he had to go after all the variety and wildness that lay beyond poor and backward Lowell. When he left for Columbia, Jack Kerouac did not have the money for a bus ticket, so a friend of his family gave him the cash.

Being near a superb library, being in classes that required him to read the *Iliad*, Sophocles, and to hear lectures by experts who had written some of the books they were using changed Kerouac's life. So did being near Harlem. The sounds of the new music he was able to discover on his trips to Harlem helped Kerouac understand what he wanted to do in writing. He wanted to write in a way that was personal, spontaneous, intellectually complicated, sexy, and very, very American. Avid to achieve what the musicians had already mastered he started to imitate their techniques for getting ready. He tried smoking marijuana, he used benzedrine, and he drank. He loved New York.

Kerouac's sense of freedom coupled with his idea of an artist's responsibility made him have to try everything new that New York offered him. Girls of a kind he had never met in Lowell, aggressive, exuberant, rich girls, exposed him to a way of seeing things that he had never even found in his wide reading. Playing football for Columbia did not dominate his freshman year. For one thing the coach did not give Kerouac many opportunities to play. When his father learned about the slights in letters, he saw signs of "politics." Using the reasoning that worked in Lowell, Leo was sure that the coach, an Italian, favored Italian players over his gifted son. Jack knew that the education he was offered guaranteed an easy future on what he saw as a rich man's inside track, and access to privileges he did not value. The following year Kerouac told the coach he did not want the scholarship any more in a move that devastated his parents. His mother had been dreaming of seeing her smart son reach life's highest attainment by one day becoming an insurance company executive.

While Kerouac was out of school, the attack on Pearl Harbor catapulted America into war. He signed up to join the Navy, but had to wait so long to be called up for his physical that he lost patience. In 1943 Kerouac joined the Merchant Marine and sailed to Liverpool on the *George Weems*.

After his return, Kerouac drew the attention of officers at his Navy physical through a distinction that did not serve him well. He was told that he had the highest I.Q. of anyone who had ever gone through the base at Newport, Rhode Island, and for that reason, he was suspected of being a Communist agent. The Navy then let Kerouac know that he was to be trained as a commando. To avoid that honor, Kerouac wrote friends of his plan to convince the Navy of his insanity, a plan that succeeded. After spending time at a Navy mental psychiatric hospital, he was discharged for having an "indifferent character." The trial put a great deal on the line because if he had been found sane, Kerouac would have faced a court-martial. From the hospital he wrote a friend that "the defeated are the strongest," a belief he would teach a generation. In that experience Kerouac also elevated outrageous behavior to being a necessary part of demonstrating personal integrity, another article of faith for his admirers years later.

Kerouac's education continued at an accelerated speed after he left Columbia for good. Knowing that he wanted intellectual depth and convinced that universities do not dispense that gift, he read and read and read. His impatience to become a writer meant that more than anything he resented having to sleep. Maybe because of his good physical condition or just from natural strength, he had been able since high school to stay up all night talking with friends, whole nights through without suffering from the loss of sleep. In New York he met intellectuals, young people who read as much as he did and who also looked for experiences to teach them what books hinted at. An aristocratic Midwesterner named William Burroughs became one of his good friends along with a would-be labor organizer and poet four years younger than Kerouac named Allen Ginsberg.

Because Kerouac came from a tight community where people expected to help the people they knew and to be helped by them, he did not look for superficial acquaintances with his new friends. As one New York friend noticed, everyone who came along was someone else for Jack to love. Part of the same circle was Lucien Carr, another wealthy Midwesterner, who was pursued everywhere by a former teacher, a man who had fallen in love with him. Ultimately Carr ended up murdering the teacher in self-defense. Counting on help from his friend, Carr went to see Kerouac, who did help him get rid of the murder weapon, a Boy Scout knife. Carr, whose wealthy family provided him with excellent lawyers, impressed the police with his own importance and social status. (He ended up serving two years after pleading guilty to manslaughter.) Kerouac noticed that his own treatment by the police showed no respect. New York cops handled Kerouac as the young tough-guy thug he looked like to them. He was taken to jail and stayed for a while because Leo refused to send his son the $100 bail he needed. By ending up in jail after throwing away terrific chances for success, Jack had dirtied the name of Kerouac, as far as his father was concerned.

Elliott Erwitt, Magnum

Jack Kerouac inspired not angry young men but weeping young men, the Beat Generation, who found the postwar American prosperity spiritually empty.

Jack's girlfriend, Edie Parker, who came from the affluent and closed community of Grosse Pointe, Michigan, tried to use her trust fund money to help him out. Her family's legal advisors explained that her money could be used to help the young man only if the couple (already living together) were married. So with the understanding that it was a means of coming up with bail, they got married. To no one's surprise, the marriage did not "take," and failed to inspire either partner to make any concession to married life such as to discontinue dating other people. They moved in with Edie's mother in rich and predictable Grosse Pointe, a place Jack found moribund and revolting. Within a year, Jack had signed up again with the Merchant Marine.

Back in New York, Kerouac met Neal Cassady, a young "jailkid" who would help the dropout become the author. Kerouac also met John Clellon Holmes, to whom he first uttered a phrase that became a label. When Holmes asked what he should call the people their age hanging out in Times Square, Kerouac baptized them "the Beat Generation," "beat" as in defeated but also as in "beatific," Kerouac would later expound.

Jack Kerouac still thought of himself as on his way to being a writer, but he had to figure out what kind. In 1948 he was already at work on a book that retold his travels with Cassady. Kerouac also admired Thomas Wolfe so much that his first book, *The Town and the City*, echoed Wolfe. In the frenzy of getting that published, Kerouac met and then married three days later Joan Haverty, who needed a reason for not going back to Albany. Very shortly before they married, Kerouac made sure that his previous marriage was annulled. This marriage lasted about as well as the first. He was holding fast to his idea that a writer has an obligation to experience as much as possible both in order to have material to write about and to understand the human soul enough to convey and "dig" what he had gone through.

As a writer, Kerouac insisted on being as thoroughly American as possible. Because he had not learned English until he was over five years old and still had halting English as late as the age of sixteen, he loved the English language in an acute way that was almost physical. The sounds of words impressed him. He heard the music of English as being exotic and having a strong beat, like the drums that he loved, and unlike the rising music of his first language. To be American and sound American he needed to see and know and hear America. Sure that he could only know what he lived, Kerouac set out to travel all over America.

With Neal Cassady, and without money, Kerouac hitchhiked. Thanks to rides from mostly marginal people they saw America and Mexico. A series of trips between 1947 and 1950 turned out to be the raw material for his next book in which he sang the craziness and variety he found and loved. Kerouac kept his habit of writing every day. As he wrote he hit upon a theory, spelling out what he had known by intuition in his college days in Columbia, the idea that in his writing he wanted to do what jazz musicians do. He wanted something that everybody gets in one sense, because it is related to beats we all feel in our bodies, earthy and pulsing. But at the same time, the music has enough form to it to tolerate very cerebral analyses. That mystery of having both truths, one obvious and one elusive, proved its art. Kerouac wanted to write what he called "spontaneous prose," not redrafted, corrected, and worked over, but something that just came out of him the way the notes came out of jazz horn players. "What a man most wishes to hide, revise and un-say, is precisely what Literature is waiting and bleeding for . . . ." as he would write his editor.

In three weeks in April 1951, on a very long roll of paper, Kerouac typed all at once the novel that he had been making in his mind out of the continent crossing trips of his earlier years. Because he had already published one novel, he expected to have less of a hard time with his second, a much more original work. He was right that a publisher would be interested, but also cautious.

It took years for the book to come out in print, even after an editor at Viking, a prestigious New York literary publisher, became interested. The editor, Malcolm

Cowley, spoke of Kerouac as first of all a French Canadian writer, a group Cowley considered "under-represented" in American literature. True enough, but very little in the book would be recognizable as French-Canadian to the people of Lowell, Massachusetts. Legal, not literary problems slowed down the book, as Cowley eventually explained, because Viking lawyers feared a big libel suit from people described in the novel, all easy to recognize. Kerouac changed their names, but anyone who knew any one of them would not be fooled for long. Cowley said he would get signed releases from two important ones, Allen Ginsberg (Carlo Marx) and Neal Cassady (Dean Moriarty). Cowley also suggested that the title be changed because *The Beat Generation* would fit better for another project of Kerouac's. So the novel of the trips around America carried the title *On the Road* when it finally appeared in 1957. Now considered an American classic, it has remained in print ever since.

Whatever else it was, Kerouac's novel had to be acknowledged as original. Its main character, who talked the way Kerouac did, came across as naive enough to be thrilled by his own daring at hitchhiking across America, sometimes riding on the back of a flatbed truck with no side rails. But the hero was so well read that he could admire and be moved by the language of the people he met. Every page had evidence of an unusual ear, someone hyper-alert to how people sounded and the words they used. Two qualities of the author explained these traits of the narrator. Kerouac's habit had long been to listen, intently and respectfully, to everyone who spoke to him. And people had always been surprised at his phenomenal memory, especially for things people said. In Lowell, Kerouac had earned the nickname "Memory Babe" from friends who swore he never forgot a thing he heard.

Being forced to wait so long—from 1951 until 1957—to see his novel in print did not keep Kerouac from writing more. Believing that he had only begun a life-long project, one long autobiographical novel that would encompass his entire life, he kept adding to his material for future works by continuing to travel. In San Francisco, where friends from New York had gone, he wrote *Visions of Cody*. Because he could live cheaply and he needed to stretch his money, he went to Mexico. In Mexico City he found plentiful and inexpensive marijuana and with its help wrote *Doctor Sax*, the title from a character he invented in a childhood game. In 1953 he wrote *Maggie Cassidy*, a novel based on his teenage love for Mary Carney, a girl he swore he loved with an intensity he would never know again. He tested that hypothesis on many, many women. Handsome enough to be an actor, but not vain, and tender in a way that women liked, Kerouac's female contacts of varying duration numbered somewhere around 250, he thought.

Many years away from Lowell and Father Morissette, Kerouac had long stopped counting himself a practicing Catholic, but his strongly developed spiritual side continued to demand more cultivation. In New York and also on the west coast again he began investigating Buddhism, so full of mysticism and so appealing to a writer with strong links to a dead older brother, Gerard. Between 1955 and 1956 Kerouac wrote *Mexico City Blues*, *Tristessa*, a novel with a marked Buddhist sensibility, and *Visions of Gerard*, his favorite novel. All of this while waiting for *On the Road* to be published.

Young people made *On the Road* a phenomenal success, buying over half a million paperback copies. People not young, especially critics, tended to have strong opinions about his writing, good or bad. The *New York Times* said *On the Road* was: "The most beautifully executed, the clearest and most important utterance yet made by the generation Kerouac himself named . . . as 'beat.'" Truman Capote passed judgment on *The Subterraneans* (1958) giving a verdict that still gets quoted for its acidity. Said Capote, "That's not writing, that's typing."

Kerouac figured out how to say what people his age believed. Postwar America burdened the young with victory, with treasures, and with opportunities of every kind. Kerouac found the best of the good life to be cold. He had hated his close up view of American wealth and privilege in Grosse Pointe where millionaires' residences made him think of funeral parlors. He could not comprehend the trade-off he was expected to make—to give up the excitement that others called instability for no reason except to conform. Because he grew up around people of great integrity and small material prospects, he had not been conditioned to making choices for other people's reasons. Making ends meet had imposed on his family as much conformity as they could stand—going to work and paying the rent just like everyone else, with not much sense of choice. Critics who saw Kerouac as throwing off middle class values had never been to Lowell, Massachusetts. Kerouac had pole vaulted out of the hard times of blue collar life to the precariousness of conscientious objectors to materialism.

So smart and so good looking, he could have had a better job, his mother used to think. As he began to be known as a writer, she learned to be proud of "Jackie," who bought her houses in Long Island and Florida, where she would protect him so that he could write. When his dubious-looking friends showed up, *Mémere* did not always let them past her.

Unlike his poet friend Allen Ginsberg, Jack Kerouac did not know how to take advantage of the media. Kerouac appeared on television on the popular, mainstream Steve Allen Show in 1958. Steve Allen proved his appreciation and his desire to help the young writer when Allen played a jazz piano accompaniment to Jack reading his poems for an LP recording. But the limelight did not add to his adventure, and did not help him write.

By 1965 after he had written *Desolation Angels* in Mexico City, Kerouac turned from America to think about his family's Breton origins. The result of that effort, *Satori in Paris*, he hand-printed on seven July nights in a row. His return to the Old World prepared him for a return to his old neighborhood. In 1966 he moved back to Lowell where he married Stella Sampas, sister of a boyhood friend. The stress—a word people had not yet learned to say—of all the nomadic years, the drugs, and the bouts of untreated phlebitis, ravaged Kerouac. His friend Neal Cassady, inspiration for Dean Moriarty, so important in *On the Road*, died in February 1968, a loss that the fat, balding, grumpy Kerouac refused to believe. Flower children were claiming Kerouac as their spiritual inspiration, while he rejected their soft path to enlightenment via mind-bending drugs. He had suffered and refused the smooth, fast track in the name of art. The following year, in October 1968, Kerouac died at age forty-seven. In his thinking, Jack Kerouac had not lived long enough to stop being young, nor lived slowly enough to start being old.

QUESTIONS FOR THOUGHT AND DISCUSSION

1. Millions of Americans grow up in ethnic enclaves like the French-Canadian community in which Jack Kerouac grew up in Lowell. How are these enclaves different from heterogeneous urban neighborhoods or more affluent suburbs? Which would you consider most "American"?

2. What sparked Kerouac's artistic talent and led him to a writing career?

3. How was Kerouac's work related to the jazz music scene of the mid-twentieth century? Was there an implicit political message in both jazz music and beat writing?

4. Was Kerouac's emphasis on accumulating more and more experience through a series of escapades, travels, and drug-induced states noble or self-indulgent? Did the 60s generation appreciate his message even more than he himself understood it?

SUGGESTED READINGS

Cassady, Carolyn. *Heart Beat: My Life with Jack & Neal*. Berkeley: Creative Arts Book Company, 1976.

Charters, Ann, ed. *The Beats: Literary Bohemians in Postwar America. Dictionary of Literary Biography*. Vol. 16. Detroit: Gale, 1984.

Charters, Ann. *A Bibliography of Works by Jack Kerouac (Jean-Louis Lebris de Kerouac), 1939–1975*. New York: Phoenix, 1967.

Charters, Ann, ed. *Jack Kerouac: Selected Letters 1940–1956*. New York: Viking, 1995.

Charters, Ann. *Kerouac: A Biography*. San Francisco: Straight Arrow, 1973.

Challis, Chris. *Quest for Kerouac*. London: Faber, 1984.

Jarvis, Charles E. *Visions of Kerouac*. Lowell, Mass.: Ithaca, 1973.

Nicosia, Gerald. *Memory Babe: A Critical Biography of Jack Kerouac*. New York: Grove, 1983.

18

Rachel Carson

More than anything, Americans believed in science in the decades following World War II. Knowledge and mastery of the terrible truths of science, after all, had produced the atomic bomb, synonym for destruction, but also, for Americans, the key to ending the war and saving American lives. No one could disbelieve science. In 1957, when the Russians surpassed Americans in putting Sputnik into space, an unmanned satellite, the sense of losing the upper hand in science sparked a concentrated effort to catch up and the "Space Race" was on. A past victory and the key to future prestige made science the most serious, legitimate and essential branch of study, in the opinion of most Americans. Only gradually, and with horror, did Americans hear reports of lapses of science. Thalidomide, for example, a nonprescription aid to sleep, suddenly had to be withdrawn from the market because women who had taken it during pregnancy gave birth to babies with shortened and malformed arms and legs.

At about the same time, a most unlikely critic of science, Rachel Carson, a former employee of a government agency, began to speak up against pesticides. Carson reminded the public that those chemicals of widely appreciated use were poisons that were allowing mankind to do something absolutely new—not to kill pests, but to alter nature. In Carson's clear vision, an idea had to change; people had to stop seeing nature as the enemy: "We still talk in terms of conquest. We still haven't become mature enough to think of ourselves as only a tiny part of a vast and incredible universe . . . . Man is a part of nature, and his war against nature is inevitably a war against himself."

AGAIN AND AGAIN, the strikes against Carson would turn out to be in her favor. Being born near Pittsburgh, one of the first American cities to be tainted by industrial pollution, Rachel Carson saw that natural beauty could be lost. The important and high-minded efforts of President Theodore Roosevelt were introducing Americans to the concept of conservation, of preserving parts of nature from development. But not where Rachel Carson lived.

181

From the time she was born on May 27, 1907, and until she went away to college, Rachel Carson's family lived in Springdale, Pennsylvania, eighteen miles northwest of Pittsburgh on a bend in the Allegheny River. In that time, she noticed, the river itself grew less beautiful as did the valley. Her family owned sixty-five acres of that valley and probably appeared prosperous to their neighbors. In fact, the Carsons were land-poor, partly because Robert Carson, Rachel's father, refused to sell off mining rights under his land to a coal company. He never really believed that the company honored the promise it made him not to mine below his land, but Carson could neither prove his suspicion, nor could he sell off his acres as house lots, as he dreamed of doing. Because the Carsons were stuck with many acres of beautiful land, they ended up having to enjoy it.

Maria Carson, Rachel's mother, had been a good enough Latinist to be able to teach before she married and had to put aside all her career aspirations, as did most women at the turn of the century. That example may have given Rachel second thoughts about marriage at the cost of more engaging intellectual work. Of the three Carson children, two daughters and a son, Rachel, the youngest by eight years, spent a great deal of time at her mother's side. Not wanting to expose her youngest to disease, Maria often kept Rachel with her, home from school, away from ailing children. A fair amount of their time together was spent out of doors, where education still went on. From Maria Carson, Rachel learned to notice what she saw in the woods—the birds, the flowers, the trees, each with its particular name and importance. That childlike sense of totally absorbed and concentrated delight never left Rachel Carson's experience of nature.

The whole family knew that Rachel deserved as much education as they could afford. They recognized her writing ability early on, not only because her teachers spotted it, but because in a writing competition she won first prize and publication in the *St. Nicholas Magazine*, a review for children, and then won twice more. When time came for college, a way had to be found to send Rachel, even on the slim financial means her family could offer for help. When the Carsons learned that tuition and expenses at Pennsylvania College for Women (later known as Chatham College) amounted to one thousand dollars per year, they knew that they could not even come close, but Rachel was offered a scholarship.

The college administrators thought Rachel Carson showed good, practical sense in deciding to major in English. She talked about wanting to be a writer, but her advisor believed that even if that plan failed, Rachel would always be able to find a job teaching; in other words, always have a livelihood. By that same reasoning, her advisors found little sense in her decision to change her major from English to biology in her junior year. Not even a woman with a degree in science could expect to get a good job; everyone knew that science jobs belonged to an entirely male domain controlled by a closed fraternity at every level. But in science Carson had found the most satisfying kind of study yet. Through science, she learned to put a structure to the labels she had learned on her girlhood nature walks with her mother. Best of all, she now thought, she had finally found something to write about.

Even in her study of science Rachel Carson held on to a poetic streak expressed in her love of the sea. A girl born and raised in Pennsylvania in a family that did not travel anywhere, she had never laid eyes on the ocean, but she loved reading about it, imagining it, and studying its creatures in books. When she graduated from college in 1929, the same professor who had influenced her change of major, Mary Scott Skinker, also helped Carson get a fellowship for graduate study at Johns Hopkins University, in Baltimore, Maryland, where she would work with R. P. Cowles, a well-known authority on marine life. Another fellowship was also arranged for Carson to spend the summer before graduate school at the highly respected Woods Hole Marine Biological Laboratory in Massachusetts. There, in the summer after college, at age twenty-two, Rachel Carson laid eyes on the Atlantic Ocean for the first time. Nothing had ever mattered so much.

Larger events in the world outside graduate school could not have been worse. The first semester of graduate school included October 1929, when the precipitous fall of the stock market sent the American economy into a tailspin. Carson, luckier than many, was able to finish her course work in graduate school and get her degree, but her family suffered setbacks along with everyone else. Her parents and then her brother, suddenly jobless, came to Baltimore to move in with Rachel. Keeping more than one household going was out of the question in the Depression. Because unemployment was the only growth in the economy, Rachel Carson knew that in October of 1929, her job prospects sank along with the fortunes of many Americans. In the thinking of the times, no good job should ever be "wasted" on a woman when it could go to a man. She managed to get a part-time teaching job at the University of Maryland to provide partial income, as she continued "living like a graduate student," economically strapped. Being forced to live with normal people, her family, while doing her scientific work no doubt forced her to talk about her work in a way that an intelligent nonspecialist could understand. Those hard times may have helped develop her talent for making science understandable to nonscientists.

Before she started at Johns Hopkins, Rachel Carson had visited in Washington, D.C., with Elmer Higgins, a scientist who worked for the Bureau of Fisheries. He recognized her seriousness, but even before the Depression did not want to give her expectations that would only be disillusioned. As a woman scientist, Higgins explained, Carson would never find a job in industry simply because those science jobs were strictly reserved for men. To be realistic, she had to see her two choices: either she could teach or she could try to find a job in government.

That was before Carson started graduate training. Now that she had her master's degree, now that the Depression was tightening belts, and now that she needed to help her family as much as she could, Rachel Carson went back to Elmer Higgins. She felt encouraged because as part of the New Deal President Franklin Roosevelt encouraged employers at every level to consider hiring women. Higgins offered her what he had, admitting that it meant taking a risk. He had never seen a word Carson had written, he confessed, but he needed someone to write short scripts for a radio program that the Bureau of Fisheries had been asked to offer. Within the Bureau, people referred to these as "Seven-Minute Fish Tales," but officially the series was called "Romance Under the Waters."

Maybe recognizing what it would mean, Higgins suggested that someone collect the scripts and turn them into "something of a general sort about the sea," to be printed together as a pamphlet from the Bureau of Fisheries. Naturally he asked Rachel Carson to prepare the introduction for the new version of collected scripts, yet when he saw what she wrote in answer to that request, he told her that it was not at all what he had in mind. Her introduction and text were much too good to be wasted in a government pamphlet. Taken aback, Rachel Carson asked for advice: what should she do with what she had written? Only because Higgins assured her that *The Atlantic* would be glad to have her work did she have the confidence to send her piece to such a highly respected literary magazine. In September 1937, *The Atlantic* published "Undersea." They, too, recognized in her the rare ability of a scientist to write about technical facts in a way that made people want to read it—not dull, not impossible to follow, but a pleasure because of the graceful, clear writing.

Because Rachel Carson was already working for the Bureau of Fisheries, she heard that a position was coming open for a junior aquatic biologist. To be considered for the job she took the civil service examination required of all candidates, a group in which Rachel Carson was the only woman—and had the highest score. Based on that result, she was hired for $2,000 per year, twice as much as her previous job paid.

The article that she had sent to *The Atlantic* pleased many of the magazine's readers, but one of them, editor-in-chief at Simon and Schuster Publishing, wanted to see that same approach to science expanded. He wrote Rachel Carson asking her to write a book for him, a book about the sea, an effort published in 1941 as *Under the Sea Wind*, the book that remained Rachel Carson's favorite. In it she experimented as a writer in a way that no "serious" scientist probably would have dared. She described and discussed the sea from the point of view of creatures in it, exploring changes in the sea as they would appear to a mackerel, or following seasons with a family of migrating shore birds. Bad luck, the only thing that detracted from the book's success, had nothing to do with Rachel Carson but with another intrusion from the world of man-made conflict. A very short time after that first book appeared, the attack on Pearl Harbor took place, an event that froze millions of careers. Suddenly, America had time for one thing only, to strengthen its war effort.

Every government agency, including her employer, the Fish and Wildlife Service (the Bureau of Fisheries changed its name in 1940), participated in the war effort. For her part, Rachel Carson, now promoted to assistant aquatic biologist, was called upon to write pamphlets to encourage Americans to eat fish. (Red meat, in short supply, had to be reserved for the fighting men, both overseas and those being trained in the United States). For a short period during the war, the offices of the Wildlife Bureau had to be moved to Chicago when government office space in Washington became scarce during the war, but other than those few months, she worked in Washington, living with her family. During her years with the Wildlife Bureau, Rachel Carson continued to advance slowly in the normal course of her work: from assistant aquatic biologist (1942–43) she rose to associate aquatic biologist (1943–45), then aquatic biologist (1945–46), and finally information specialist (1946–49). This record establishes her credentials as a scientist, a fact that her later critics would ignore in their efforts to detract from her name as well as the seriousness and validity of her writing.

While she maintained her government job Rachel Carson continued to work at her writing. Had she been free to choose, she would have devoted all of her time to it, but circumstances took that luxury away. In 1935 Rachel Carson's father died, leaving her mother in the charge of Rachel and her sister Marian. Because Marian had divorced and returned "home" with her two children, Rachel and her sister were already acting as parents to Marjorie and Virginia. When Marian died in 1937, Rachel and her mother had to take over the sad duty of raising the children. More than ever Rachel depended on her predictable government paycheck.

World War II made the oceans more important, or made it necessary to have more detailed and precise information about them than had ever been pursued or collected. When the United States found itself fighting in two oceans at once, facts about those oceans proved crucial in gaining and maintaining military advantage. After the war, the government possessed copious new data that expanded the world's understanding of what went on beneath the surface of the sea. Rachel Carson, trained as an information specialist within government, found it natural to want to make public the wealth of such vast new knowledge. Her next book, *The Sea Around Us*, repeated the clear, strong language of her first book which this new effort now let her revive. (Her readers found *The Sea Around Us* such a treasure that they went back and rediscovered *Under the Sea Wind*.) Within weeks the new book ranked at the head of the best seller list and remained there for eighty-six weeks, spending thirty-nine weeks in first place.

The financial success of *The Sea Around Us* changed Rachel Carson's life. First, it meant that she could give up her government job and still take care of her inherited family. Her unpretentious way of life let her live on her royalties for years while she wrote her next book. Carson allowed herself two luxuries from those profits, two things that she had wanted for a long time. As a scientist, she splurged on a high quality binocular-microscope. Then, as a lover of the sea, she built a cottage in Maine, on an island near Boothbay Harbor, where she would explore beaches and tidal pools in bliss for years.

The Sea Around Us bought Rachel Carson freedom beyond her financial liberation from her government job. As a civil service employee, like all the others, she had been required to take a loyalty oath that bound her not to participate in activities that would be subversive to the government of the United States, an oath that also constrained civil servants from being critical of government policies. Now that she no longer worked as a civil servant, Rachel Carson could say in public what she saw happening under President Eisenhower. People she had worked with, competent career scientists, were being let go while untrained political appointees took their places. Dwight Eisenhower appointed as Secretary of Agriculture Douglas McKay, a man who brought to that post a background in selling used cars. On the side of business—and farming was growing rapidly into a huge business—he had no use for conservationists, a group McKay labelled "long-haired punks." Writing a letter to the *Washington Post* in 1953 to protest such appointments, Rachel Carson was only beginning to oppose her former employer, the United States government.

In the years following World War II, scientists worked to find civilian applications for chemicals that had been developed as part of the war effort. America and other countries wanted to see science turn away from "military ends," the polite

The Bettmann Archive

Soft-spoken Rachel Carson ignited violent social criticism from opponents who ignored her credentials as a scientist.

euphemism that allowed people not to mention the atomic bomb and nuclear fallout. The Atoms for Peace program was typical of the new mentality, along with efforts to "convert" chemicals to peacetime use. In one case, a chemical that had been known for its destructive properties became a hero, a universal problem solver.

Dichloro-diphenyl-trichloro-ethane, known as DDT, had first been synthesized in Germany in 1874. Its use as an insecticide did not occur until 1939, an application so appreciated that the scientist who discovered it won the Nobel Prize for his find. Suddenly, with a great sense of power, farmers felt that they could destroy any "pest" that endangered their crops and their profits. A chemical able to kill insects on contact, without being ingested, attracted other professionals and led to new herbicides. Highway engineers saw that roads no longer had to be blemished with wild "brush" growing at roadside; a modern highway could have a modern look. In operations called "chemical plowing" a large scale spraying could take away all vegetation to any desired height, four feet or eight feet, and it was cheaper than mowing. Fruit trees could be sprayed to guarantee bug-free produce. Acres of farmland could be sprayed inexpensively from airplanes with a powder believed to be harmless—except to insects. All the arguments were concrete and irrefutable, in economic terms: more food, smaller losses, and higher profits. In postwar America everyone recognized progress.

Rachel Carson, an advocate of "the web of life," as she called it, wrote about the interconnected and subtle system that linked insects, birds, flowers, fish, and on up the food chain to man. People did not yet use the word "environment," nor did they need to because the public did not know how to think about "nature" and "man" as part of one concept, as being on the same side. Man was conquering nature. Man was winning again and again, thanks to chemicals, the new gift of science, and the predictor of assured progress.

As early as 1945 Rachel Carson had known differently. In that year she had first proposed an article in *Reader's Digest* on the subject of the hidden dangers of DDT. She also knew that its success was not absolute, that new insects were developing, resistant to chemicals that succeeded only in killing off lesser, relatively harmless strains. In other words, nothing was being gained in many cases. Carson never wrote that article because the magazine rejected her proposal. Patience, a quality that research both required and developed in her, let Rachel Carson accept that setback, sure that in time the true information would reach the public. In 1957 she had not lost interest in the harmful effects of DDT when she started receiving letters from Olga Huckins in Duxbury, Massachusetts, describing the deathly transformation of salt marshes after extensive sprayings with DDT.

At the point when Rachel Carson would have started a book based on her observations and knowledge of the effects of pesticide, sadness took over her family life again. In 1957 the niece she and her mother had raised died, leaving her son, Roger Christie, five years old, whom Rachel adopted. With a small child at home she could not think of starting another book. Rachel Carson knew better than anyone that each effortlessly graceful book she had written took years of concentrated effort. Meanwhile, magazines turned down her proposals for articles from the author of a best-selling book on science. Even *Good Housekeeping*, with its potential for reaching a huge audience of women, refused her proposal to write about insecticides, speculating that such a message would cause "unwarranted fear." Such reluctance, in Rachel Carson's view, proved that she must do a book on the new and unwelcome knowledge. By 1958 she had made the decision that she had to go ahead with a project she expected to provoke a controversy.

Before *Silent Spring* appeared as a book, an achievement that took research over many years, *New Yorker* magazine published it in installments starting June

15, 1962. Even this small dose alerted chemical manufacturers to the problem that was brewing. Hoping to contain their troubles, Velsirol Chemical Corporation wrote a five-page letter to Houghton Mifflin, Carson's publisher, to urge that the book never be published because, they suggested, she represented a Communist plot to reduce the food supply of the West. Unconvinced, Houghton Mifflin brought out *Silent Spring* as planned in late September 1962.

Immediate and loud public reaction greeted the book, both praise and dismay, as opponents made far more noise than Rachel Carson's fans. Carson detractors recognized the most menacing aspect of the book in its meticulous research; with every assertion Carson included sources to verify it. As Carson's publisher astutely noted, the ferocity of the attack made no sense if it came simply as a response to criticism of DDT, a chemical that represented only a small share of the companies' considerable profits. A far more troubling criticism, the industrialists understood, came in Carson's questioning of how Americans allowed technology to destroy nature in the name of progress. She was objecting far less to new chemicals than to the new thinking, an attitude that allowed scientists to alter natural relationships, to change nature forever. Did mankind intend or want to diminish nature's variety? Had anyone put a value on clear lakes or on their loss? Did people understand that rivers, the place where runoff went, combined in their waters chemicals that no scientist would have mixed in a laboratory, mixtures that were unpredictable and beyond control?

To the delight of Houghton Mifflin, the chemical industry reacted to Carson's book as if to a publicity problem: they spent money. In their attempt to discredit *Silent Spring*, The National Agricultural Chemicals Association spent well over a quarter of a million dollars (a fortune in 1962), far more than any publisher could have devoted to making a new book known. Because its author happened to be a woman, words like "hysterical" and "emotional outburst" appeared in critical reviews. In general, criticism downplayed the fact that the "hysterical woman" had training and experience as a scientist, but the public already knew her earlier books about nature, written beautifully and with authority.

Chemical companies also recognized that to fight what had to be acknowledged as scientific charges, they needed good publicity and a scientist of their own to assure America that no proof linked DDT to any health hazards. In that role Dr. Robert White-Stevens, an executive of American Cyanamid Company, travelled around the United States denouncing Rachel Carson. Industry bombarded Americans with every possible kind of assurance that science created benign products for the public good. A famous propaganda photograph from the 1960s shows children on swings in a playground engulfed in a cloud of DDT, which they ignore, as proof that everyone accepted DDT as harmless. Rachel Carson's charges that agricultural workers were being sickened by chemicals days after spraying did not merit serious answers. White-Stevens said her claims were "gross distortions of the actual facts." (Some readers might have remembered that CBS News had documented the general mistreatment of such workers in Edward R. Murrow's famous documentary, "Harvest of Shame.")

Precisely because she had always been shut out of the man's world of science jobs in industry, Rachel Carson as an outsider could see what was not obvious from the inside. Not at all in a position of weakness, she now found that her excluded view gave her the credibility of an objective, unbiased observer. Because Rachel Carson researched her claims, argued persuasively, and wrote beautifully, her book was not easy to demean. As her opponents' behavior soon taught her, in such cases, attacks become personal.

Portrayed as a woman who cared more about insects than about people, Rachel Carson was ridiculed as a proponent of a world so tolerant of pests it could no longer feed itself. If her beliefs were put into action, America would "return to the Dark Ages." In fact, as she publicly repeated, *Silent Spring* does not urge the ban of all pesticides and herbicides, only of their widespread use. Because she had never married, critics mocked Carson for even caring about genetics or about future generations. "Isn't she a spinster?" As a former government employee, she felt the insult of an attack headed by the United States Department of Agriculture, but could not have been surprised. When she set out to write the book, Carson understood that she would face formidable opposition precisely because so many spraying programs were paid for by the government. She was taking on two strong allies, the chemical manufacturers plus the United States government.

"Silent Spring Is Now Noisy Summer," a *New York Times* headline said to describe the uproar surrounding Carson's book. Not just her readers but the American public needed to know what to think. CBS television, recognizing the disturbing confusion created in the atmosphere of accusation and denial, invited Rachel Carson to speak to America, to tell the public what she had written, what she had found. "The Silent Spring of Rachel Carson" presented an interview of Carson by the respected journalist Eric Sevareid. (Equal time was given to her attacker, Dr. White-Stevens.) Americans saw and heard the shy, soft-spoken scientist whose critics had compared her to Carrie Nation, the hatchet-carrying crusader for temperance. But the importance of Carson's book had inspired others to compare her to Charles Darwin, whose scientific writing also changed how people thought about the natural world. That television appearance demanded a great physical effort from Rachel Carson, as had the completion of the book, from the author weakened by cancer. Knowing that she would never witness any change brought about by the book, Carson could not keep from writing it "because I knew what I did."

President Kennedy had been reading Rachel Carson and taking her seriously. As a result of *Silent Spring*, he appointed a Pesticides Committee, source of a later report vindicating Rachel Carson, giving her credit for making the public aware of a new danger. By the end of 1962, Congress was at work on forty bills to regulate pesticides.

When Rachel Carson died in 1964, proof of her important work was beginning. In that same year a quiet and monumental change occurred when the legal requirements in cases of chemical questions shifted, a subtle but crucial difference directly attributable to Carson's *Silent Spring*. In the past, the burden of proof had been on the government, the partner of industry, to prove that chemicals were hazardous. Now, manufacturers were required to prove the safety of their products before they would be allowed on the market. In 1970, the year of the first Earth Day, the federal government created a new kind of regulatory body, the Environmental Protection Agency, unimaginable a generation earlier. Rachel Carson's idea of the web of life, delicate and interdependent, had migrated to the public consciousness, and conscience.

QUESTIONS FOR THOUGHT AND DISCUSSION

1. How was Rachel Carson able to rise and achieve distinction in the male-dominated scientific community? In what way could you or would you describe her as a pioneer?

2. Does Carson's fascination with the ocean and aquatic life seem an obsession? Are career obsessions more acceptable in men than in women? How was the fact she was a woman used against her by her later adversaries?

3. Why was Carson's crusade to challenge the widespread use of the DDT pesticide labeled a communist plot?

4. Carson's *Silent Spring* helped touch off the modern environmental movement that some say has gone too far. What should the appropriate balance be between protecting the environment on one hand and preserving business and landowner rights on the other? What would Carson's advice be in this regard?

SUGGESTED READINGS

Brooks, Paul. *The House of Life: Rachel Carson at Work*. Boston: Houghton, 1972.

Carson, Rachel. *Silent Spring*. Boston: Houghton, 1962.

Freeman, Martha, ed. *Always, Rachel: The Letters of Rachel Carson and Dorothy Freeman, 1952–1964*. Boston: Beacon, 1995.

Graham, Frank, Jr. *Since Silent Spring*. Boston: Houghton, 1970.

Jezer, Mary. *Rachel Carson*. New York: Chelsea, 1988.

Rossiter, Margaret W. *Women Scientists in America*. Baltimore: Johns Hopkins UP, 1982.

Sterling, Philip. *Sea and Earth: The Life of Rachel Carson*. New York: Crowell, 1970.

Whorton, James. *Before Silent Spring: Pesticides and Public Health in Pre-DDT America*. Princeton, N.J.: Princeton UP, 1974.

19

César Chávez

*I*n 1963 California became the state with the greatest population, pulling like a magnet from all the states to its east. More than a place, California had become the Oz of a new consciousness for America, especially for young Americans. Anything would be possible for those who could get there. So many things that mattered came from California, and in some cases from nowhere else. Movies came from California, but so did other kinds of entertainment, pleasure, and what seemed to be an unstoppable prosperity. With so many people, so much competition, and superb universities, California generated a new variety of well-being associated with a new natural resource, the talent of highly skilled and highly trained people. The future mattered far more than the past. The aerospace industry occupied a place that would gradually be taken over by the new wonder machines known as computers. California led the nation in being modern, with a version of the ecstatic, almost show-off attitude of its for-pleasure-only mascots, the surfers, heroes of songs that praised a way of life most Americans never got near.

More elemental things also came from California, as well, things such as food from the nation's leading agricultural state. So successful were California farmers, known as growers, that some crops were not even worth producing commercially anywhere else. For a long time people in the East did not know at what cost California fed the continent. César Chávez changed all of that, coming as a spokesman for agricultural workers and eventually founding a union. When he started his work as an activist, the average farm worker earned less than $1.50 an hour. Chávez never left the fields, even as he rose to national prominence and influence. The man Robert Kennedy called "one of the heroic figures of our time" allowed himself a salary of five dollars a week, to keep himself from forgetting how his brothers suffered.

To MANY PEOPLE and in many ways, what he did made no sense. César Chávez, so intelligent, so hardworking, so knowledgeable about leadership and building support, a David against the Goliath of California growers, and such an unusual individual, might have made a wonderful life for himself and his family, and might have grown rich. He might have risen high in any organization, an example of how far Mexican Americans could go. He might have easily avoided a lot of the trouble he put himself to, being arrested, and investigated as a suspected Communist. But Chávez deliberately chose not to rise above his origins, knowing exactly how he could have done it. His brother, for example, was doing all right for himself, until César persuaded him to quit his job and come and work for "*La Causa,*" the cause, as if there were only one; for César, there was. When his incredulous relatives asked him what he was doing for money, he told them that he had none, that he usually found enough to eat for his family of eight children, but that he did not go out of his way to get money, and never cared about it. Even the results of his work were dubious. In the end, he succeeded in organizing only about twenty percent of the 200,000 farm workers of California. And to many of those people, to the people who knew him, this man of few and limited successes was a saint. Many farm workers still think of him as in their midst, as not gone away after his death because he remains their messiah.

Part of the simplicity of César Chávez lies in the explanation of why he chose a hard life and an impossible task for himself. No mystery surrounds his motive, as plain as most things about him. His motive was memory—memory of his childhood and memory of his mother.

The Chávez family that welcomed Césario at his birth on March 31, 1927, owned property and had already been in Arizona for a long time. His parents, Librado and Juana, had married later than many Mexican couples—he was thirty-eight and his bride was thirty-two. In the North Gila Valley where they lived, the Chávezes claimed over 100 acres as homesteaders. Césario's father and his grandfather had cleared the land and had worked on it bringing firewood to the site of the building of a federal dam. Césario's father, one of fifteen children, was the only one who stayed on the family farm. In 1925, a year after he married, Librado Chávez bought a business nearby, about a mile from his parents' ranch, as farms in the west are still often called. With a grocery store, a garage, and a pool hall, Chávez was a small businessman. Many of his customers were close relatives, including his brothers and sisters who lived in the general vicinity, each with large families of their own. In that valley at least 180 nephews, nieces, and cousins of Césario started growing up together. That large, extended family made for a very rooted community for the children. On the way to school and on the way home Césario and his brothers and sisters, five in all, would stop and visit aunts and uncles, a natural part of staying in touch.

The Chávez family thought of that valley as theirs, not only legally, but humanly as well. César (as he was called by an English-speaking teacher as soon as he started school) knew that his father and grandfather had homesteaded that land three years before Arizona became a state. That sense of connectedness made him resent insults he would hear later in his life from people telling him that he should "go back to his own country." Arizona was his country.

Librado Chávez understood the land well enough to be able to feed his family of five children and help relatives. To run a store and take care of the extended family did not always add up to good business, but no one thought twice about extending credit. After the Depression started, money became so scarce that all the relatives asked for—and got—credit from the store. With more relatives than cash, Chávez had found himself in a corner with his whole store out on credit, while he lacked the cash to pay off his creditors. With no choice, he sold out his business in 1932, two weeks before Franklin Delano Roosevelt was elected, for $2,750, an amount that turned out to be just about what he needed to pay off the people he owed.

Even when the family with five children moved in with their grandmother they did not experience disgrace nor resentment. As grownups, the children retained a sense of having been better off than a lot of other people in those days, and they were. In general, people on farms weathered the Depression less ravaged than people in cities or even towns. On farms people had everything they needed—except money. Even without money, they ate well because they could still grow food and raise small animals. César Chávez remembers that his family early in the Depression got a little cash by selling eggs to neighbors, sometimes for as much as five cents a dozen. As the Depression went on, they could not find buyers even at that price when people did not have the five cents. His own family ate pretty well, often eating chicken, for example, but not always having salt to put on it. Even in the worst days, as a matter of belief, they found enough food to give some away to people they knew or people they heard about who had no food at all.

In the culture that gave the world the word and the concept of *macho*, that sense of visible masculinity based on pride and toughness, a quality that must be proven and defended, César Chávez's mother insisted that her sons never fight. The tiny woman, Juana Estrada, who was born in Mexico but had lived in Arizona since the age of six months, exercised great moral authority within her family, over her large and powerful husband as well as her sons. When she declared that the family would give away the last of what they had, no one prevailed over her. With her example and preaching, her children did not know selfishness and did not see any value put above regard for one another. One piece of candy given to one child meant one thing, that it would have to be divided into five parts. When the children worked and had money, she insisted that they not lend it to each other because lending put too much importance on the money itself. The one who had the money should give it, in a view that considered money as something like rain, a necessity you hoped would be there when you needed it, but that no one could be foolish enough to pursue.

Juana Estrada Chávez never learned to speak English and never learned to read or write any language. Like many people who cannot rely on writing to hold on to things, she developed a powerful memory. Her technique for teaching her children and for expressing principles she thought worth repeating relied on proverbs or *dichos*, short sayings that convey great truths economically. The one her sons heard most often went, "It takes two to fight, and one can't do it alone." In a more extreme form, probably reserved for more serious fights, she taught, "It's better to say he ran from here than to say he died here." That conviction against violence, so useful for a small woman, remained with her diminutive son Cesar for the rest of his life.

When the Chávez children went to school they needed the help that their mother's principles gave them. César Chávez had only bad memories of school, the place where he learned to expect to be spanked for speaking Spanish. His sister Rita, a good student, showed her ability to follow written instructions and fill out grown-up paperwork. As a girl she helped many of their neighbors by making out orders for the Sears catalog, yet because of the hard times of the family later on, she would never advance past seventh grade. School did not cost the family money, but Rita expected to go to school wearing shoes, a necessity that cost more than her parents could manage the year she would have gone to eighth grade. Her brother César would always see his talented sister as proof that poverty means losses not for the individual but for the whole society, when he thought of the contribution she might have made with a decent education.

As the Depression worsened, the Chávez family relied on what they had at hand to take care of what they needed. In 1933 Juana had another baby, a daughter. The family's money had run out but the doctor had to be paid and he was— with a few tons of watermelons. With dim hopes the Chávezes saw things take an unbelievable turn downward when their valley had its first drought since 1867. Even the expertise of Librado, his knowledge of how to cultivate arid land so that it did not lose its moisture, and even his little secrets could not make thin crops grow. The whole family remembers 1937 as the year the taxes on the land came due. No more grace period. That year Librado left Arizona when he went ahead of his family to Oxnard, California. His willingness to leave Juana and the children even for a short time proved to everyone his desperation.

As a grown man César Chávez remembered with pain his adventures when his mother, the children, and two relatives struck out for Oxnard as soon as Librado sent for them. Terror came when they reached the border to California where two cars of border guards stopped the Chávez car, terrified his mother, and questioned the family for five hours. The Chávezes had set out in darkness to be able to cross the desert before heat made it unbearable, but being detained for so long meant they were forced to drive in the hottest part of the day in a car crammed with eight people who were accused of somehow smuggling concealed, illegal Mexicans across the border. Juana relied on her saints and her grit to get her family to where her husband was working. On that first foray into California, the Chávezes stayed only a short time while they still dreamed of getting their land back.

Because legal notice is required when land is to be sold at auction, Librado Chávez first learned in print that his land, the acres he had cleared with his father and had cultivated with his sons, was being put up for sale. He read the announcement in February 1939, in the Yuma newspaper. The only other people who had lived on it, all relatives, had no means and no intention of bidding against him for it. On the day of the auction two interested parties appeared: Librado Chávez, because he still considered the land his own and wanted a last crack at it, and Archibald Griffin, a prosperous farmer who owned huge tracts of land adjoining the Chávez acres. Griffin wanted his property lines evened out and had no reason to expect trouble with bankers. Librado Chávez made a bid of $12,300 and got thirty days to come up with the money. No banker or other lender came through in time, and Griffin got the land for under two thousand dollars. Ultimately, César Chávez and his brother watched tractors sent by Griffin come to wreck their corral and take over their land. They ended up giving away their horses only because no one they knew of had any money at all to buy them.

The loss of the farm made an abrupt and radical difference for the Chávez family. Accustomed to being broke, they were now poor. With no property, they left the farm and Arizona and piled into a Studebaker headed for California. For Librado Chávez, the loss of the land had meant an end to the job he had known all his life, but a farmer without a farm goes by a different name. Librado Chávez now joined the huge and itinerant population of migrant workers.

When the Chávez family left everything they had called home in pursuit of the hope of work in California, they repeated what some 300,000 other desperate people had done ahead of them. The drought that ruined the Plains states had forced many farmers off land they could no longer farm. "Okies" from Oklahoma belonged to the same exodus that America would read about in horror in John Steinbeck's novel, *The Grapes of Wrath* (1939), and then see as a classic film. In California the huge numbers of people arriving gave a great boost to farm business, agribusiness as it would be called, a new word needed for the new huge scale of farming. California already enjoyed the two huge advantages of good land and a superb growing climate. For generations farmers there had been saying that if you stuck a broomstick into the ground in California, it would grow. Now, the added advantage of surplus labor created a boom—for the growers. For farm workers, the influx of people meant two things. First, work would be harder to find than usual because so many people wanted to be hired. Worse, from the workers' perspective, wages would be lower for the small amount of work that could be found. Stiffer competition insured a lower payoff.

In their new place in a growing underclass, the Chávez family saw that the marginal way of life of migrant workers requires mastery of hazards that face all the members of a family on the road. Since such families are by definition homeless and since children could help parents in harvesting some crops, quite often hiring involved signing up whole families, not just male workers. Children and grown-ups had to adjust to the new life, a transition that took the Chávez family about one year, one full cycle of growing seasons, before they could recognize the hazards. Much worse than the obvious hardship of not finding any work, they had to learn about labor contractors, an expensive, humiliating, sometimes infuriating lesson that marked the family's apprenticeship. Middlemen between growers and farm workers, labor contractors specialized in spotting migrant families. What could be easier than to notice an anxious-looking family crowded into a car stuffed with children and belongings piled all over it? The first labor contractor the Chávezes met showed them exactly what to expect from the rest. Appearing to have inside information, labor contractors tell a family that they have heard that there is work in some town not too far away, and the pay is good. Good housing, too.

César Chávez and his parents heard about Oxnard where they could pick walnuts, lots of work, the contractor said. What they found soon turned out to be only the usual pattern. The pay was lower than they heard, there was less work than it sounded like, and the housing was "always a pigpen." Anyone driving in rural California in a nonharvest season might still see and not recognize the housing for what it is. Lots of small buildings together, abandoned looking, too ramshackle to be garages, a little too big for doghouses, such dubious structures serve as migrant housing. Most of the time for the Chávezes there was no running water and no electricity. One faucet for 50 to 100 families would be typical. The shelters were so small that life was lived outside, with no possibility of privacy for any reason. Sanitation or the lack of it, more like India than the United States, was provided to farm workers, their wives, and children of all ages. Many times there was no work for anyone because growers used *braceros*, workers from Mexico being brought in under a federal law that allowed them—when there was no local help available.

Unlike many families, the Chávezes, no doubt under Juana's influence, always sent their children to school in the towns where they were working, even if they only stayed for three days, even for one. With so much irregularity in attendance, the family considered it a true accomplishment when César at age fifteen completed eighth grade. His proud mother took that success as reason to encourage her son, so full of promise, to go on to high school. But when Juana was still working in the fields at age fifty, César put his foot down and insisted that he stop school for the time being so that his pay could free his mother from field work. Librado had been in a car accident and everyone in the family knew how much they needed the money that César could add to what they had. He never went back to school.

Except for two years he spent in the Navy in World War II, every minute of it hated, César Chávez continued as a farmworker, an experience that gave him great patience and accustomed him to seeing progress made in tiny increments. (The price paid for cotton was two-and-a-half cents per pound, for peas it was about the same price for a hamper.) He also learned the price the body pays for spending whole days bent doubled at the waist. He learned to mistrust promises of labor contractors who cheated workers on the weighing of what they picked, especially cotton, and who sold workers things they needed—not just cigarettes but also rides to work—at outrageous prices. His parents had been forced to pay twenty-five cents per day for a ride to the fields, whether or not they got work once they arrived. And there were days when they earned no more than twenty-five cents. He learned what it was like to sleep in a tent during the rainy season. He learned that when contractors withheld part of what workers earned, trouble would follow.

In a worked-out system, labor contractors would pay workers only part of what was coming to them in order to make sure that they finished out the season. As the season went on and there was less work, and less of the crop to pick, the great fear of growers was that the workers would leave before completing the harvest. To keep the workers around, therefore, labor contractors made promises of a bonus, money that was really only what the workers had coming. But then some labor contractors disappeared before any workers got their bonuses. Families in desperation sometimes asked labor contractors for loans so that they could feed their children, and the labor contractors would loan money—at 100 percent interest.

By the time César Chávez was twenty-five years old and met Fred Ross, a trained labor organizer in his early forties, Ross did not have to waste much effort

UPI/Bettmann
Most people who knew César Chávez still count him as a saint, while Ronald Reagan saw him as the leader of a dangerous uprising.

explaining to Chávez why he opposed the practices of growers. Ross had been sent to find and recruit leaders for the CSO, Community Service Organization, and he knew Chávez had the experience that gave him the conviction leaders needed. Chávez knew by then that the growers of California had accumulated political influence as estimable as their land holdings. Public officials at every level were afraid of them. But what Ross said made sense to Chávez, and he wanted to give his ideas a chance. Just before meeting Ross, Chávez had made friends with a Catholic priest named Donald McDonnell who liked to discuss books with Chávez, and who would give him books so that they could discuss them. In a biography of Saint Francis, for example, Chávez first heard of Gandhi, a leader who sounded a lot like Chávez's mother in his strong position favoring nonviolence. The idea of winning in the name of a cause against a hugely powerful organization, like the British Empire, impressed Chávez and planted a seed. Gandhi's example of nonviolence would become a model for Chávez, as would his practice of fasting to focus spiritual energy.

In the years when "back east" civil rights activists were taking great risks in order to register people to vote, Ross was instructing Chávez in the same methods. For years Chávez repeated the few simple steps Ross taught him, doing the same slow work over and over, in a rhythm he knew from the fields, always another row, always knowing that in a few weeks the same thing would need to be done somewhere else. After years and years of migrant work, Chávez saw no hardship in constantly going from one town to the next in this new work of "organizing," as he always referred to what really amounted to converting people's thinking. In every town it would start with a home meeting, gathering a small group in the living room or kitchen of a cooperator. Only after he had talked to or organized every poor worker in the town, would Chávez have a general meeting. As he met with people he would get deputies assigned from the local registrar of voters to help sign people up to vote. Next, he would start offering citizenship classes. He read about labor unions, read about laws that affected workers and employers and immigrants. He made himself known to local officials of the Farm Placement Service. He would stay after meetings to give people whatever kind of help it was they needed: dealing with an employer who refused to pay, showing an injured worker how to file a compensation claim, assisting a poor family without burial insurance. And Chávez knew that the people he helped were automatically part of his movement, "*La Causa*."

After he returned from World War II, Chávez married Helen Fabela, a girl he had met in Delano, California. Helen had seen enough of the conditions of farm workers to understand why Chávez wanted to help. A few years later he had a steady job at a lumberyard in San Jose, the largest Spanish-speaking settlement in California outside Los Angeles, when his organizing efforts started to overshadow his job. He figured out that there were days when he could do what was needed for the cause only if he did not go to work. Before long a general layoff at the lumberyard left him without work. His efforts attracted the eyes of organizers he had never met. Saul Alinsky, who described himself as a "professional radical," knew about Chávez from Ross and a few years later hired him to work at organizing farm workers. Alinsky thought it was only fair for CSO to give Chávez a salary, in view of the long hours he put in away from his family and without pay. When he started paying Chávez $4,000 a year, Alinsky received a letter from Chávez reporting on his efforts and adding that he thought he was being overpaid. Alinsky assured him that he was more than earning his salary, but was not good at one duty—he never filled out expense accounts for his time away. Chávez would ask to be paid back what he had spent for gas, but did not ask for anything for food when he traveled.

César Chávez worked so hard that inevitably he had to be given more responsibility in the organization he was helping to create, but he was still in his twenties and looked even younger. Wearing a mustache made him look old enough for his role, or at least older than he was, or so he thought. Because he was young and had not been to college, or even high school, Chávez did not always understand how much he risked, as he readily admitted himself. In the 1950s, still in the era of Senator McCarthy and the terror he created about Communists, Chávez found himself being investigated by the FBI on suspicion of being a Communist. He found out that the investigation got help from middle class members of the local CSO board, Mexicans who felt drawn to help their less fortunate brothers, men and women who had not gotten out of the fields as they had. That sense of betrayal made Chávez decide never to allow any middle class members of CSO to have positions of influence. He trusted farm workers more than their educated betters.

The Community Service Organization began to attract the attention of labor in the classical sense of labor unions. An organization called Agricultural Workers Organizing Committee, or AWOC, tried to get help from organized labor. Chávez mistrusted the influence of unions he feared would not have the interest of his workers at heart. Finally he formally resigned from CSO on his thirty-fifth birthday, March 31, 1962.

César Chávez knew that if he continued the kind of effort he had been making, using the same technique of house meetings, general meetings, and the rest, he would be able to form a union. But more than anything he feared mistakes that come from impatience. The point of forming a union, he reasoned, was not to force growers to offer contracts the minute the union came into being. His much more sophisticated plan involved a period of waiting, of development, and of strengthening. Only after the union had existed for a while—five years he thought when he started—would it make sense to call a strike. Only then would a union be strong enough to have a successful strike, and there had been many, many that did not succeed. He learned about them by talking to old timers from earlier movements and earlier strikes. In California, the history concerned failure every time because growers worked with local, even federal, officials against the workers.

When Chávez finally judged that the time was right, this union, called Agricultural Farm Workers Association, called its first strike. Thinking through every step, reflecting on his experience, Chávez orchestrated one crucial day brilliantly. He found out that strikers were going to be arrested. Making practical use of his advance knowledge, Chávez started driving north so that he would be at the University of California at Berkeley before noon, aiming to speak at Sproul Plaza, a large open space at the center of the campus reserved for speeches, often political. (Just a year before that space had served as the platform for what would become the Free Speech movement.) He announced to politically aware students that forty-four strikers had already been arrested, a fact he checked with a phone call he made after he got there. Chávez asked that the students give their lunch money to help *La Causa*, help pay bail, and help support the strikers. Then he crossed the bay and went to San Francisco State University and made the speech, then down the Peninsula to Palo Alto to give the speech at Stanford University. On the way back to Delano he had over six thousand dollars, in one dollar bills. The success of the speeches confirmed for Chávez his idea that the public was willing to support *La Causa*, if only they knew about it. Encouraged with what he had seen, Chávez decided to take on the growers even more directly.

In October 1965, after a strike of grape growers had begun, Chávez expanded the effort into a boycott. Besides table grapes, much of the produce was destined for wineries. The technique planned in the beginning was to position picket lines wherever the picked grapes were sent, because only nonunion workers were still picking. Some grapes and picketers ended up on the docks of San Francisco. When the longshoremen saw the picket line, they knew how to show union solidarity. They refused to load the nonunion grapes onto ships and walked off the job. An important, established union had become involved. That unplanned addition of strength multiplied the force of the boycott.

Visits by labor leaders and well-known political figures also added weight and significance to the strike. When the AFL-CIO meeting happened to be in San Francisco, Walter Reuther, president of the United Auto Workers, attended the conference and asked to visit the picket lines of the farm workers strike. Chávez was able to persuade Reuther to talk to local authorities, a hugely important step when the growers had refused to talk to Chávez, insisting that his union did not represent the workers, who were happy, according to the growers. Reuther talked to the Mayor of Delano, California, with a simple message, that he tell the growers that sooner or later "these guys are going to win." Reuther spoke from his own experience with Ford Motor Company which had fiercely resisted his union for years—until they had no choice. Soon after that the Senate Subcommittee on Migratory Labor came to California for hearings. Senator Robert Kennedy from New York came, too.

Suddenly the entire country knew about César Chávez and what he was doing. When people saw Chávez on the news, they heard him described with a term they knew, "nonviolent," the same word being used at the time by Martin Luther King, Jr. Because Chávez stayed with the picketers, because he marched 300 miles from Delano to Sacramento, he saw the strength of the movement grow town by town, knew that he had huge public support. With that confidence he understood that the boycott could inflict more than economic harm on the companies they opposed. Their boycott of Schenley's, a huge wine-producing company and a big grape customer, did not cost Schenley much in lost business. But when they saw how much their name had suffered by association with the strike, the company ended up inviting Chávez to the president's home in Beverly Hills to negotiate. The president, with the intuition of any good businessman, knew that the value of their image could be diminished irreparably:

settling was the best move for both sides. When the strike started, the average farm worker was paid less than $1.50 an hour. Now, thanks to Chávez, wages were getting better. At its height, seventeen million Americans boycotted grapes coast to coast.

In the end, Chávez achieved what he had promised his supporters. The grape boycott became national, then international. The growers saw that they had to negotiate, even in a state whose governor had traditionally been their ally. The former governor, Edmund Brown, was terrified in the face of the political power of the growers. On July 30, 1970, having lost millions of dollars, the growers acknowledged Chávez's union. Governor Ronald Reagan, elected in 1966, found little merit in Chávez's goals because he saw his duty as governor in protecting the industries of California. Reagan referred to the actions of Chávez's union as "an uprising." He could see no reason for a union based on what he knew about conditions in the field.

When the son of Governor Brown, Edmund G. Brown, Jr., became governor, legislation did favor the farm workers in many ways. In 1972 Brown outlawed the use of the short handled hoe, the tool of cultivation and also of oppression, from the farm workers' point of view. Largely because of Chávez, California's legislature passed the first collective bargaining act outside Hawaii to include farm labor. In 1974 Governor Brown signed the Agricultural Labor Relations Act, a landmark bill. Finally there would be insurance, finally farm workers would not be excluded from the law. But a subsequent change of governors also changed the fortunes of farm workers for the worse. With the arrival of Governor George Deukmejian in 1983, ground was lost, quickly and forcefully.

Overall, Chávez had created America's first successful union of farm workers. But by the time of his death, old problems were coming back, and technological changes were starting to make new problems that threatened his creation. The problem of *braceros* or their equivalent reappeared as many new illegal immigrants came to California to work for less than the unionized farm workers would consider. New machinery eliminated old labor-intensive jobs, machines that could vibrate whole walnut trees to make the walnuts fall off, machines that could do entire rows in a fraction of the time workers needed.

Chávez had changed the atmosphere, the climate, the range of possibilities of what growers could expect. Yet he never considered his job done. In 1993, at the end of a seven-day fast, Chávez was in Arizona where he was called to help in a trial involving a lettuce grower who was suing workers. In the night, alone in a motel, Chávez died. He had become well-known but had never achieved the kind of success that people ordinarily expect as a reward for hard work, not much in the way of material comfort, no expectation of taking it easy a little. He had even rejected the American dream in his refusal to leave the fields, to rise above the misery that claimed so much of his childhood. Materially, Chávez could have done much better. The Teamsters Union would have known how to compensate him, for example. Yet many people think of him as a saint. At his funeral thousands of people marched, not all of them mournful looking, as they honored the smiling man they had regarded as their own messiah.

QUESTIONS FOR THOUGHT AND DISCUSSION

1. How did the experiences of César Chávez's family influence his rise to champion of the United Farm Workers? Were the growers and labor contractors who profited from the Mexican migrant workers morally evil or merely smart businessmen?

2. Why were the California growers able to maintain control over the migrant workers year after year? How did Ronald Reagan, as California governor in the late 1960s and early 1970s, view the plight of the migrant workers and the rise of the UFW's national boycotts?

3. Why did Chávez not use his personal talents to make himself a successful living as a business owner or professional? Was his preoccupation with "La Causa" a noble devotion? Was he, as some claimed at his death, a saint?

4. As happened to Rachel Carson and Martin Luther King, Jr., some critics labeled Chávez a communist for his unionization efforts. Was what Chávez sought for his people akin to the worker ownership of production, or something less dramatic? In a country which celebrates rugged individualism, is someone like Chávez who promotes worker solidarity a dangerous collectivist or a necessary counterforce?

SUGGESTED READINGS

Garcia, F. Chris, ed. *La Causa Política: A Chicano Politics Reader*. South Bend, IN: U of Notre Dame P, 1974.

Horowitz, George D. *La Causa. The California Grape Strike*. New York: Macmillan, 1970.

Levy, Jacques E. *César Chávez: Autobiography of La Causa*. New York: Norton, 1975.

Numerous *New York Times* articles, an important source for the day-to-day record of Chávez's political work, may be found in the *New York Times Index* under "Chávez."

20

Martin Luther King, Jr.

*I*n *the 1940s and especially during World War II, African-American leaders, principally through the National Association for the Advancement of Colored People (NAACP), began to step up their efforts to end racial discrimination. One forum was the United States Supreme Court, where NAACP lawyers won a number of victories. In 1941, the Court ruled that separate facilities for black and white railroad passengers were unconstitutional; in 1944, the justices ruled that the all-white primary election, which excluded blacks from voting in any significant election in the South, was unconstitutional. Blacks also began to use new tactics to protest segregation: in 1943, the Congress of Racial Equality (CORE) launched its first sit-in at a Chicago restaurant, with black protesters sitting in places reserved for whites.*

Since the Civil War, when ten percent of all Union troops were black, American wars had temporarily improved black economic opportunities. Expanding military forces in World War II included one million African Americans, most fighting in segregated units. In 1948, President Truman ordered desegregation of the armed forces. But segregation prevented blacks from gaining wartime jobs in defense plants despite labor shortages until A. Philip Randolph of the Brotherhood of Sleeping Car Porters threatened a march on Washington, D.C., in 1941. President Roosevelt issued an executive order banning racial discrimination in defense industries. A million blacks moved North during the war and the Supreme Court continued to strike down legal barriers in the late Forties and early Fifties. Black clergy joined lawyers and union leaders demanding an end to discrimination, especially in public places and transportation. The stage was set for twenty-five-year-old Martin Luther King, Jr., a third generation Baptist minister to organize the first mass protest by blacks in Southern history.

NOTHING IN MARTIN LUTHER KING, JR.'S childhood suggested that he wanted to become a fundamentalist Southern Baptist minister, organize black clergy and their congregations, and lead the first black mass protest movement in the world, earning himself the Nobel Peace Prize. Until his senior year in college, Mike King (he was born Michael like his father, and his father later changed their names) seemed only to aspire to a comfortable middle-class life with enough money to support his expensive taste in clothes. Until then, the question was, would he become a doctor or a lawyer in Atlanta's well-heeled Auburn Avenue black district. Maybe he did not incline to the life of a Baptist minister because he had to spend much of his life in church.

His paternal grandfather had been a cotton sharecropper from Stockbridge, Georgia. The mule-drawn wagon that carried the body of Martin Luther King, Jr. after he was assassinated was, in the Deep South, an unmistakable reference to the family's post-slavery poverty. After the Civil War, white landowners rented hard-scrabble farms, shacks, and seeds to landless black families, supposedly dividing crops equally with the black sharecroppers, but since the white owners kept the records and owned the only stores, many illiterate blacks were easily exploited and stayed bemired in debt.

Born into this system in 1899, rugged Michael Luther King, Sr., one of ten children, at age sixteen walked twenty miles to Atlanta to seek a better life. Working at odd jobs, he went to school at night. He managed to get himself accepted to Bryant Preparatory School. He studied hard, carrying books wherever he went. He won admission to Morehouse College, a private, all-black men's college in Atlanta, and he fell in love with Alberta Williams, daughter of the pastor of Atlanta's largest black church, Ebenezer Baptist Church. Reverend Williams, born into slavery a year before the Emancipation Proclamation, was a founder and president of the Atlanta branch of the NAACP, which he organized after witnessing the brutal race riots of 1906.

At the time Mike King, Jr. was born in 1929, the black community of Atlanta was already the most prosperous and advanced in the South. Lined with black churches, black-owned businesses, and many fine homes owned by successful African Americans, it was strung out along Auburn Avenue, but it was still a segregated community. Whenever its residents left the black neighborhood, they instantly realized that they were walled off from the whites. Signs on public facilities read, "For Whites Only," "Colored Entrance," and "Negroes and Dogs Keep Out." Blacks used separate drinking fountains, restrooms, playgrounds, schools, and seats on buses and trains.

The Reverend Williams had helped to build up Atlanta's strong black community, which accounted for forty percent of the city's population and forty-five million dollars worth of real estate (today at least ten times that) by World War II. It also boasted the nation's first black daily newspaper, the *Atlanta World*. He had made the local NAACP a force to reckon with. When the city fathers proposed a bond issue to build new public high schools for whites only, the NAACP organized a protest movement. One of the city's newspapers, the Hearst-owned *Georgian*, denounced NAACP leaders as "dirty and ignorant." Reverend Williams began the family tradition of protest by organizing a boycott of the *Georgian*: six thousand black Atlantans canceled their subscriptions in a single day. Eventually, the paper folded. Atlanta got a new all-black high school, Booker T. Washington High.

Marrying into this leading black family, Michael King, Sr. became assistant pastor to Rev. Williams and moved into a spacious Victorian frame house at 501 Auburn Avenue. Mike King, Jr.'s childhood could not have been more ordinary for an all-American boy. His days were filled with sandlot baseball and football on a nearby vacant lot, basketball at the hoop in the King's backyard, rollerskating, shooting marbles, flying kites, and riding bikes. There was school, of course, and he liked to sit in the shade of an oak tree out back and read as he got older. He could fight when he felt he had to, frequently resorting to wrestling. He was moody, and when he could not talk someone out of a fight, would settle it violently. Once, his brother A.D. remembered, Mike hit him over the head with a telephone receiver. If there was anything distinctive about him, it was his singing voice. From the age of four, his mother took him to church all around Atlanta where he sang solos. There seemed to be nothing unusual about Mike King except that during the Depression he was much better off than most black children and many whites in the South.

But Mike soon became painfully aware of racial barriers. When he started school, two white boys his age he had always played with went to a different school and their mother no longer let them play with him. One day, his father took him to a white-owned shoe store. They took seats in the front of the store. A salesclerk told them to move to back seats. His father became furious. "We'll buy shoes sitting here, or we won't buy any shoes at all." They walked out. His father was no more intimidated by the white police. Once, when police stopped his car, the officer ordered, "All right, boy, pull over and let me see your license." His father responded, "That's the boy there, I'm a *man*. I'm Reverend King." His father was in the forefront of rights demonstrations as young Mike grew older. When Mike was six, Reverend King led a thousand blacks on a march from Ebenezer Church to City Hall demanding voting rights. When he was seven, their Auburn Street house was the meeting place for black teachers planning protests against unequal pay. Frequently, there was "hate" mail from white supremacists. One letter came with a picture of his father laid out in a coffin.

When Mike was twelve, Ebenezer Church expanded and his family moved into a larger house. Mike was transferred from Daniel T. Howard Elementary School to an experimental school at Atlanta University for seventh and eighth grades. When the school closed, he transferred again, this time to the high school built by his father's crusading. His wide reading enabled him to skip ninth grade. His interests were expanding: he learned to play the piano and the violin. Mike's parents demanded his almost-constant attendance at church services. One Sunday, when he was twelve, he sneaked out of a Woman's Day speech given by his grandmother to go to a parade. While he was away, his grandmother suffered a fatal heart attack. Bereft, Mike tried to kill himself, jumping out his bedroom window. He only slightly injured himself.

Hearing hundreds of sermons had given him a good ear for rhetoric and language. In eleventh grade, he won a statewide oratory contest with a speech, "The Negro and the Constitution." His joy was short-lived. On the way home, when whites came aboard the bus, he had to give up his seat. He and his voice teacher had to stand "in the aisle for the ninety miles to Atlanta," King later recalled. "That night will never leave my memory. It was the angriest I have ever been in my life."

When he was only fifteen, King, benefitting from a Ford Foundation program that liberated talented blacks from segregated high schools, was admitted to Morehouse College as a freshman, skipping twelfth grade. Active in student affairs, he sang in the glee club and, despite his small stature, played football aggressively. His classwork was mediocre: he earned a "C" in philosophy his freshman year. He helped to found the college's Youth Chapter of the NAACP and served on Atlanta's integrated Intercollegiate Council. It was his first sustained black-white relationship. It "convinced me that we have many white persons as allies, particularly among the younger generation." At Morehouse, Mike earned a second nickname, "Tweed," because of his elegant dressing style. Since he had delivered two routes of newspapers as a boy, he had always indulged his taste for expensive clothes. He was also popular with girls from a peer school, Spelman College. "I couldn't keep up with him," his younger brother, A.D., said, he was "just about the best jitterbug in town."

It was Morehouse's Harvard-trained religion professor, President Dr. Benjamin Mays, who began to turn King into a serious young man. Dr. Mays, a close friend of Mike's father, every Tuesday morning lectured Morehouse's 400 students at chapel. Mike got in the habit of dropping by his office to discuss the sermons. In the summer of 1947, he joined schoolmates who went to a Connecticut tobacco farm near Hartford to earn spending money. He saw how differently blacks could live outside the South. Until then, he had wavered between becoming a doctor or a lawyer who would fight segregation through the courts. That summer, King seems to have undergone some kind of religious awakening. He had long ago decided he did not want to follow in his father's assured footsteps at fundamentalist Ebenezer Church. He was tired of the "Hallelujah, praise the Lord" school of down-home preaching and interacting with the congregation, so it came as a shock to his father when he announced his intention to become a clergyman. A large crowd packed Ebenezer for his first sermon. Young King, wearing a white surplice, surprised people with his powerful, well-reasoned sermon. In February 1948, in his senior year in college, he became a licensed clergyman.

Graduating at nineteen, he applied to Crozer Theological Seminary in Chester, Pennsylvania, explaining on his application that he felt "a sense of responsibility which I could not escape." One of only six blacks among 100 students, he began what he later described as "a serious intellectual quest for a method to eliminate social evil." Abraham Muste, a visitor to the campus, profoundly influenced him. He was executive secretary of the Fellowship of Reconciliation, a prominent figure among pacifists and early civil-rights activists, and was known as the "American equivalent of Mahatma Gandhi," the famous pacifist father of independent India who had just been assassinated that January. On a Sunday soon afterward, King went into neighboring Philadelphia to hear Dr. Mordecai Johnson lecture about his recent trip to India to attend the World Pacifist Conference: the meeting had been delayed because of Gandhi's death. Gandhi's lifelong and successful campaign to rally his people to end social injustice moved young King. He bought all the books he could find about Gandhi. "As I read, I became deeply fascinated by his campaigns of nonviolent resistance."

In June 1951, King was graduated valedictorian of his Crozer class with a straight "A" average. He won a fellowship to the divinity school of his choice. He chose Boston University. He drove to Boston that Fall in a new Chevrolet given him by his parents and began Ph.D. studies in systematic theology. In Boston, he met Alabama-born Coretta Scott, a graduate of Antioch College studying voice on a scholarship to the New England Conservatory of Music. King proposed marriage to her on their first date. They married nearly two years later and rented an apartment in Boston while she completed her studies in music education and he finished his courses.

Just as King was finishing his course work, Chief Justice Earl Warren in 1954 announced the opinion of the U.S. Supreme Court in *Brown v. Board of Education of Topeka*, the milestone civil rights case which ruled that "separate educational facilities are inherently unequal." King had his choice of several church appointments in the North and South. He decided to accept a job at the Dexter Avenue Baptist church in Montgomery, Alabama, in the shadow of the first capital of the Confederacy. King believed that "something remarkable was unfolding in the South."

He didn't have to wait long. On December 1, 1955, a forty-three-year-old black woman, Rosa Parks, weary from a day of sewing, boarded a crowded bus in Montgomery and sat in an aisle seat directly behind the section reserved for whites. Soon all the seats were filled and a white man stood waiting over her. She refused to budge. Rosa Parks, married to a union organizer, had been carefully trained at a Highlander, Tennessee, camp where activists learned the tenets and techniques of Mahatma Gandhi's doctrine of passive resistance. She had been selected at a meeting of black leaders to resist the next attempt to enforce the Montgomery bus segregation law. The driver warned her, "Look, woman, I told you I wanted the seat. Are you going to stand up?" She answered, "No." Taken to the police station, she was arrested, fingerprinted, and booked, the fifth black woman arrested that year.

The civil rights movement in Alabama had been growing since the *Brown* decision. In August 1955, African Americans in seven Black Belt farm counties had petitioned the State Department of Education to desegregate their county schools. Many stunned whites believed it was as a result of a plot by the NAACP. That autumn, white supremacists were busy organizing White Citizens' Councils: between October and December 1955, membership in Alabama grew from a few hundred to 20,000. Tensions grew when Congressman Adam Clayton Powell, the only black man in Congress, traveled from Harlem to speak to Operation 5000, a black grassroots movement organized to register black voters in Montgomery.

That weekend, at the Dexter Street church, Dr. Martin Luther King, Jr., joined with the Women's Political Council and the local Brotherhood of Sleeping Car Porters, the black railroad workers' union, to form a city wide boycott of Montgomery buses. King and his secretary ran off 7,000 mimeographed leaflets distributed by scores of women and teenagers, that said:

> Don't ride the bus to work, to town, to school, or any place Monday . . . . Another Negro woman has been arrested and put in jail . . . . Don't ride the buses . . . . If you work, take a cab, or share a ride, or walk . . . . Come to a mass meeting Monday at 7:00 P.M . . . .

On Sunday, black ministers repeated the instructions from their pulpits. On Monday morning, the buses, mostly used by black domestic workers, were virtually empty. That night, hundreds packed the Dexter Street church, hundreds more stood outside, listening to twenty-six-year-old Dr. King on loudspeakers:

> We are here this evening to say to those who have mistreated us so long that we are tired–tired of being segregated and humiliated, tired of being kicked about by the brutal feet of oppression. Protest courageously and yet with Christian love . . . We are not here advocating violence . . . . The only weapon that we have . . . is the weapon of protest . . . The great glory of American democracy is the right to protest for right.

King's sixteen-minute speech turned the boycott into the beginning of a thirteen-year religious protest movement. Forming the Montgomery Improvement Association, King and fellow pastor Ralph Abernathy set up car pools that used church basements as transportation depots. Black-owned taxicab companies gave rides at cost. Automobile owners arranged carpools. Some 50,000 black workers, students, and shoppers shunned city transport for more than a year.

King's life was threatened and his home was bombed but King, organizing the Southern Christian Leadership Conference, continued to insist on nonviolent protest. City leaders indicted King and more than 100 protest organizers for operating an illegal, unlicensed bus company. King was the first to be tried. He was convicted and sentenced to 386 days at hard labor. On appeal to the Federal District Court, the Montgomery city bus system was declared in violation of the Fourteenth Amendment. This time, the city appealed to the U.S. Supreme Court. On November 13, 1956, the high court declared Alabama's state and local segregated transportation laws unconstitutional.

The Montgomery bus boycott made King America's most famous civil rights leader before he was thirty. He wrote a book based on the Montgomery boycott, *Stride Toward Freedom*. He was touring bookstores autographing copies when he was attacked and stabbed in a New York department store by a mentally-disturbed black woman who plunged an eight-inch letter opener into his chest, narrowly missing his heart. After a long convalescence, King and his wife accepted an invitation from a Quaker group, the American Friend Services Committee, to visit India, where King studied Gandhi's tactics of nonviolent protest. To capitalize on the prestige he had gained, King and the SCLC decided to broaden the non-violent movement into a nationwide struggle against racism and discrimination. In 1960, King moved from Montgomery to Atlanta to devote more time to SCLC and he became copastor of his father's church. That autumn, beginning in Greensboro, North Carolina, black college students began sit-ins at lunch counters refusing to serve blacks. An inexpensive booklet entitled *Martin Luther King and the Montgomery Story* inspired hundreds of students spreading the sit-ins through the South. Students and young black ministers were trained by SCLC.

On February 16, 1960, King told a packed meeting of representatives from North Carolina colleges that the SCLC would support them: "You have the full weight of SCLC behind you in your struggle." The sit-ins spread to Nashville, Tennessee, where they were organized by divinity students. In Orangeburg, South Carolina, 1,000 black students marched through the streets on March 1. When

Archive Photos

Shown here after delivering his famous "dream" speech to nearly 300,000 on the Washington Mall during the 1963 Freedom March, Martin Luther King, Jr. would be gunned down by an assassin only five years later.

they marched again two weeks later in the freezing cold, police drenched them with high-pressure hoses. In Atlanta, where student Julian Bond helped to bring on the protests with "An Appeal to Human Rights" in all three remaining Atlanta papers, King encouraged student activists even as he fought a fresh legal challenge. A Montgomery jury charged him with perjury for not reporting all his income. Wherever he went, Southern police dogged him. He was arrested for driving a borrowed car with an expired driver's license and he was placed on probation for one year. Meanwhile, he lent his support to the founding of the Student Non-violent Coordinating Committee (its first president was Fisk University student Marion Barry, later the controversial mayor of Washington, D.C.). King arranged temporary offices for SNCC ("Snick" as it became known) and outlined his "Strategy for Victory" in a speech in Raleigh, North Carolina's City Auditorium.

Each years' protests kept pressure on Congress to enact civil rights reform legislation and on the Supreme Court to widen its antidiscrimination rulings. Under the 1960 Civil Rights Act, the Civil Rights Commission, set up after earlier protests, was given broad new powers to help blacks register to vote. King also conferred that June with Democratic presidential candidate John F. Kennedy, in a ninety-minute meeting urging strong presidential leadership in civil rights.

That fall of 1960, King and student leaders targeted the Rich Department Store in Atlanta for a sit-in and urged black consumers to close their charge accounts. When King joined Julian Bond and students in the sit-in, he was arrested. This time he was held in jail because his probation on the traffic charge forbade any violations of state or federal laws. He was sentenced to six months in the state penitentiary at Reidsville. To her amazement, Coretta King answered the phone one day and heard John Kennedy reassure her of his help. His brother and campaign manager, Robert Kennedy, meanwhile called the DeKalb County judge and arranged King's bail. Republican candidate Richard M. Nixon remained silent. At a televised welcome-home ceremony in Atlanta, King's father, a strong Republican, told the throng, "Take off your Nixon buttons! If I had a suitcase of votes, I'd dump them in John Kennedy's lap." In the close 1960 election, the heavy black vote proved decisive for Kennedy .

After Kennedy's election, however, King grew impatient with the slow pace of civil rights progress. Early in 1963, King and the SCLC launched a massive demonstration in Birmingham, Alabama, considered by them one of the South's most segregated cities. Police Chief "Bull" Connor used dogs and high pressure fire hoses to drive back peaceful marchers, including children, many of whom were bitten and beaten as the national television audience watched. Arrested again and jailed, King wrote his famous "Letter from Birmingham Jail." Smuggled out of the jail, it explained why King insisted on intruding in other cities. "I am in Birmingham because injustice is here . . . Injustice anywhere is a threat to justice everywhere."

The national outcry over Bull Connor's tactics and King's jailing put pressure on President Kennedy to introduce a far-reaching civil rights bill in Congress. To increase that pressure, King and other civil rights leaders organized a massive Freedom March on Washington that would highlight high black unemployment. On August 28, 1963, nearly 300,000 black and white Americans gathered at the Lincoln Memorial to hear King give his stirring "I Have a Dream" speech, which eloquently spelled out the moral basis of his nonviolent civil rights movement. In 1964, shortly after Kennedy was assassinated, his successor, Lyndon Baines Johnson, pressed the Kennedy bill toward overwhelming Congressional passage. The Civil Rights Act of 1964, King's greatest triumph, outlawed racial discrimination in public places and mandated equal opportunity in employment and education. On December 10, 1964, King received the Nobel Peace Prize.

King's final victory for nonviolent protest as well as his break with more militant black leaders came in 1965 at the time of the Selma-to-Montgomery, Alabama, protest marches. Demonstrators protested the practice of white registrars arbitrarily denying most blacks the right to vote. When several hundred demonstrators ignored King's advice and crossed the Edmund Pettus Bridge into Selma, state and local police, many of them on horseback, launched a bloody attack, once again televised. The indiscriminate use of clubs, tear gas, and dogs revolted many Americans. As SNCC, CORE, and other black groups called for another, larger march on Selma, King urged only a token procession to the Pettus Bridge and back without a fresh confrontation in the Alabama capital. Many black leaders now grew disenchanted with King, but King's nonviolent approach was rewarded when President Johnson delivered a speech to a joint session of Congress:

> It is wrong—deadly wrong—to deny any of our fellow Americans the right to vote . . . . (Black leaders) have called upon us to make good the promise of America. Their cause must be our cause, too . . . .

Now, King was ready to lead another march to support Johnson's bill. Now, 30,000 Freedom Marchers set off on the fifty mile march; 25,000 finished the historic pilgrimage, with King, his wife, and their parents heading the procession. A few months later, Congress passed the Voting Rights Act of 1965, ending all local and state barriers against African Americans' right to vote.

By this time, King had become convinced that black leaders should shift their attention to the economic problems of all poverty-stricken Americans, black and white. Other black leaders, especially after continued attacks on Northern voter registration volunteers in Mississippi, wanted a more aggressive and confrontational movement and, following SNCC's lead, took up the cry of "Black Power." It became clear that King no longer spoke for all African Americans. In 1967, he worried that the Vietnam War would drain away the efforts, manpower, and resources to correct economic problems and convinced that poverty was as great an American problem as racism, King called for an end to the Vietnam War.

Calling for a redistribution of the nation's wealth from the rich to alleviate the suffering of the poor, he launched a Poor People's Campaign to unite poverty-stricken blacks and whites for another march on Washington in the summer of 1968. While he worked on the plans, he agreed to make a brief visit to support a lingering strike of all-black city garbagemen in Memphis, Tennessee. On the night of April 3, 1968, the thirty-nine-year-old Nobel Laureate gave a hauntingly prophetic speech in the city's Masonic Temple. Although he had never worried about his safety, not even after he had been stabbed ten years earlier, he said in his ringing, tremulous voice:

It really doesn't matter with me now. Because I've been to the mountaintop. I've looked over and I've seen the Promised Land. I may not get there with you, but I want you to know tonight that we as a people will get to the Promised Land. So I'm happy tonight. I'm not worried about anything. I'm not fearing any man.

The next day, as he stepped out onto a balcony outside his room at the Lorraine Motel, he was shot through the neck by an assassin's bullet. He died instantly. For one last time, thousands marched behind him as a plain sharecropper's wagon pulled by a single mule carried his body to South View Cemetery in Atlanta. Later, he was moved to his final resting place at Ebenezer Baptist Church. On his tombstone were carved the words he had proclaimed five years earlier during the Freedom March on Washington: "Free at last, free at last, thank God Almighty, I'm free at last."

QUESTIONS FOR THOUGHT AND DISCUSSION

1. How did Martin Luther King, Jr. first gain national exposure as a leading advocate of the civil rights movement? Was he ready for such instant fame?

2. Was King's use of nonviolent civil disobedience the proper tactic for the modern civil rights movement? What were its advantages and disadvantages?

3. What major effort was King in the midst of planning at the time of his assassination in 1968? How did it reflect a change in emphasis from his earlier civil rights activities?

4. King, Malcolm X, and Medgar Evers were all assassinated in the 1960s. Were they to reappear in the United States today, what do you think would be their verdict about the potential for racial harmony and equality?

SUGGESTED READINGS

Branch, Taylor. *Parting the Waters: America in the King Years, 1954–68*. New York: Simon, 1988.

Garrow, David J. *Bearing the Cross: Martin Luther King, Jr. and the Southern Christian Leadership Conference*. New York: Morrow, 1986.

King, Coretta Scott. *My Life with Martin Luther King, Jr.* London: Hodder, 1970.

Lewis, Arthur Levering. *King: A Biography*. 2nd ed. Urbana, Ill.: U. of Illinois P, 1978.

Patterson, Lillie. *Martin Luther King, Jr. and the Freedom Movement*. New York: Facts on File, 1989.

21

Robert S. McNamara

When John Fitzgerald Kennedy ran for President in 1960, he insisted that the United States was facing a time of great peril in its relations with Communist powers. To be an American in the 1960s, he predicted, would be a hazardous experience: "We will live on the edge of danger." Kennedy could point to the recent victory of Fidel Castro's revolutionaries in Cuba to stir Americans' latent paranoia about the Red menace, which had subsided somewhat in the five years since the Army-McCarthy Communist infiltration probes had ended. Kennedy also insisted there was a gap between the U.S. and the Soviet Union in intercontinental ballistic missiles: Americans had recent, painful memories of being caught unprepared when the Russians launched their Sputnik space shot.

Trumpeting a call to "move forward" to confront Communism, Kennedy declared that the issue was no less than the "preservation of civilization." The world, he declared, paraphrasing Abraham Lincoln, could not exist "half slave and half free." Narrowly defeating Vice President Richard M. Nixon to become thirty-sixth president, Kennedy assembled a "brain trust," a team of brilliant corporate executives and Ivy League scholars. None would take more literally his marching orders to whip the United States military into shape and confront the Communist menace than the forty-four-year-old president of Ford Motor Company, Robert S. McNamara. Over the years, the Vietnam War would become synonymous with his name—"Mr. McNamara's War"—and the can-do, problem-solving Harvard Business School mentality.

ROBERT STRANGE MCNAMARA was born June 9, 1916, the son of a shoe salesman, in an ethnically mixed, middle-class neighborhood in the San Francisco Bay community of Piedmont. His earliest memory, he wrote in *In Retrospect* (1995) was of a "city exploding with joy." It was November 11, 1918. He was only two years old and this child whose memories as an adult would become both his blessing and his curse would never forget the impression of San Francisco celebrating "not only the end of

World War I but the belief, held so strongly by President Woodrow Wilson, that the United States and its allies had won the war to end all wars." In his controversial memoir he added that "they were wrong, of course . . . . The Twentieth Century was on its way to becoming the bloodiest, by far, in human history: during it 160 million people have been killed in wars across the globe."

Robert McNamara was part of a World War I baby boom that crowded class-rooms by the time he attended first grade. A privacy-loving man who talked little about his family, he was the son of an Irishman, Robert James McNamara, sales manager for a wholesale shoe company, and Clara Nell Strange, of Scottish and English extraction. By the first grade, the frail, nearsighted boy could read as well as most thirteen-year-olds. He relished competing with "ethnic rivals," as he put it, for honors in school.

If classes, in a shack as he remembers it, were crowded, and accommodations "poor," his teacher was superb. "At the end of each month she gave us a test and reassigned our seating based on the results." The pupil with the highest score sat in the front seat on the left row. "I was determined to occupy that seat." While the class was "predominantly WASP" (white Anglo-Saxon Protestant) his competitors were "invariably Chinese, Japanese, and Jews" who would, after working hard all week, go to ethnic schools on the weekends and study their ancestral languages, absorbing "ancient and complex cultures." McNamara would spend his weekends playing with his neighborhood friends. He did not mix with his ethnic rivals, who would return to school on Mondays "determined to beat their Irish classmate." They rarely did.

Neither of McNamara's parents had gone to college. It is difficult to learn any hint of what they thought they should do with their brilliant son, who had a phe-nomenal memory. At Piedmont High School, he earned a straight "A" record. McNamara thinks his drive for academic influence was a result of the fact that his father had not gotten beyond eighth grade. His parents, he says proudly, were "fiercely determined" that he would be the first in his family to go to college. "Their resolve shaped my life."

Graduating from high school in 1933 in the Great Depression, when one in four adult males in the U.S. were out of work, was what McNamara considered a "defining" influence in his life. Violent strikes were frequent throughout the coun-try, especially in the Bay area, where there were waterfront strikes from 1934 to 1936. McNamara remembered seeing as a teenager machine-gun emplacements on roofs along the San Francisco waterfront. He also remembers his shock at see-ing a longshoreman chase a man he believed was a strikebreaker, knock him down, and shatter his leg by stomping it against the curbstone.

McNamara's choice of colleges was limited by his parents' means. He entered the local public university which, fortunately for him, was the University of Cali-fornia at Berkeley, with tuition of fifty-two dollars per year. He quickly distin-guished himself and was elected to the Phi Beta Kappa honor society as a sopho-more. Majoring in economics and minoring in philosophy and mathematics, he revelled in "intellectual ferment." Never happier than on a college campus, he would have preferred to spend his life among scholars. He remained impressed all his life by the achievements of Berkeley scholars who, despite the fact that the uni-

versity was totally dependent on the archconservative, farmer-dominated state legislature for funding during the *Grapes of Wrath* era, managed to make Berkeley
famous for its liberal intellectual atmosphere. "My four years there exposed me to
concepts of justice, freedom and the balancing of rights and obligations."

During his first week as a college student, McNamara met Margaret
McKinstry Craig, a vivacious girl from Alameda who taught him patience as well as
bringing "balance, strength and joy" to his life. Margaret was all that the bookish,
shy McNamara was not: "warm, open, gentle, extroverted and beloved by all." To
help pay his way through college, McNamara took a summer job in 1935 that gave
him firsthand knowledge of the working conditions that were prolonging maritime
strikes on the West Coast. He shipped out as an ordinary seaman on the tramp
steamer S.S. *Peter Kerr*. He had worked out and made Berkeley's rowing team and
he liked to climb the mountains of Northern California: he was in tiptop shape. Yet
nothing prepared him for what he had to endure to earn a pitiful twenty dollars a
month. There was "no running (fresh) water in the crew's quarters, the bunks were
so infested with bedbugs that one morning I counted nineteen bites on one leg."
The food was so inedible that the already-skinny collegian lost thirteen pounds.
Summer stints as a sailor took McNamara through the Panama Canal, to the Far
East, and four times to Hawaii.

He also had his first brush with the military at Berkeley, where, because it was
a land grant college largely paid for by taxpayers, all male students were required
to join the Reserve Officers Training Corps (ROTC) for at least two years. McNamara applied for the optional four-year Navy training program but was rejected
because of poor eyesight. He served his two years in the Army ROTC. What he
learned was that "nobody took the military seriously." Like so many of his classmates in those pre-World War II days, he saw the Army as a "pointless ritual irrel-
evant to our world."

After Berkeley, McNamara won a scholarship to the graduate School of Business Administration at Harvard University, where he completed his degree
requirements for an M.B.A. in two years. Homesick for Margaret, he returned to
San Francisco and took a $125-a-month job as an accountant with Price Water-
house. The next summer Harvard offered him a junior faculty job teaching statistics. McNamara told the dean he would only accept it if Margaret, now a school
teacher in California, would marry him. First he had to track her down. She was on
a cross-country vacation with an aunt. In a phone booth at the Baltimore YWCA,
she accepted his proposal after a seven-year courtship. They lived in a single room
in Cambridge for a year, washing their dishes in the bathtub.

Five weeks after their first child was born, the Japanese bombed Pearl Harbor.
In early 1942, Harvard signed a contract with the Army Air Corps to train statistical control officers to help track men, supplies, and munitions and plan the myriad
details of managing a worldwide war. A young New York investment banker,
Charles B. "Tex" Thornton, pioneered a control system that could account for the
day-to-day status of planes, men, and missions, enabling statistical predictions of
the chances of success or failure of an attack on the enemy and pinpointing problems that could be corrected. McNamara was excited to join the team at Harvard
teaching this sophisticated new problem-solving approach to logistics.

In early 1943, McNamara was invited to go to England to work with the Eighth Air Force as it stepped up its daily bombing raids over Nazi-occupied Europe. In the next three years, he served in England, India, China, the Pacific, and at three U.S. bases. A brilliant logician who never saw men die in battle, McNamara came to see war as a supply problem, its outcome determined by sufficient men and material: he did not see it as a moral question. He also became enamored with being surrounded and praised by high-ranking officers and welcomed their praise. He was promoted to lieutenant colonel by war's end.

Although McNamara had helped revolutionize the way the Air Force had to keep track of every dollar, he could not afford to celebrate the end of this war. He and his wife both were stricken by polio in the summer of 1945. McNamara recovered quickly, but his wife's case was so severe that she appeared permanently crippled. Moved from Harvard to a hospital in Baltimore, she faced years of expensive treatments and therapy. McNamara had hoped to return to a quiet life on the Harvard faculty but so high were his wife's medical expenses that he could no longer afford the meager academic pay. When his old military boss, "Tex" Thornton, recruited him as part of a management team to go to the Ford Motor Company, he reluctantly said yes.

In the next few years, applying the statistical approach they had learned in the military, McNamara and his nine teammates, dubbed the "Whiz Kids" because of their cerebral, youthful approach to the 1,000-man Ford management maze, moved up quickly in the car company's ranks. Named manager of Ford's offices of planning and financial analysis in 1949, McNamara became Ford controller. He earned the reputation of "knowing where every buck is spent." Four years later, he became assistant general manager of the Ford division. There, he argued, since the average income in the U.S. was increasing, cars of the future should appeal to high-income as well as low-income buyers, a departure from Henry Ford's original philosophy. As a result, Ford developed the low-slung, elongated 1957 Ford, which quickly became the best-selling American car.

Named general manager of the Ford division in 1955, he was promoted to vice president of all car and truck divisions only two years later. His meteoric rise had come primarily because of his use of statistics and his introduction of computer analysis coupled with psychology and sociology to predict the car-buying tastes of Americans years in advance. He was responsible for changing the Ford Thunderbird from a two-to a four-seater to make it a family luxury car, tripling its sales, and he also developed the compact Falcon. He never did understand why, however, Americans preferred glitzy, gas-guzzling cars with fins and lots of chrome over the austere, stripped down, economical Falcon. He also introduced and promoted safety features, most notably the seat belt, and introduced the 12,000-mile or twelve-month warranty. In 1960, he became the first Ford Motor Company president who was not a member of the Ford family, despite the fact he had earned a reputation as a maverick by refusing to join the super-rich Ford car royalty of Grosse Pointe Farms, Michigan, choosing to live instead in a modest house near the University of Michigan campus in Ann Arbor.

Less than a month later, newly elected President John F. Kennedy offered McNamara the post of Secretary of Defense. The offer came as a shock not only to the Ford top brass but to McNamara, who had never met Kennedy and had voted Republican as often as he had voted Democrat. To take the $25,000-a-year Defense post would mean foregoing three million dollars in Ford stock options over the next four years and a salary equivalent to two million dollars a year in today's money. Far from impoverished, McNamara would receive $618,750 in bonuses he had already earned and sold his accumulated Ford stock for another $1.1 million, putting the proceeds in a blind trust. Twice before, he had been approached about assistant secretary's jobs under both the Truman and Eisenhower administrations. "I felt I wasn't ready, financially or otherwise." There was a degree of fatalism now in his acceptance. "At some particular point I felt I would have to do it if I was asked. You just can't go on saying 'no' all your life."

Agreeing to take the job if he could have a completely free hand to modernize the Pentagon, he left tranquil Ann Arbor for Washington, D.C., where he instantly informed the press of his plans to streamline the huge Pentagon civilian bureaucracy. He had brought statistical analysis from the World War II military to peacetime corporate America. Now, marrying it to the new computers, he brought corporate tactics back to the military on the eve of the Vietnam War. Developing a planning-programming-budgeting system, he established a Systems Analysis Office that scrutinized all costs and plans. Introducing cost-benefit analysis at the Defense Department as he had at Ford, he devised systems of estimating military needs and costs ten to fifteen years into the future.

To meet the Berlin Wall crisis in 1961, he created a "flexible response" system that increased American troop strength in Europe in the short run, and theoretically at least, gave the military more adaptability worldwide. Increasing requests for Defense Department spending even as he closed obsolete World War II bases, he took the bureaucracy out of the hands of generals and put it under civilian control, antagonizing not only the Joint Chiefs of Staff but their powerful allies in Congress.

Working long hours, he became known in Washington for arriving at his office before any of his assistants. "Senior members of [McNamara's] staff," one reporter noted, "would hurry to the Pentagon on Sunday mornings [to] feel the hood of the Secretary's car to determine by its temperature how long he had been at work." Yet not everyone admired this hard-driving architect of a new, modern military. Some senior military men found him two-faced and loyal only to his superiors. One-on-one, he was warm, responsive, and understanding; in a group of people, he became authoritative. Everyone believed he was a committed Cold Warrior. "There is no true historical parallel to the drive of Soviet communist imperialism to colonialize the world," he told the Senate Armed Services Committee. The Russians, he believed, were seeking "not merely conquest but the total obliteration of the enemy." He believed, like President Truman, that Communism must everywhere be contained by American military might. He firmly believed in the "domino theory" formulated by former Secretary of State John Foster Dulles and espoused by President Eisenhower. As he said in a 1995 *Washington Post* interview, he believed that unless the Soviet Union and the Chinese Communists were everywhere resisted, there would be "a fall of the dominoes." In Southern Asia, this would mean, after the fall of, say, Vietnam, "then we'd lose Thailand, Malaysia, Cambodia, Laos, Indonesia, and possibly

Archive Photos

A brilliant star at Ford Motors before being appointed Secretary of Defense, Robert McNamara would long remain loyal to President Lyndon Johnson's Vietnam policies despite his own growing misgivings.

India, and that would in turn weaken the forces of the West in NATO and our relationship with Japan."

Modernizing American forces, McNamara ordered new fleets of supercargo planes, new squadrons of B–52 long-range bombers, formed an airmobile division with hundreds of new helicopters, and ordered ten new Polaris long-range nuclear submarines. Using statistical studies of America's NATO allies as well as intelligence reports of Soviet forces, he made sure American and allied forces equalled Soviet and allied forces worldwide and in every category of weapon, in the process setting off a mammoth East-West arms race.

No test of this doctrine ever came so close to igniting a nuclear war as the Cuban Missile Crisis of October–November 1962. In part, the showdown between the U.S. and the U.S.S.R. came as a result of McNamara's tightening of the nuclear ring around Soviet territory. In October, the U.S. turned over new missile systems to the Turkish military within easy striking range of Moscow. When the Soviet Union began to install intermediate-range ballistic missiles in Cuba, ninety miles from American shores, President Kennedy startled the world in a nationwide TV address, disclosing his decision to issue an ultimatum to the Russians that their missiles must be removed.

In a thirteen-day-long nightmare of national hysteria, Americans learned that Cuban-based Russian missiles could reach virtually any American city or town. McNamara persuaded President Kennedy to call up the nation's National Guard reservists, and sent aloft nuclear-armed long-range bombers. Then he played the dove in the meetings of Kennedy's executive crisis committee. He argued against demands by military leaders to invade Cuba or to bomb the missile sites. He suggested instead imposing a naval blockade of all Russian ships approaching Cuba. This was an act of war. Even though Russian ships carrying missiles stopped dead in the water, military pressure continued to mount. McNamara urged prudence to allow the Russians a diplomatic escape from the crisis. His argument that the military "hawks" could not guarantee they could knock out all Russian missiles and prevent an attack on American cities eventually prevailed.

The crisis finally abated when the Soviets agreed publicly to remove their missiles and President Kennedy secretly agreed to pull American missiles out of Turkey (their presence on the southern border of the U.S.S.R. had not been known by the American people). How close had the world come to nuclear holocaust? "It is perfectly clear now," McNamara said in 1987, "that Cuban and Soviet leaders at that time believed the U.S. was intending to invade Cuba." McNamara believed the Russians were more determined to protect Communist Cuba against American attack and thus preserve their base in Latin America than to try to alter the balance of nuclear power worldwide. He said he never believed the Russians would risk total destruction just to move forty missiles closer to the U.S. But "it makes no difference whether you're killed by a missile fired from the Soviet Union or from Cuba," he contended. "A missile is a missile."

In the early days of the Kennedy administration, McNamara was not involved in the growing conflict in Southeast Asia. In mid–1961, he attended his first Vietnam-related meeting in Hawaii. At the time, he was more worried about a spreading civil war in Laos. He came away from the July 1961, meeting talking of "tremendous progress" toward phasing out American involvement in Southeast Asia and publicly predicted a complete victory by anti-Communist South Vietnamese forces by 1965. U.S. military advisors to the South Vietnamese Army (ARVN) numbered about 10,000 in Vietnam at this time, but there were no U.S. troops in combat. In fact, he ordered 1,000 American advisors withdrawn in the spring of 1962 and secretly recommended to Kennedy that 200,000 U.S. combat troops be sent to Vietnam even as he concluded that military might could not build a stable regime in Saigon. One reason for his de-emphasis of the use of military advisors was that they were telling him what he didn't want to hear: that the South Vietnamese Army was faction-ridden and passive and had little will to resist the highly-trained North Vietnamese, who had thoroughly beaten the French. But

McNamara's own doubts that the ARVN could win were growing, though he chose to keep such thoughts to himself.

After another Vietnamese visit in December 1963, shortly after the assassination of Kennedy in Dallas and the collapse of the Diem regime in Saigon, his secret report to the new President Lyndon Johnson was chilling: "The situation is very disturbing. Current trends, unless reversed in the next two or three months, will lead to a neutralization at best and more likely to a communist-controlled state." In March, 1964, McNamara agreed with military leaders that U.S. military support for the South Vietnamese army must be increased. With a new president in office, it was the perfect moment to reevaluate American participation in the Vietnam War, but it was a presidential election year and President Johnson had assumed the Kennedy mantle. Besides, McNamara sensed that Johnson believed in continuing American involvement more than Kennedy had; he would later maintain that, had Kennedy lived, the U.S. would have pulled out of Southeast Asia much earlier.

In any case, Lyndon Johnson ignored McNamara's new cautionary note. Indeed, at the height of the 1964 election campaign, Johnson used the pretext of a supposed attack by North Vietnamese torpedo boats on two American destroyers, the *Maddox* and the *C. Turner Joy*, to ram through Congress the Tonkin Gulf Resolution, which declared that "the U.S. regards as vital to its national interest and to world peace the maintenance of national peace and security in Southeast Asia." At the same time, Johnson made peace in Vietnam a principal campaign theme, overwhelmingly defeating Republican Barry Goldwater, who called for the use of nuclear weapons to stop the Communists.

Many liberal Democrats supported Johnson on the Tonkin Gulf Resolution, apparently unaware that he would consider it a declaration of war that gave him *carte blanche* as Commander in Chief. On February 6, 1965, only weeks after Johnson's inauguration, the Viet Cong launched a small-scale attack on U.S. advisors at Pleiku, an air base in South Vietnam. Johnson used the Pleiku incident to justify "escalation," a policy of drastically increasing U.S. forces in Vietnam. He also ordered the bombing of North Vietnam. On April 20, McNamara met with top military officers and Johnson Administration officials in Hawaii. The floodgates opened. First, 40,000 U.S. reinforcements were to be sent in, including combat troops for the first time. Two months later, the number was raised to 75,000. After McNamara toured Vietnam again in June 1965, he recommended sending in more U.S. troops by the end of 1965, as many as 300,000 by the end of 1966. At a White House meeting in July 1965, he even proposed a call-up of reserves, but this would have provoked a Congressional debate. Johnson wanted to avoid giving Congress the chance for a thorough debate over whether to continue to fund the war or to continue his Great Society domestic programs. He wanted both.

As General William C. Westmoreland, U.S. commander in Vietnam, called for more and more troops, promising that there was "light at the end of the tunnel," enlistments lagged and the quotas were filled by the draft, usually a measure reserved for wartime. McNamara had told Westmoreland not to "worry about the economy of the country, the availability of forces or public or Congressional attitudes." Westmoreland was to ask for whatever he thought he needed; McNamara would put pressure on Washington to accommodate him. Primarily, McNamara pressured the Army, causing the serious depletion of U.S. forces in Europe, and used up the strategic reserve he had created in the U.S. At the same time, each American troop increase led to a Communist response and an increase of tensions as many Americans feared that the Chinese and the Soviets would become openly involved. By late 1966, large-scale infiltration of battle-seasoned North Vietnamese troops into South Vietnam to assist the Viet Cong began. In November, 1965, after another Saigon visit, McNamara recommended raising troop strength to 400,000. Only months later, it would reach 542,000 combat troops.

But by October 1966, when McNamara, on orders of Johnson, once again toured Vietnam to assess the war effort, McNamara came away persuaded that the South Vietnamese could not win the war with any level of U.S. aid. He told Johnson the odds were now two-to-one against an American victory. Yet he did not disclose this growing conviction to any other Cabinet officers or to the public. In his report, he said, "I see no way to bring the war to an end soon." Reporting heavy enemy casualties, he added that there was "no sign of an impending break in enemy morale." Yet, far from recommending American withdrawal, he urged freezing U.S. ground forces at 470,000 men. Time after time, he hesitated from telling Johnson or anyone else that the U.S. must withdraw or risk disaster. He continued to propose problem-solving solutions, feeding Johnson and his Cabinet optimistic figures based on estimates of enemy dead fed him by field commanders telling him what he wanted to hear.

As student protests against the draft turned into a national antiwar movement, McNamara refused to speak out against the war or its futility. Nor did he offer to resign. He did begin to quietly oppose expansion of the war even as he continued mass bombing raids on North Vietnam. McNamara, who had helped facilitate massive bombings in Europe and Asia in World War II, clung to the belief that the North Vietnamese could be bombed to the negotiating table. In Cabinet meetings, away from the public eye, he pointed out that the huge amount of money being spent by Americans in Vietnam was leading to runaway inflation in the U.S. and was further destabilizing Vietnam. For most of 1966, McNamara was locked in arguments with the Joint Chiefs of Staff and Congressional hawks over his reservations about further escalation.

The confrontation led in July 1967, to McNamara's final Vietnam tour of inspection. General Westmoreland had called for another 100,000 troops. McNamara saw for himself that the war had shifted from a guerrilla war to main-force battles. When he returned to Washington, McNamara testified before the Senate Preparedness Committee on August 25, 1967, for the first time openly contradicting Johnson's Vietnam policies. On October 31, he met personally with LBJ; in a private memo the next day he called continuation of Johnson's war policies fruitless. He urged turning the war over to the South Vietnamese and announcing there would be no further escalation. On December 18, 1967, after polling his principal advisors, Johnson, assured there was little support for McNamara's position, formally rejected his advice. But by then, he had already decided that McNamara must go. On November 22, 1967, LBJ nominated McNamara as president of the World Bank. McNamara quietly left the Pentagon in February 1968, receiving the Medal of Freedom from Johnson at the White House. Forced out as Secretary of

Defense, he did not make public his own terrible second thoughts about the war, which dragged on for eight more years.

Serving for eighteen years at the World Bank, McNamara refused to speak out against the war for twenty-seven years after his resignation. Not until 1995, the twentieth anniversary of American withdrawal from Saigon, did the seventy-eight-year-old McNamara decide to break his long silence. He sought, he said, "to put Vietnam in context," to counter "the cynicism and even contempt with which so many people view our political institutions and leaders." The two administrations he had served had made wrong decisions—"we were wrong, terribly wrong"—because of "an error not of values and intentions but of judgment and capabilities." He maintained that the U.S. Vietnam policy was based on two contradictory premises: first, the "domino" theory, which overstated the threat to U.S. security and world peace if the North Vietnamese won; second, a belief that the South Vietnamese were not committed to defending themselves and that no other nation (or the United Nations) could do it. In his 1995 memoirs, McNamara took responsibility for resolving that contradiction. Even in 1995, he avoided taking personal responsibility for bloodshed in Vietnam despite his admission that he had concluded as early as 1962 that the war could not be won by the South Vietnamese.

McNamara argued that the U.S. fought in Vietnam "for what it believed to be good and honest reasons: We were captives of our experience. [We] had all fought in World War II. After we ultimately won the war against Germany and Japan, the Soviet Union took Poland, Czechoslovakia and Hungary . . . . During my seven years in the Defense Department, in August of 1961 we had an attempt by the Soviet Union to take Berlin. A year later they put nuclear warheads in Cuba . . . It was a terrible threat . . . We misjudged that threat, but it was a real threat. And we, part of the World War II generation, were very sensitive to that."

In admitting that he and the government were "wrong," McNamara said he meant "strategically" wrong "from point of view of pursuing the interests of this nation, to insert 500,000 into Vietnam and carry on combat there. I think we could have protected the security of the nation without it and therefore we were wrong to do it." But was he morally wrong to keep his misgivings to himself while an estimated three million soldiers and civilians died? I would love to discuss the morality of it," he told the *Washington Post*, "but it opens up such a field. I can't get into it." Many of McNamara's critics would not accept this answer: the *New York Times*, in a stinging editorial, called McNamara "morally bankrupt."

Yet McNamara remained confident that he had represented the wishes not only of two presidents but of a majority of the American people through much of the Vietnam era and he urged the U.S. to continue its leadership role among nations in a system of collective global security. The lesson of Vietnam, he warned in his book, *In Retrospect*, was that the U.S. "clearly cannot and should not intervene in every conflict arising from a nation's attempt to move toward capitalism." He had learned in Vietnam that "military force has only a limited capacity to facilitate the process of nation building."

QUESTIONS FOR THOUGHT AND DISCUSSION

1. In what ways was Robert McNamara ideally suited to join the Kennedy "brain trust" as Secretary of Defense in 1961?

2. Why was McNamara's number-crunching, systems-oriented genius insufficient in meeting the military challenges of U.S. involvement in the Vietnam conflict?

3. Why did McNamara refuse to publicly express his growing doubts about the U.S. ability to win in Vietnam? Did he owe President Johnson such loyalty, or do you sense he was covering his own tracks?

4. In his autobiography, *In Retrospect*, McNamara admits that he and the other leaders who promoted our Vietnam commitment at its most critical stage were wrong. How does this belated acknowledgment strike you? Why do you think the *New York Times*, as well as many veterans' groups and old antiwar activists all responded angrily to McNamara's *mea culpa*.

SUGGESTED READINGS

Herring, George. *America's Longest War: The United States in Vietnam, 1950–1975*, 3e. New York: McGraw-Hill, 1990.

Kagan, Donald. *On the Origins of War and the Preservation of Peace*. New York: Doubleday, 1995 (see "The Cuban Missile Crisis," pp. 437–565).

Karnow, Stanley. *Vietnam: A History*. New York: Knopf, 1984.

Kinnard, Douglas. *The Secretary of Defense*. Lexington, Ky.: UP of Kentucky, 1980.

McNamara, Robert S. *In Retrospect: The Tragedy and Lessons of Vietnam*. New York: Times, 1995.

_____. *The Essence of Security: Reflections in Office*. New York: Harper, 1968.

Sheehan, Neil. *The Pentagon Papers*. New York: Random, 1975.

_____. *A Bright Shining Lie*. New York: Random, 1985.

22

Richard Milhous Nixon

*I*n 1968, the U.S. was in the greatest turmoil since the Civil War, divided by race riots, assassinations, and antiwar protests. The Tet offensive by the Viet Cong revealed, contrary to government claims, that the unpopular war in Vietnam was far from over. The antiwar movement was only part of a growing generation gap. The murder of Martin Luther King, Jr. triggered riots that left fires blazing within sight of the nation's Capitol. A clear sign of the massive disenchantment with President Johnson's "war of containment" in Southeast Asia came in the New Hampshire primary, first of the presidential election year. Senator Eugene McCarthy's near-victory was quickly followed by Johnson's surprise announcement that he would not seek a second term. Into the void raced charismatic Robert F. Kennedy, who was shot on the day he won the crucial California primary. Almost by default, the Democrat's nominated Vice President Hubert Humphrey, whose disorganized, underfunded campaign was further weakened by the third party candidacy of segregationist Alabama Governor George Wallace.

Sensing victory, the Republicans rejected a compromise candidate and nominated former Vice President Richard M. Nixon, a tough, unscrupulous, controversial campaigner who had lost the 1960 presidential election, the 1962 California governor's race, and had been long considered politically dead, blaming his demise on a hostile press. The resilient Nixon had built his political career on Red-baiting during the Cold War. Not above lying about the supposed Communist ties of Democratic rivals, he had been caught with an illegal slush fund in the 1952 presidential election, but his use of television, his family, and even his pet dog to appeal for support had kept him on the ticket. Appealing to right-wingers, special interests, and the "silent majority," claiming he had a secret plan to end the Vietnam War, he narrowly defeated Humphrey in the most astonishing comeback in American political history. Within five years, however, he brought unparalleled disgrace on the White House. Accused of lying and covering up a host of crimes, he became the only president to resign.

IN THE MID–1950s, when Richard Nixon was serving as Vice President to the enormously-popular President Dwight D. Eisenhower, he liked to talk about his ancestor John Nixon, painting him as a hero of the American Revolution. He told interviewers that this long-ago Nixon had been the sheriff of Philadelphia in 1776 who had the honor of reading the Declaration of Independence in public for the first time to a crowd gathered at Independence Hall. When Nixon became President, he made much of this ancestral link, coming to Independence Hall and, as mounted police kept crowds of antiwar demonstrators several blocks away, announced he had written a "Second Declaration of Independence," his latest overstated euphemism for his plan to share some Federal tax revenues with the states and cities.

The truth about Nixon's family background was, as so much of what he said, a little less dramatic than what he felt compelled to make it. John Nixon was a revolutionary soldier *asked* by the sheriff to read the Declaration aloud, he was never the sheriff. Nixon left out the complicating fact that John Nixon had been expelled by the pacifist Quakers for fighting, but that might have qualified somewhat his frequent campaign references to his mother's proud Quaker origins. Through fifty years of political life, Nixon, a history major in a Quaker college, worked hard at rewriting his own history.

As controversy continues about his place in American history, some facts are indisputable. He was born January 9, 1913, in Yorba Linda, California, a town about thirty miles southeast of Los Angeles. Though no poorer than many cashless Americans living through the Great Depression, through most of his life, Nixon was anxious about having enough money and said he had grown up in poverty, which was untrue. He liked to talk about the Nixon family's struggle for survival. In fact, his father's frequent smalltime business failures were offset by his mother's grim frugality, as she set out to put three sons through college. His Ohio-born father, Frank, had quit school in the fourth grade and had gone to work as a farmhand. Restless, quarrelsome, and hot-tempered, he wandered from job to job and state to state, working as a housepainter, glassworker, potter, sheep rancher in Colorado, telephone lineman, oil field roustabout, and trolley car motorman. Starting out as a Democrat, he became a Republican when President William McKinley complimented him on the horse he was riding. He raised cattle for awhile and named them after movie stars.

It was as a motorman in Ohio that he had his only other brush with politics, and that was as a labor agitator. In bitter Ohio winters, he had to stand outside in an open vestibule, his feet freezing. Organizing the other motormen, he campaigned at the Ohio statehouse for better working conditions. There were two results. He was out of a job and he spent the rest of his life holding forth about politics, rarely letting his son Richard interrupt him. Frank Nixon migrated to Southern California in 1907, working as a motorman on red trolleycars that linked suburban Whittier with Los Angeles. A Methodist, he settled in the Quaker town of Whittier, where he met Hannah Milhous, an Irish Quaker whose family had helped found the town. Hannah's family was famous among Quakers, immortalized in Jessamyn West's novel, *The Friendly Persuasion*, the story of her grandfather, a redheaded Quaker who scandalized his Meeting by buying an organ. Frank

Nixon married Hannah Milhous in 1908 and, for a while, managed the Milhous ranch. Itching for his own ranch, he moved them to the San Joaquin Valley; when that venture failed, they moved to Yorba Linda, where he planted a lemon orchard. Richard Milhous Nixon was born in a small frame house there in 1913. There was oil under the land but luckless Frank Nixon moved again before it was discovered. He took the family back to Whittier and opened a small grocery store with a gas pump out front.

There were only two distinctions in Richard Nixon's childhood. One was that he was never late for school. The other: at age three he fell out of a buggy on his head, the wagon wheel opening a gash that took twenty-five stitches after he nearly bled to death during the twenty-five-mile ride to the nearest hospital. Quiet, obedient, and repressed, he preferred reading newspapers to books, yet he managed to finish four years of work in his three years of school in Yorba Linda. At Whittier High School, his favorite subjects were history and civics. He went out for football and spent year after year sitting on the bench, waiting fruitlessly to get into a game. He had to attend Quaker services at midweek and three times on Sundays and he dutifully practiced violin and piano. After school, he had to work in the produce section of his father's market and pump gas.

From seventh grade on, Nixon loved to debate. That year, he took the affirmative in his first debate: "Resolved—That insects are more beneficial than harmful." He won. At Fullerton High School, he won the Constitutional Oratorical Contest for the first time as a sophomore and was the West Coast representative in the National Oratorical Contest. In one debate, he argued that "it is our duty to protect this precious document, to obey its laws, to hold sacred its mighty principles . . . " His success in school received a jolt in his junior year when, at fifteen, he had to transfer to Whittier High and work longer hours in his father's store. Perhaps the most traumatic experience of his boyhood came when his mother left his father and the two young boys behind and went to Arizona for two years to nurse the oldest boy, Harold, who suffered from tuberculosis. He missed his mother terribly and felt deserted by her; he also had to take over her bookkeeping duties. Life had been austere with his mother. He once told a reporter, "We had very little. I wore my brother's shoes, and my brother below me wore mine. We never ate out—never." Without his mother, he was starved for affection, signing one letter to his mother, "Your good dog, Richard." During summer vacations, Richard joined her, working part-time as a barker for the Wheel of Fortune at the Slippery Gulch Rodeo in Prescott. His mother came back after Harold died.

After driving to the Los Angeles public market every morning to buy fresh fruit and vegetables, Richard went off to school, where he found appreciation, in his junior and senior years maintaining an "A" average and winning for a second time the Constitutional Oratorical Contest. In an intelligence test where the norm was thirty-five, he scored fifty-nine. He won the Harvard Award for "best all around student" but had to turn down the chance to apply for a Harvard scholarship because he could not afford to go away to college. At seventeen, he became a freshman at Whittier College, won several national debating awards and, already fascinated by politics, became president of the student body of the all-Quaker school on a platform promising "A Dance a Month." The Quaker college had always barred dancing, but Nixon convinced officials that mixers would keep students from sneaking off to Los Angeles dance halls. He rarely went out on dates—dates cost money and he had none.

Graduating in 1934 during the Depression, he won a full scholarship to Duke University School of Law in Durham, North Carolina. In his letter of recommendation, Whittier's president predicted that Nixon "will become one of America's important, if not great, leaders," only qualifying his praise by adding that Nixon lacked sophistication. At Duke, Nixon entered school politics and became president of the student law association. He helped meet his expenses by doing research for thirty-five cents an hour under the New Deal's National Youth Administration's work-study program. Called "Gloomy Gus" by classmates, he nevertheless won election to the Order of the Coif, the national law honor society, and ranked third in the 1937 graduating class of forty-four students.

Yet it was the Depression and there were few jobs. Nixon applied for a job with the Federal Bureau of Investigation and was rejected. He traveled to New York and was advised to go home to Whittier and start working there. He went back to California and joined a Whittier firm on a piecework, per-case basis, specializing in constitutional law. He became a partner and began to make money. He lost some of it when he invested in a frozen orange juice business that failed, but at age twenty-six he was elected the youngest member of Whittier College's board of trustees.

Nixon met Thelma Catherine Ryan shortly after he returned to Whittier at a neighborhood theater audition for *The Dark Tower*: both were fond of acting and starred in the leading roles. Born in a Nevada copper mining camp and nicknamed Pat because she was born on the eve of St. Patrick's Day, she grew up on a California farm. Her mother died before Pat finished high school, but she managed to work her way through low-tuition University of Southern California. She was teaching typing and shorthand at Whittier High when Nixon met her. They married two years later on June 21, 1940.

When World War II broke out, Quaker Nixon was exempt from military service, but he decided that he wanted some part in the war effort. The young couple drove to Washington, D.C., where Nixon found a job as a tire rationer with the Office of Price Administration. He decided that he wanted to seek political office after the war. Without military service, he correctly reasoned, his chances would be few. He sought an officer's commission and joined the Navy as an ensign in October 1942. He served as a rear-area transport specialist in the South Pacific Combat Air Transport Command, distinguishing himself mainly for his ability to swap anything to get the supplies he needed and for his uncanny ability at poker playing. He was able to accumulate a rumored $10,000 in winnings by war's end, a huge take for the time and the grubstake he needed to run for Congress.

After his discharge in 1946, Nixon returned to Whittier, where Republicans were looking for a "new face" to run against five-term New Deal Democrat Congressman Jerry Voorhis. Nixon the debater and recently promoted Navy lieutenant commander managed to persuade them he could unseat Voorhis, although GOP leaders gave him little hope. Campaigning aggressively, Nixon implied that Voorhis was a Communist, although there never was any evidence to prove that he was. A strong end-the-New-Deal tide was running and Nixon managed to paint Voorhis as "soft" on Communist expansionism. The massive swing to the right that year helped the GOP to capture the House for the first time in sixteen years. With the help of his Red-baiting, Nixon won.

In the House of Representatives, Nixon was appointed to the Un-American Activities Committee, where he further exploited the rising tide of anti-Communism. His first target was Alger Hiss, a former State Department official accused of passing classified documents to a Soviet spy ring during the 1930s. It came down to a question of belief: whether Hiss or his principal accuser, *Time* editor Whittaker Chambers, a confessed former Communist courier, was telling the truth. Nixon believed Hiss was lying. Many Republican committee members wanted to drop the matter but subcommittee chairman Nixon insisted the charges be proven or disproved. Nixon helped raise the issue of Communist infiltration of the government to a frenzied pitch. One result was that, when he was nominated for an honorary doctorate at Duke, his law school, the faculty voted to deny him his LLD.

But the hysteria of the Cold War surrounding the Soviet detonation of an atomic bomb, which Americans thought was their exclusive secret, and Hiss's conviction by a Federal District Court jury for perjury in denying that he had given secrets to Soviet agents, made Richard Nixon a shining new Republican star. His Red-hunting overshadowed his other Congressional activities. He was proudest of working on the committee that established the Marshall Plan. As a member of the House Education and Labor Committee, he also helped to write the Taft-Hartley Act, setting federal limits on labor union activities. A dedicated Cold Warrior, he voted for aid to Greece and Turkey and a peacetime military draft.

Easily reelected to the House in 1948, Nixon decided to run for the U.S. Senate in 1950, as Americans reeled from the unexpected Communist invasion of South Korea. Nixon opposed Congresswoman Helen Gahagan Douglas, a New Deal Democrat, taking up charges first levelled at her during the Democratic primary that she did not understand the Communist threat. Nixon went further. He flooded the state with 500,000 "pink sheets" that sought to link Mrs. Douglas's voting record in the House with the goals of the Communist Party. Dubbing her the "Pink Lady" and implying that she sympathized with Communism, he carried out a vicious campaign, accusing her of being "pink down to her underwear." He, in turn, earned the lasting sobriquet of "Tricky Dick" from a small newspaper, the *Independent Review*, but Nixon won one of California's most savage elections by a huge 700,000-vote margin. At thirty-eight, he was the youngest Senator.

In two years in the Senate, he served on the Permanent Investigations Subcommittee chaired by Senator Joseph McCarthy of Wisconsin, actively joining in its Red-hunting inquests. He worked hard traveling the country to support GOP candidates at GOP fundraisers. In 1952, he won the Republican nomination for Vice Presidential running mate to Dwight Eisenhower because GOP managers convinced "Ike" that Nixon could effectively use the "soft on Communism" issue on the stump. Ike had his doubts, but agreed. Only one month later, in mid-campaign, the *New York Post* broke the story, under the headline "Secret Nixon Fund," that Senator Nixon had an $18,000 secret "slush fund," set up by private Nixon supporters in California to cover Nixon's out-of-pocket expenses. Nixon maintained that he had only used the money for political purposes and, facing being dumped from the GOP ticket, went on radio and television on September 23, 1952 to state his case. In an emotional thirty-minute speech that became infamous as his Checkers speech, he detailed his personal finances and said that "Pat doesn't have a mink coat, but she does have a respectable Republican cloth coat." He admitted accepting gifts for his daughters, Tricia and Julie, but vowed to keep Checkers, the cocker spaniel given to the girls. "I just want to say this, right now," he said mockingly, "that regardless of what they say about it, we are going to keep it." He asked Republicans to wire or write GOP national headquarters to indicate whether he should stay on the ticket or withdraw. The tidal wave of letters ran 350-to-1 in favor of Nixon. The next day, Ike put his arm around the thirty-nine-year-old Nixon and said, "You're my boy."

A ruthless campaigner now considered the Republican hero, Nixon accused his Democrat opponents, Governor Adlai Stevenson of Illinois and Senator John J. Sparkman of Alabama, of "fellow traveling" with Communists and insisted that a vote for a Democrat was a vote for continued socialism at home and surrender to Communist domination worldwide. Sweeping to victory, Eisenhower gave Nixon unparalleled influence in his government, working not only as his Congressional fence-mender, but sending him on goodwill visits to some sixty nations. He also allowed Nixon to preside over Cabinet and National Security Council meetings during his frequent absences. When Eisenhower suffered a heart attack in September 1955, Nixon carried out his normal duties, held Cabinet meetings and kept the government running smoothly. When Ike was hospitalized with colitis in June 1956, and a stroke in November 1957, Nixon again played the successful understudy. His smooth standing-in may explain why, when there was talk of dumping Nixon from the GOP ticket in 1956, Eisenhower fumed: "Anyone who attempts to drive a wedge of any kind between Dick Nixon and me has just as much chance as if he tried to drive it between my brother and me."

In his second term, Nixon's frequent overseas missions—he visited every continent but Antarctica—brought him face to face with danger and enormous publicity. Venezuelan mobs yelling "Yanqui go home" pelted his limousine with eggs and rocks, smashing the windows and rocking the car. In Lima, he was spat on. In July 1959, at a U.S. trade mission "typical home" exhibit in Moscow, Nixon and Soviet Premier Nikita Khrushchev argued economic systems in a highly-publicized "kitchen debate." There was little doubt that Nixon was being groomed as Eisenhower's heir-apparent: at the 1960 GOP national convention, Nixon won the nomination on the first ballot.

The 1960 campaign was the first that made effective use of television—to Nixon's great disadvantage. The popular, Hollywood movie star image of John Fitzgerald Kennedy was pitted against the slightly-jowly, five o'clock shadow of Nixon in the first televised national presidential debate. As most American voters listened to their radios or watched on TV, Nixon seemed to win the four debates on points, but on television, tired and haggard from his grueling campaign, he was no match for the charismatic Kennedy. In a photo-finish election, Kennedy won the White House by only 114,673 votes out of a record sixty-nine million amid charges of massive vote count fraud, especially in Democratic-controlled Chicago.

Returning to practicing law after nearly two decades in politics, Nixon decided to run for governor of California in 1962. He won the primary but split the party, failing to win conservative support. Incumbent Democratic Governor Edmund G. (Pat) Brown drubbed Nixon by 300,000. Nixon, who had grown increasingly paranoid, believed his political career was over and that he had been destroyed by the press. He took out his frustration at a press conference, insisting reporters were

> so delighted that I had lost. For sixteen years, ever since the Hiss case, you've had a lot of—a lot of fun—that you've had an opportunity to attack me ... but as I leave you I want you to know—just think how much you're going to be missing. You won't have Nixon to kick around anymore, because, gentlemen, this is my last press conference.

In 1963, the Nixons moved to New York City, where Nixon practiced law. He sat out the 1964 presidential election but, in 1966, evidently decided to attempt a comeback, earning political IOUs by campaigning in scores of House and Senate races. The stand-off between Nelson Rockefeller and Ronald Reagan in 1968 ended when Senator Strom Thurmond of South Carolina wooed Southern delegates away from Reagan to Nixon. Taking an early lead against Democrat Hubert Humphrey, Nixon ran on a promise to end the draft and said he had a "secret plan" to end the war in Vietnam. Giving no specifics, and only appearing in ten closed TV filmings with selected Republican audiences, he pledged to solve "the crisis of our cities." He appealed to a "silent majority" by vowing to restore "law and order," an obvious allusion to suppressing antiwar activists. At the same time he pledged to stop the bombing in Vietnam, and suggested he had a secret plan to end that war. By a thin 600,000 vote margin, he defeated Humphrey in the most amazing political comeback in U.S. history.

During 2,027 days in the White House, Nixon frequently took credit for an array of events and achievements that occurred because of the efforts of others. During his administration, as the civil rights movement bore fruit, more Southern schools were desegregated than under any other President. The space program initiated by President Kennedy came to its spectacular climax on July 20, 1969, when Apollo II astronauts Neil A. Armstrong and Edwin E. Aldin, Jr., became the first people to walk on the moon. After a strong environmental movement swept the country in the late 1960s, Nixon signed legislation creating the Environmental Protection Agency.

Nixon kept his promise to end the draft, but not for five years, during which time it appeared that, far from ending the Vietnam War, he was expanding it. Soon after his inauguration, as peace talks in Paris stalled, he announced his policy of *Vietnamization*, ordering speeded-up training for South Vietnamese forces so they could gradually take over the war effort. Amid massive student protests that Nixon's policy was too slow, Nixon ordered U.S. troops in 1970 to invade Cambodia on the pretext of attacking North Vietnamese supply bases there. While Nixon insisted this would shorten the war, hundreds of protests broke out on college campuses, culminating in the killing of four demonstrators by National Guardsmen at Kent State University in Ohio. Undeterred, Nixon imposed a Navy blockade of North Vietnamese ports and, on Christmas 1972, ordered the bombing of Hanoi, the North Vietnamese capital.

AP/World Wide

Even as he was departing the White House in disgrace on the day of his resignation, Richard Nixon flashed his habitual campaign smile and gave his reflexive "V for Victory" sign.

At the same time, however, Nixon's Secretary of State, Henry Kissinger, made a dramatic diplomatic breakthrough in relations with China and the Soviet Union. In 1969, Nixon removed some restrictions on American travel to China to encourage the resumption of trade between the two countries, which had ceased during the Korean War in 1950. In 1971, he approved limited exports to China and sent Kissinger to undertake secret talks in Beijing. In February 1972, as his reelection campaign began, Nixon made a widely publicized "journey for peace" to China for seven days, the first U.S. president to visit there. Later that year, he visited the Soviet Union, signing agreements with Soviet leader Leonid I. Brezhnev to limit nuclear weapons.

Easily winning renomination in 1972, he won the greatest landslide in American history, polling eighteen million more votes than his opponent, Senator George S. McGovern, and receiving 520 electoral votes to the Democrat's 17. Only one week after his inauguration, the U.S. signed agreements to immediately stop the fighting in Vietnam, at the same time finally carrying out his pledge to replace the draft with an all-volunteer army.

But Nixon's vaunted foreign-policy record was soon overshadowed under the Kleig lights of the two-year-long Watergate scandal, the gravest U.S. political crisis since the Civil War. On June 17, 1972, five employees of Nixon's Committee to Reelect the President (CREEP) led by a former CIA agent were arrested in the act of burglarizing the Democratic National Headquarters at the posh Watergate Complex in Washington. Their address books linked them to White House aides and $100 bills they were carrying were traced to funds raised in the Midwest by Nixon campaigners and "laundered" in a Mexican bank account. Dismissed by the White House as a "third-rate burglary attempt," the break-in touched off a chain of events that unravelled the worst political scandal in U.S. history and for the first time forced a president to resign in disgrace.

Over the next two years, scores of misdeeds committed by or in the name of Nixon were disclosed by investigative reporters, most notably Bob Woodward and Carl Bernstein of the *Washington Post*, and followed up in hearings by the Senate Select Committee on Watergate, chaired by Democrat Sam Ervin of North Carolina. Among the charges were that Nixon campaign officials had installed eavesdropping devices inside Democratic headquarters as part of efforts by a Republican "dirty tricks" squad to sow dissension among Democratic candidates. White House officials including Nixon were accused of authorizing the payment of "hush money" to Watergate defendants as part of a conspiracy to cover up the break-in: the coverup included an array of criminal acts, including shredding important evidence and obstructing justice. Journalists and Senate investigators discovered that a White House "plumbers unit" created to plug leaks of sensitive political information had burgled the office of the psychiatrist of Daniel Ellsberg, the former White House aide who had distributed to the press the Pentagon Papers, a top-secret study of the Vietnam War. The Nixon Administration had also drawn up an Enemies List: according to a White House memo, it was "use the available machinery to screw our political enemies." That machinery included the IRS and the FBI. The list included members of Congress, CBS newsman Daniel Schorr, and celebrities Bill Cosby, Jane Fonda, Paul Newman, and Tony Randall.

Time after time, Nixon denied any involvement or wrongdoing, but White House counsel John Dean testified that, even if Nixon had not personally authorized the Watergate break-in, he directed the coverup. The evidence of Nixon's direct involvement came, ironically, from a secret White House taping system installed in 1971 by Nixon, supposedly to allow him to reconstruct the events of his presidency for his memoirs. Vowing his innocence, Nixon nevertheless refused to turn over the tapes to the Senate investigating committee, claiming executive privilege. Only after the Supreme Court unanimously ordered the release of the tapes did he comply, but one tape had a mysterious eighteen-and-a-half-minute gap: sound experts agreed it had been erased. The tapes, replete with his foul language, completely discredited Nixon.

Pursuing an independent investigation, special Watergate prosecutor Archibald Cox was prosecuting Nixon officials. In addition to the five original burglars and John Dean, fourteen White House or CREEP officials, including former attorney general John Mitchell, were indicted and Nixon himself was named as an unindicted co-conspirator. When Nixon fired Cox, a broadbased movement to impeach Nixon gathered force in Congress.

In July 1974, the House Judiciary Committee, after reviewing the evidence, voted to recommend three articles of impeachment. The committee, after dramatic televised hearings, charged Nixon with obstructing justice, abuse of presidential powers and disobeying subpoenas. Printed transcripts of his taped conversations went on sale to the public, demonstrating that Nixon had approved a coverup on June 23, 1972, only six days after the Watergate break-in. Republican leaders now warned Nixon that he faced certain impeachment by the House and conviction by the Senate. On August 6, 1974, a red-faced Republican Senator Barry Goldwater told Vice President Ford that "the best thing that he can do for the country is to get the hell out of the White House." Goldwater told White House Chief of Staff Alexander Haig, "He has lied to me for the last time and lied to my colleagues for the last time." On August 8, 1974, Nixon ended the two-year-long crisis by announcing his resignation.

In his last speech to the assembled White House staff, crowding into the East Room, Nixon, speaking without notes to a vast television audience, was still defiant: "We can be proud of it—five and a half years." Shaking his head vigorously, he claimed that "no man or no woman ever profited at the public expense or the public till . . . Mistakes, yes, but for personal gain, never. You did what you believed in. Sometimes right, sometimes wrong. And I only wish I were a wealthy man." Then he reminisced about "my old man . . . And then he was a grocer" and then turned and stared off, "Nobody will ever write a book about my mother . . . My mother was a saint." Free associating, Nixon was shaking as he rambled on about his disappointments. Finally, he ended it with a last piece of advice for the nation. "And so, we leave with high hopes, in good spirits and with deep humility and with very much gratefulness in our hearts." Moving downstairs, then outside with his family, Nixon was the last to board the helicopter that would carry them away: for the last time, he gave his reflexive V-for-victory sign.

Less than one month later, the new president, Gerald R. Ford, granted Nixon a "full, free and absolute" pardon for all federal crimes he "committed or may have committed or taken part in."

For the next twenty years, until his death in 1994, Nixon carried out a ceaseless campaign as author of eight books and as a behind-the-scenes advisor of presidents to win back a measure of respectability. Some old rivals, such as George McGovern, whose campaign had been ruined by Nixon's "dirty tricks" practitioners in 1972, came to revise his opinion of Nixon over the years. "I saw Nixon struggle to regain his position. I developed a kind of grudging respect for him." But others, like former President Harry Truman, were less forgiving: "Richard Nixon is a no-good lying bastard. He can lie out of both sides of his mouth at the same time, and if he ever caught himself telling the truth, he'd lie just to keep his hand in." President Jimmy Carter worried about the long-range effects of Nixon's presidency on American history. "In 200 years of history, he's the most dishonest president we ever had. I think he disgraced the Presidency."

QUESTIONS FOR THOUGHT AND DISCUSSION

1. In what ways, if any, did Richard Nixon's background shape his political style and philosophy? Would you say his upbringing was exceptional or average?

2. On what issue did Nixon as a young congressman first make his mark as a national figure? Do you think his passion on this issue was sincere?

3. Why did the nation turn to Nixon in 1968 and elect him President? Was he suited for the presidency? What were his principal successes in office?

4. In his famous farewell speech to his White House staff on the morning of his resignation, Nixon made some remarkable references to his mother and father, as well as to the (questionable) fact that he was not a wealthy man. What do you think he was getting at here, and do you think it might hold a clue to his downfall?

SUGGESTED READINGS

Ambrose, Stephen E. *Nixon*. 2 vols. New York: Simon, 1987–1989.

Anson, Robert S. *The Unquiet Oblivion of Richard M. Nixon*. New York: Simon, 1984.

Brodie, Fawn M. *Richard Nixon: The Shaping of His Character*. New York: Norton, 1981.

Kutter, Stanley I. *The Wars of Watergate*. New York: Norton, 1990.

Morris, Roger. *Nixon*. New York: Holt, 1989.

Nixon, Richard M. *The White House Transcripts*. New York: Bantam, 1974.

Woodward, Bob and Carl Bernstein. *The Final Days*. New York: Simon, 1976.

———. *All the President's Men*. New York: Simon, 1974.

23

Sandra Day
O'Connor

In 1981, when Ronald Reagan announced his nomination of an Arizona judge, Sandra Day O'Connor, as the first woman on the United States Supreme Court, only five percent of judges were women. That same court in 1873 had declared that "The natural and proper timidity and delicacy which belongs to the female sex evidently unfits it for many of the occupations of life." Because the conclusion had to include a positive assertion, the court went on to specify that the "paramount destiny and mission of women are to fill the noble and benign offices of wife and mother. This is the law of the Creator." The case was Myra Bradwell v. State of Illinois, *a decision in which Bradwell lost. Ronald Reagan, not usually associated with feminist politics, chose astutely when he recognized O'Connor's unusual gifts. The questions the whole country dreaded and knew would come to the court again and again needed a woman's insight—a minefield to legal scholars surrounded the question of abortion; cases involving discrimination against women were growing more complex as women watched their own economic and political stakes rise. Reagan might have been boasting about his own good judgment when he hailed O'Connor as "a person for all seasons."*

IN A CAREER THAT still goes on, no one can give the verdict on what matters most in the legal thinking and decisions of Justice Sandra Day O'Connor, whether it is that she is a woman or something else about her, a question that she does not claim to be able to answer herself. As the court has become polarized following recent appointments, a pattern is now emerging in which her vote breaks deadlocks and therefore carries great weight. Her decisions show consistently independent thinking and reasoning that cannot be dismissed as merely ideological. As much as anything, maybe, O'Connor can be looked at as a product of the West, as a person who would have turned out very differently if she had come from a different region of the United States. Her grandfather, Henry Clay Day, a Vermonter, had moved out West, in an emigration that made him resemble so many other sons of New England, much like the parents of Myra Bradwell who moved West when that meant going to Illinois.

The Day family did not stop before reaching Arizona where her grandfather protected his land from attacks by Apaches, sometimes led by Geronimo.

As a girl Sandra Day hoped to grow up to be a cattle rancher. The way of life that formed her on the unpretentious Lazy B ranch, then a spread of some 246 acres, taught her about effort and more importantly than anyone knew at the time, taught her to work alongside men on projects larger than any one person could do alone. By the age of four she had learned to read—by the light of a coal-lamp. By the time she was eight Sandra knew how to shoot a rifle, brand cattle, and drive a tractor. For years she kept a bobcat as her favorite pet. But being alone was part of childhood on a ranch with so few children around.

That early experience of pitching in with cowboys, of learning to repair fences, to ride a horse, to drive a truck long before she could legally have a driver's license, all prepared the bright girl for more hard work. Her parents recognized Sandra, their oldest child, as too good a student to be left to the chancy education of rural schools around Duncan, Arizona, where they lived, near the New Mexico border. In the solution that they found, Sandra went to live with her grandmother in El Paso, Texas, so that she could attend the Radford School, a good private school for girls. So far from home, young, and in surroundings totally unlike ranch life, Sandra became so homesick for the Lazy B that her family had her come home for a year and go to school in Lordsburg, New Mexico, roughly twenty miles from the ranch. On country roads, the relatively short commute meant getting the school bus before daylight and returning home after dark, an experience that Judge O'Connor would later recall when the Senate committee in hearings leading to her confirmation asked about busing children to schools. Her answer came from what she had gone through, but showed her self-control: "The transportation of students over long distances can be a very disruptive part of any child's educational background." After that school year she returned to Radford for one more year, then on to Austin High School. At age sixteen she graduated.

Harry A. Day, Sandra's father, had dreamed of going to Stanford University himself. Now his daughter, who had seen California along with most of the states west of the Mississippi with her parents on family trips, wanted to leave the ranch for Stanford. Still a good student, she majored in economics, a perfect fit for her very practical, nuts-and-bolts cast of mind, yet rigorous enough in its abstract concepts to satisfy her precise and analytical approach to problems. More than any economics course, a seminar in ethics turned her head in a new direction. The course happened to be taught by a professor who had been trained as a lawyer. Seeing what that kind of training did, Sandra Day wanted to try it for herself. Because her academic record was strong and because she had already done enough course work, she was allowed to start Stanford Law School as a first year student in what would have been her senior year. In 1950 she had her B.A., *magna cum laude*.

Normally people spend three years to complete the program at Stanford Law, as in most other law schools. Sandra Day finished in two. In 1952, after five years she had completed the work that would have taken seven years for an ordinary student, or even a good one. Going through quickly had not meant doing anything in haste or shoddily. She was elected to the Order of the Coif, the honorary law soci-

ety, and also worked as an editor of the *Stanford Law Review*. By the time of graduation she ranked number three in a class of 102 students. Her classmate who
claimed the distinction of first place would turn up later among her associates; that
student was William H. Rehnquist. While at Stanford and working on the *Law
Review* Sandra Day also met a student named John Jay O'Connor III from San
Francisco, son not of a rancher, but of a physician. He belonged to the class after
hers, and they waited until after her graduation to be married.

The young woman who completed seven years of university work in five years
and finished near the top of her class now had a new set of tests to face. Like other
aspiring lawyers she read announcements on bulletin boards at Stanford, especially the ones that asked for students with good academic records. Her professors did
nothing to help her to get interviews, but neither did they do much to help her
classmates, or so she perceived, with no sense of unfair treatment. In California, at
least in Los Angeles and San Francisco where she looked, major law firms took no
interest in her academic accomplishments and offered her very few interviews
because in 1952 they had never hired a woman lawyer. One Los Angeles firm
offered an interview, went over her impressive resumé and did in fact make her an
offer—to work for them as a legal secretary. She courteously declined. (One member of that firm, William French Smith, would be Attorney General of the United
States when Sandra O'Connor finally joined the Supreme Court.) Wanting to get
on with finding work more than she wanted to fight prevailing practices, O'Connor
understood that since the private practice of law seemed closed to a woman lawyer,
she would have to look for work in the public sector. Sandra O'Connor found work
on the staff of the county deputy attorney of San Mateo County, California, a job
with the advantage of being not far from Stanford, while she was waiting for her
husband to finish his legal training.

When her husband served in the Army's Judge Advocate General's Corps in
West Germany for three years, Sandra O'Connor accompanied him there and
found work as a civilian lawyer with the Quartermaster's Corps. When the couple
moved back to the States, Arizona was home. When Sandra had her first son, she
continued working in her own suburban practice, but when she had her second
baby, she decided to take time off to be with her family. For five years she was away
from the law, a break that she feared would mean that she might never work again.
To keep in touch with her profession in some way, she did a lot of volunteer work,
always looking for projects that had a legal aspect. She graded state bar exams, she
helped judges as a referee in bankruptcy and other cases, and she served as an
administrative assistant at the Arizona State Hospital, a mental institution confronting legal problems because of the outdated laws setting the criteria and regu-
lating procedures for admitting patients for mental treatment. At the same time
she worked for the Republican Party.

After her five years off, Sandra O'Connor found work as assistant attorney
general of Arizona from 1965 to 1969. Her aim, she explained, was to work so hard
that she would be thought of as indispensable. She was not, of course, she modest-
ly claims, "but they thought I was." In that position she had to strike a deal, again
in the interest of her young family. She agreed to be paid for half-time, but would
work two-thirds or even three-quarters time, just to be allowed the privilege of

part-time work. She still believes that in order for women to be able to have careers and still give their families the time they need, arrangements have to be worked out for more flexible work hours for those years when children are young. Because of her own choice to have a career and have a family, she says, in her matter-of-fact way, she never had "any free time or any spare time." Not a complaint, but an observation.

While she served on the attorney general's staff, the good fortune of another woman resulted in a new turn to Sandra O'Connor's career. Isabel Burgess, a member of the Arizona State Senate from O'Connor's district, chose to leave Arizona for Washington, D.C., when President Nixon named her to the National Transportation Safety Board in 1969. Possibly because that vacancy was left by a woman, but possibly not, the governor of Arizona, Jack Williams, thought of Sandra O'Connor as perfectly suited to take over the senate position. As a member of the attorney general's staff she had already done legal work for legislators. From her volunteer work and her years of living in Arizona she knew all about the problems the legislature faced.

After filling out that state senate term, O'Connor went on in the next year to be reelected. Running again in 1972 she won the senate seat and then served as the Majority Leader in the state senate, the first time that a woman in any state legislature had held that position. Not all state senators favored her analytic approach to problems, especially when their efforts failed to win her cooperation. One frustrated Arizona state senator, sure he was delivering the last word, said to O'Connor, "If you were a man, I'd punch you in the mouth." Cool-headed and smiling, the Majority Leader replied, "If you were a man, you could." O'Connor's influence grew in Arizona Republican circles: she attended the 1972 Republican National Convention as an alternate delegate and cochaired the Arizona Committee to Re-elect the President.

With experience in the attorney general's office and the state legislature behind her, O'Connor had served in two branches of government. At the end of her second term in the senate, she decided that she was ready to try the one remaining branch and pursue a judicial post. Her careful plan, worked out in advance, connected the pieces of her experience, just like building a fence once the posts are in place. The year was 1974 and the post was judgeship of Maricopa County Superior Court. At a time when the women's movement was getting up steam, the candidacy of any woman for any position elicited strong voter reactions, as much to the idea of women running as to the particular candidate. Phoenix was growing and changing so rapidly, facing so many new problems that voters, looking for change in a judge, elected O'Connor.

O'Connor had voted in the Arizona senate in favor of the Equal Rights Amendment, but her profile did not match the ideologically motivated feminists of the time. In 1974, when she was still senate majority leader, a measure was proposed to amend the University of Arizona stadium construction bill, a humdrum measure that included a provision that would make abortions less available. O'Connor opposed the bill, not as a proabortion feminist but for her own reasons, having to do primarily with a point of law. As she would explain later, her aim had been to discourage senate bills with riders on them that did not pertain directly to

Reuters/Bettmann

Supreme Court Justice Sandra Day O'Connor has both a family and an estimable career but does not remember ever having had spare time.

the bill, a ploy that sometimes lets legislators masquerade explosive bills as being harmless. While she defended the rights of women regarding property, such as their right to manage it with their husbands, and supported changes to the state constitution to end discrimination against women in labor practices such as the number of hours they could work, she generally voted like a Republican, but a moderate one. Her decisions protected the natural environment and encouraged bilingual education. True to her origins, not forgetting the isolation and danger of ranch life, she also opposed gun control. She voted to restore the death penalty, to limit government spending, and to reform tax laws to help even out the finances of economically dissimilar counties. Eventually, her record made her noticed in high places.

As part of his presidential campaign, Ronald Reagan promised in October of 1980 that he would appoint "the most qualified woman I can possibly find" to fill one of the first vacancies on the Supreme Court. Not much time passed before the seriousness of that promise would be tested as it was when Justice Potter Stewart announced in mid-June 1981, his plan to retire. Not even a month later, on July 7, 1981, President Ronald Reagan, seven months into his first term, announced that he had nominated Sandra Day O'Connor, an Arizona judge, to fill the position. Women's groups who had resented Reagan's earlier opposition to the Equal Rights Amendment now thought better of his view of women. The National Organization for Women publicly announced its pleasure with the nomination. But so did Barry Goldwater, the conservative Republican Arizona Senator, as did Republican Senator Strom Thurmond, and Democratic Senator Edward Kennedy. It looked as if O'Connor's nomination had appeased both political parties.

Then the Moral Majority, who had strong influence in the right wing of the Republican party, spoke up strenuously against O'Connor, vowing to try to block her confirmation because they read her record as proof that she favored ERA and, in their view, approved of abortion. The case they probably had in mind and that apparently misled them—because the real issue was not abortion—concerned the Arizona stadium bill, and its nongermane rider.

Her professional colleagues did not wholeheartedly cheer at O'Connor's nomination, but expressed reservations in an oddly quirky way. The American Bar Association, in particular its committee on the federal judiciary, gave O'Connor its qualified endorsement. According to the committee, she did not have the kind of court experience that they thought would suit "the highest standards of judicial temperament and integrity." O'Connor had served as both a trial and appellate judge in Arizona, and had been respected by her colleagues when "rated" on whether she should be renewed in that position. The ABA's assessment leaves out these facts and other pertinent information that may have surprised newspaper readers who were suddenly given second thoughts about Reagan's choice. Among Supreme Court justices, the 101 "brethren" who preceded O'Connor, many lacked judicial experience. In the fifty years right before her nomination, for example, only half of the twenty-eight justices named had any judicial experience, and of those, half had served five years or even less time as judges.

President Reagan's decision, no doubt, had been strengthened by Judge O'Connor's article that appeared in the *William and Mary Law Review* in the Summer 1981 issue, the printed version of her participation in a symposium in January of that year on the topic, "State Courts and Federalism in the 1980s." The thinking expressed in that paper matched the legal perspective Ronald Reagan valued in a judge. In clearly reasoned arguments O'Connor showed her support for state courts as she pointed out that federal courts should expect state judges to have done a good job: "It is a step in the right direction to defer to the state courts ... on federal Constitutional questions when a full and fair adjudication has been given in the state court." Federal judges needed to remember where the fences between state and federal jurisdiction had been put and why. No doubt O'Connor was speaking from both her experience as a state judge and from her high esteem for her colleagues when she observed that, "When the state-court judge puts on his or her federal-court robe, he or she does not become immediately better equipped intellectually to do the job." From her work in the Arizona senate, she also thought federal courts, including the Supreme Court, should respect state legislatures by hesitating to undo their efforts. Building on those views, her article went on to recommend that the work of federal courts should be lightened by having those courts intervene less often in state and local questions. The guidelines of how to avoid federal intervention might come from the policies that the newly elected president, Ronald Reagan, had already recommended. Reagan had found his associate justice.

The voting record of Justice O'Connor, from her first session up to the present, shows a general reliance on the principles that President Reagan wanted to guide any appointee of his. More often than not, O'Connor has voted with Rehnquist and, until his resignation, with Chief Justice Warren Burger, both considered to be in the conservative wing of the court. In the cases on which she has not voted with them, notably including cases on women's rights, her convictions show a depth and rigor that depend more on the particulars of each case than on her general political disposition.

The 1985–86 Supreme Court term, for example, showed sixty-nine cases on which the voting split along the line of conservative wing (defined as Burger and Rehnquist) against liberal wing (defined as Brennan and Marshall). In most of those cases, fifty-three out of sixty-nine times, O'Connor voted with the conservative wing. Even so, sixteen times she did not line up with them. Her record since that time tests the cliché, or the received wisdom in Washington, that the experience of being on the Supreme Court changes the thinking of associate justices, that the ones who start out conservative become more liberal. When her record from 1987 to 1992 is examined, for example, she shows a strong likelihood of voting with Chief Justice Rehnquist as she did 79.4 percent of the time and with Justice Kennedy 79.3 percent of the time. (To help interpret this alignment, one might compare that pattern to the alliance between Justices Marshall and Brennan, who voted alike 94 percent of the time, or that between Justices Scalia and Thomas, voting together 85 percent of the time.)

Supreme Court watchers have studied Justice O'Connor's record in cases that involve the civil rights of women or deal with sexual discrimination, a record that deserves serious consideration because of the ways in which it departs from what might be expected. Even when it meant parting with her colleagues, for example, Justice O'Connor took a stand against giving women an automatic advantage in educational opportunity. In the 1982 case of *Mississippi University for Women v. Hogan*, a man had claimed that his civil rights were violated because he was not allowed to attend a federally-funded nursing school that admitted women. In O'Connor's thinking, the question very much resembled discrimination based on race, even though the Supreme Court had already ruled in such decisions as the famous 1978 case of *University of California Regents v. Bakke* that sex-based discrimination did not have to be treated by the same "rigorous standard" as distinctions based on race. O'Connor insisted that equal protection under the laws meant equal, in both directions, a position that could not tolerate a man's exclusion from nursing school. On the precise point of equal protection, she wrote, "It must be applied free of fixed notions concerning roles and abilities of males and females."

The convinced tone of O'Connor's language comes in part from her knowledge based on experiences working beside men on her family's ranch.

Some women's groups might have expected Justice O'Connor to find it impossible to see any need to give explicit help to a man, in the face of the historical record of systematic and repeated discrimination against women. In Justice O'Connor's thinking, however, what matters most is the concept of equal protection, even when "equal" favors a man. She had faced questions of discrimination before, particularly when the Arizona legislature had debated the Equal Rights Amendment. In that debate O'Connor herself came under the pressure of heavy lobbying from both sides, an experience that taught her how profound and intense the differences are, and left her with the belief that any issue that is debated with such passion cannot be expected to result in affirmative or positive legislation.

The cases that reach the Supreme Court often concern questions on which lower courts disagree in different parts of the country. At the present time, such cases regularly involve abortion. In *Madsen v. Women's Health Center* (1994) the Supreme Court had to review the decision of a trial judge in Florida who forbade anti-abortion demonstrators to be within thirty-six feet of a particular clinic. The protesters claimed their First Amendment rights to free speech were violated, while the Florida judge had intended to protect the privacy rights of clinic patients. In the end, the Supreme Court upheld part, but not all, of the injunctions created by the lower court judge, a decision that evoked bitter dissent among justices. O'Connor voted with Rehnquist and the majority. Her comments, focused with laser precision on the arguments, speak to the presentation of facts by the attorney for the protesters, without preaching or partisan generalizations.

In a comment that has provoked much discussion, Justice O'Connor said that she sees *Roe v. Wade* (the 1973 decision that gave women the right to obtain a legal abortion during the first trimester of pregnancy) as being "on a collision course with itself." That remark, which does not necessarily mean that O'Connor would predictably vote one way or another on abortion cases, conveys her belief that technology will alter the legal debate because it will on the one hand reduce risks to mothers later into the pregnancy and, on the other hand, make possible the survival of a fetus outside the mother earlier in the pregnancy. That imaginative vision of a moral and legal question being complicated by the influence of technology shows the thoughtful and subtle way in which O'Connor sees each decision as an element in the ongoing, never completed "dialogue" as she calls it, between the constitution and the country, through its courts.

That idea of dialogue may offer a useful guide to understanding Justice O'Connor's thinking. Naturally the woman confirmed for appointment to the Supreme Court in a 99–0 Senate vote will continue to attract media attention in all her decisions, and under scrutiny will likely continue to show herself a product of her Western upbringing. From her background on a ranch, a sparsely populated world in which survival depended on cooperation in the face of hard tasks, O'Connor learned self-reliance. As lawyer, legislator, and judge she always relied on preparation to win debates, and could not be beaten. Her view of the relation of federal to state courts, that one cannot assume itself superior to the other belongs to a cast of mind that respects serious effort regardless of rank. The plain talk and remarkable clarity of her decisions show an impulse toward a dialogue with future readers of the important record she is helping to write.

QUESTIONS FOR THOUGHT AND DISCUSSION

1. How do you account for Sandra Day O'Connor's rise in Arizona politics? Would you describe her as a feminist?

2. What led President Reagan to appoint O'Connor to the U.S. Supreme Court in 1981? Was her appointment a wise choice?

3. Do you agree that O'Connor's background as a Westerner has a profound impact on her judicial thinking? Is there such a thing as a regional way of viewing the Constitution and judging cases?

4. Is having a woman on the Supreme Court necessary to reflect a "woman's point of view"? Is there a discernible "woman's point of view"? Is it a relevant concern that the nation's highest court loosely resemble the entirety of American society? Are one or two women out of nine on the Supreme Court enough?

SUGGESTED READINGS

Lewis, Anthony. *Gideon's Trumpet*. New York: Random, 1964.

Linford, Orma. "Sandra Day O'Connor: Myra Bradwell's Revenge," in LeVeness, F.P. and Sweeney, J.P., eds., *Women Leaders in Contemporary U.S. Politics*, pp. 117–135. Boulder, Col.: Rienner, 1987.

Moritz, Charles, ed. *Current Biography*, pp. 297–301. New York: Wilson, 1988.

New York Times, July 8, 1981, p. 1; September 22, 1981, p. 1; September 26, 1981, p. 8.

O'Brien, David M. *Supreme Court Watch—1994: Highlights of the 1993–1994 Term, Preview of the 1994–1995 Term*. New York: Norton, 1994.

_____. *Storm Center: The Supreme Court in American Politics*. 3rd ed. New York: Norton, 1993.

24

Toni Morrison

From the day she started school in Lorain, Ohio, Toni Morrison knew about different kinds of children. She was the only black child in her class, and the only child who could read. That may have been the first time she noticed that her family was giving her important skills and advantages. Raised by both her parents, Morrison learned about loyalty to her family and to her community of black people. She still acts on that sense of loyalty in her writing and in her teaching as she shows her students at Princeton that African Americans have always been a presence in American literature, there from the beginning. From her novels, from her historical knowledge and moral insights, readers find a sense of a past that did not always figure in official records. Her most famous novel, Beloved, *lets readers look straight at a subject that made most writers avert their eyes, a subject they found too abhorrent and indecent to deal with—the damage done by slavery.* Beloved *made an American evil real to the minds of millions of readers. Besides reconfirming Morrison's extraordinary talent,* Beloved *proved her courage and soared. Fittingly, Morrison received the Nobel Prize for Literature in 1993.*

BECAUSE OF HER INTEGRITY, because she is what people used to call "together," Toni Morrison knows and admits the tremendous influence her family has had on her writing. The past, of a culture, of a country, of one person, must be confronted, she thinks, as part of growing up, even if parts of that past turn out to be unpleasant. Seeing in the past a source of strength, she thinks our relation to it needs to be "more affectionate," an attitude she works at achieving through her books.

Not much about the Robert Goheen Professor of Humanities at Princeton University, Morrison's present post, resembles the girl born on February 18, 1931, in Lorain, Ohio, nothing but the essentials. Chloe Anthony Wofford, second daughter in what would be a family of four children, knew that she mattered a great deal to the people around her. George Wofford, her father, held three jobs at the same time to be sure to provide what he and his wife, Ramah, considered necessary for their children, but the Wofford idea of necessities did not all come from stores and catalogs. Knowing how to read counted for so much that Chloe's grand-mother taught her to read at home at age four. By the time she went to first grade, Morrison recalls, she noticed two things when she looked at herself alongside other first graders: she was the only black child and the only one in the class who could read.

At home she read a great deal, but probably heard as many stories as she read. Everyone in the family, parents, aunts, uncles, and cousins, all had stories to tell, usually describing the part of the South they had left and why and how it happened that they were in Ohio. The memory of these thrilling stories gave Morrison an idea she still holds, that every black person is interesting because of these person-al narratives they have. Even though she never saw the South as a girl, Morrison heard what it was like, or had been like. Her mother's family had started in Greenville, Alabama, where they owned land; after they lost it they were forced to become sharecroppers. Her father's people had lived in Georgia. Besides the fam-ily's stories about itself, the children grew up hearing other stories as well, some folk tales, and what Morrison remembers as "thrillingly terrifying" stories with ghosts in them and people who could fly.

From Lorain, Ohio, where she graduated from high school with honors, Chloe Wofford went to Washington, D.C., to attend college at Howard University where she majored in English with a minor in classics. Possibly because of some sense of the dramatic she absorbed from the exciting stories she grew up hearing, she found herself drawn to the college theatrical group, the Howard Repertory Theater. An accidental part of that connection turned out to be a personal revelation when Toni, as people had now started calling Miss Wofford, traveled with that theater company to the South. Now she saw for herself places that up to that time had a mythical reality, not exactly the Promised Land yet almost what "the old country" was for European immigrants. African Americans in the North, of course, could claim two old countries, Africa and the South. What opened her eyes on that trip was not so much the difference between North and South, even though she was raised in northern Ohio, as the familiarity of what she saw. The way of life of black people, whether living among Yankees or in Dixie, in a vocabulary she would never use, showed all the tiny continuities that proved it was one culture, its own culture, not nonwhite, but something in itself. That same experience started Morrison thinking along lines she would explore for years, reflecting on and analyzing the culture that she knew so well from home, from all those stories. But she did not find that reality discussed or considered in books. Where was the literature to help interpret that way of life, her own experience before she went to college?

When she graduated from Howard University in 1953, Chloe "Toni" Wofford had a strong enough academic record to be accepted for graduate work in English at Cornell University. As a subject for her master's thesis she concentrated on two writers not usually thought of in the same breath: the American Southern novelist William Faulkner, still alive at the time, and the British feminist critic and novelist Virginia Woolf. No one knew then—except maybe the master's candidate her-self—that those two very different sensibilities would both turn out to be strongly present, along with something else, in the books of Toni Morrison. Like Faulkner, she would evince a philosophical but also gut-level and sensual appreciation of the

depth and ennobling side of pain in the most ignorant and inarticulate Southerners, an anger at not being able to say how things feel, or not knowing what things
mean. A universe away, like the well-off, well-connected Virginia Woolf, a dazzling
and brilliant beacon exposing dark corners in genteel lives, Morrison would also
write to delineate emotions in her universe and recognize nuances of spirit in
places no one had ever thought to look.

But before graduate school there had been other milestones—and for a writer
in embryo reading a book counts as a pivotal experience. As an adolescent Chloe
Wofford read Dostoyevsky and Tolstoy. Even in Lorain, Ohio, she would connect
in her mind with the worlds these writers described. More importantly, she understood why, knew that the precision, the concreteness and particularity of how they
wrote made their world alive and that she, as a reader, was "available" (a favorite
word in a very precise sense) to it. That presentation of a world, a culture, in a
novel left her reeling. She wanted to do exactly that.

Teaching jobs, predictably, followed graduate school. In 1955, Texas Southern
University in Houston hired Wofford as instructor; then in 1957 she returned to
Howard University as an instructor. While there she met and married Harold Morrison, an architect whose origins are in Jamaica. While at Howard she also started
to work on her writing and joined a writers group. She remained married for seven
years. In 1964, at the time of her divorce, Toni Morrison already had one son,
Harold Ford, born in 1962, and was expecting another. Her second son, Slade
Kevin, was born in 1966. While she thought over exactly what to do next, Morrison
returned home to Lorain, Ohio, long enough to know she did not want to remain
there with her children. Many years later, reflecting on those big adjustments in
her life, Morrison speculates that had she remained married she probably would
not have started writing, which her next job allowed her to attempt.

L. W. Singer, a division of Random House, with offices in Syracuse, New York,
was looking for a textbook editor. In the political climate of 1965, Morrison understood the potential influence of textbooks for "sensitizing" young Americans to
new cultural concepts. She welcomed the opportunity she saw in working for a
publisher. At night, after she had put her children to bed, she made time to work
on a story she had started earlier, an account of a young child, a black girl, whose
greatest wish in life was to have blue eyes. The question that fascinated Morrison
centered on how it could happen that a child would rather be a freak than herself.
Who had given that child such a message about her own ugliness? While Morrison
worked over this story white Americans were proclaiming in wonder new discov-
eries they had made. The radical slogan "Black is Beautiful" had not been widely
heard before then. Serious and amazed people wondered where all these good-
looking black people were coming from. Where had they been? Morrison understood that a big cultural perception was transforming itself. She kept re-writing
and reworking her story.

After an important job promotion, Morrison moved from the text to the trade
(nontext) division, from L. W. Singer to Random House, from Syracuse to Manhattan. While at Random House, Morrison kept writing, and Holt, another New
York company, published her expanded story as her first novel, *The Bluest Eye*, in
1970. (A convention in the publishing industry dictates if editors have work of their

own to publish, they bring it out with a company other than their employer.) That first effort did not make Toni Morrison famous as a writer. While still at Random House she was able to work at the same time as a university lecturer first at Yale, then at State University of New York at Purchase, and at Bard College.

When her next novel, *Sula*, appeared in 1974 more people noticed Morrison's unusual voice, her originality in story-line and characters. Sula, the character in the novel, did not remind readers of anyone. A rebel, Sula broke everyone's rules, even the important ones of her own community about loyalty to friends. As in *The Bluest Eye*, Morrison told the story in her own way, not the way stories are supposed to go. She reexamined such basic features as beginning at the beginning, then having a middle and an end. Chronology has its uses, but it does not always help tell a story. Morrison used far more sophisticated strategies in letting her stories organize themselves, sometimes letting the past of one character explain one piece of what happened, but then going farther back, even to a different generation, in another character's past. When Morrison manipulates the idea of personal history, the telling makes sense, in a new way. *Sula* was nominated for the National Book Award.

When Morrison wrote about her grandfather Solomon, she borrowed her title from the Bible and called the novel *Song of Solomon*. In it a black man, Milkman Dead, behaves like heroes in the literature of other cultures: he goes in search of his father, passes difficult tests, hunts for treasure, outwits evildoers, deciphers a riddle, makes a sacrifice for a friend, flies, and becomes mythical. At times he even behaves like a relative of Huck Finn. Finally the public caught on and Morrison's third novel sold over three million copies as the book held its own on the *New York Times* bestseller list for sixteen weeks. Book-of-the-Month Club chose *Song of Solomon* as its main selection. (The only other black author to win that distinction was Richard Wright with *Native Son* in 1940). *Song of Solomon* won the Fiction Award of the National Book Critics' Circle, and Morrison received the award of the American Academy and Institute of Arts and Letters. In 1977 President Carter named Morrison to the National Council on the Arts.

Tar Baby, published in 1981, was an instant success, jumping onto the *New York Times* bestseller list. Morrison's picture appeared on the cover of *Newsweek* and her happy publisher arranged a huge promotional tour. She had become a prominent literary figure. In that book a black woman enjoys material success and fame but has great difficulty in a personal relationship with a black man who sees the ancient aspects of African culture as far more important than money or fame. In the end, the couple fails to reconcile the two views and fails to be a couple. Today, readers see that Morrison recorded a debate that confronted blacks in the 1970s. In telling the story with her characteristically strong sense of place, this time on a fictional Caribbean island, Morrison comes down on the side of ancient and enduring values.

Because of the solid commercial success of *Song of Solomon* and of *Tar Baby*, Toni Morrison could leave her job as senior editor at Random House after twenty years. No black woman before her had been named to so high a place in publishing. In 1984, the same year, the State University of New York at Albany named Morrison to the Albert Schweitzer Chair in Humanities. Then she risked everything.

Ulf Anderson/Gamma-Liaison

Nobel laureate Toni Morrison writes novels that explore the American soul in our history.

Toni Morrison already had made a name for herself before she wrote *Beloved*, so strange a work that probably only an established writer could have convinced a publisher to accept it. In its bare bones, *Beloved* tells the story of a slave and is about slavery. But the experience of reading that book involves so much beyond its story that it is a distortion to say that it (or any book of Morrison's) is about any single subject. The inspiration for *Beloved* came from a true story that Morrison found while working on another project while at Random House. Not as author but as editor, Morrison had been in charge of something called the *Black Book*, published in the early 1970s, which attempted to show what life had been like for African Americans from slavery to the 1940s, not famous or outstanding individuals, but the ordinary ones. Its documents included photographs, scrap books, and commercial records such as bills of sale for people, for slaves, along with sheet music for songs. Among the newspaper clippings Morrison reviewed as she prepared the book was the story of Margaret Garner, a slave who ran away from Kentucky and escaped to freedom in Cincinnati, Ohio. What made her story appear in the newspaper happened later, when a slave catcher came after Garner and caught up with her. As he was on the point of capturing her children along with Garner to return them to slavery, their mother snapped. Deliberately and brutally she murdered her own baby in order to save it from a life of slavery.

Years later, still wondering about that incident, Morrison turned its central event, the murder, into what would become *Beloved*, a book she says she had to write to try to understand how such a crime could come about. Of all instincts, a mother's urge to protect her own children has always been revered as sacred, as beyond violation, beyond a moral duty. As in all her works, in *Beloved* Morrison was trying to answer a question.

While *Beloved* tells the story of a slave, it tells a great deal about slavery, not in the way of history books. Even today, even after *Beloved*, Morrison sees a great danger in the desire of many Americans to forget the parts of their past that they find "unpleasant." What could be more unpleasant than slavery? In the novel Morrison shows a woman suffering because she cannot put her own past together in a way that makes sense. She has trouble remembering and, of course, there are no books to help. The terror of the character's memory scrambles the chronology, takes many attempts to figure out where it began, in a story that finally goes from 1855 to 1874. But Morrison's novel does not tell the story of slavery in numbers nor in general statements, although the author dedicates her book to the "Sixty Million and more" victims of slavery.

The suffering and the diminished life of one family tells truths that would not change if they were "enhanced" by numbers. Morrison's story does not depend on details of how many Americans—slaves and owners—lived and died in a degraded way because of slavery. But she studies and analyzes how knowledge of that past lingers and continues to cause suffering. Her novel looks at the lasting damage done by the memory of slavery, a radically antifamily institution that allowed for the selling off of family members. In *Beloved*, one woman remembers her two daughters she learned had been sold off one day, before they got their second teeth. The murdered child returns as a ghost whose name is "Beloved," the one word her mother could "afford" to have engraved on the tombstone. She paid with her body.

Serious novelists, except in horror writing, do not include ghosts among their characters. But to tell the story of a dark secret that will not go away, will not leave alone the conscience of the living, Morrison's story needed to show people being haunted, and needed a ghost. Finally, an American writer had talked about slavery as belonging to a human past that tries to hold on, that wants to punish us, that we must confront, not drown in statistics and summarizing. The wild story of a repulsive murder told by having a ghost participate could have made for a pitiful book and an unfortunate attempt. But Morrison made it work. In 1988 *Beloved* won the Pulitzer Prize.

Over time, Morrison looked at *Beloved* as the first in a series of books that would look at the lives of African Americans at different moments in history. The next one after it, *Jazz*, published in 1992, talks about Americans early in the twentieth century in Harlem. It may be impossible to think of any cultural expression that is more American than jazz, but that is not why Morrison wants to explore the world of early jazz in her book. She noticed that to talk about American music at all and omit the contribution of African Americans would leave something not only incomplete, but incoherent, a story that could not hold together. That same incoherence she sees as a feature of any attempt to talk about America and leave out, for reasons of racism, the contributions blacks have made. In *Jazz* she also depends on the language of African Americans, not as a substandard or deficient version of English, but as a lively and inventive part of the language of America.

To readers outside America, Toni Morrison has come to represent a new voice from America, a new interpreter. She talks about love in all her books, but not in its egocentric, self-indulgent romantic form. For her characters, love is an elusive answer not so much to hate as to chaos, an expression of faith in the effort to make a kind of sense out of our experience, a constructive emotion. Toni Morrison's effort, her lifetime contribution to literature, won for her the Nobel Prize for literature in 1993, an honor accompanied by $825,000.

Disagreement, even debate about the meaning and importance of Morrison's books proves their significance. Black male writers criticize her for the mediocre men she creates in her work. Even after Morrison received the Nobel Prize, one African American author said he hoped the prize would inspire her to write better books. Another saw the decision to give the prize to Morrison as "a triumph of political correctness."

Morrison herself found out about the award when a Princeton colleague watching the *Today Show* heard the news and telephoned her friend. When Morrison got that call she was sure it could not be true, but that maybe her name had been read for being on a list of nominees. Later, when the fact was confirmed, Morrison said, "I'm so glad my mother is alive and I can share this with her." Her publisher invited her to have a press conference in New York, which Morrison would not do. Instead, she unplugged her telephone by 10:00 a.m. to take a bath and later went to teach her undergraduate seminar on "American Africanism."

Two weeks after the award ceremony, Morrison suffered a shock when her four-story frame house in Grand View-on-Hudson burned for five hours, defeating the efforts of 100 firefighters, every writer's nightmare. The Schomburg Center for Research in Black Culture, with a stated interest in Morrison's papers, also fearing an absolute loss, found some comfort that the loss turned out to be less cata-strophic than was feared. For a time, Morrison could talk only to other people whose houses had burned.

As part of the acceptance ceremonies in Stockholm, Nobel Laureates give speeches. For her acceptance, Morrison presented a "prose poem" that reminded people of the corresponding speech given by William Faulkner in 1950. (The Nobel Prize was first awarded in 1901, and Morrison was only the eighth woman to receive one.) As a sample of the talent that had put her there, Morrison told a story that opened with one of the oldest of lines, "Once upon a time." In her story, she describes a difficult question asked of an old woman who was black and was blind. The question concerned a small bird that, the story explains, represents something of tremendous value to humankind, namely language. In reply to a trick question about the bird, the old woman says to her young questioners, "It is in your hands." To Morrison, nothing could matter more. "We die. That may be the mean-ing of life. But we do language. That may be the measure of our lives."

QUESTIONS FOR THOUGHT AND DISCUSSION

1. How did Toni Morrison's upbringing prepare her to establish a writing career?

2. In relating stories such as *The Bluest Eye* and *Beloved,* do you think Morrison's primary motive was artistic expression? personal catharsis? desire to change the social consciousness of her readers?

3. In her Nobel Prize acceptance speech, Morrison suggests that language "may be the measure of our lives." What do you think she was getting at?

4. Should Morrison be thought of primarily as a woman writer, an African-Amer-ican writer, an American writer, a modern writer, or simply as an outstanding writer? Does categorizing her work diminish her achievements or merely reflect the focus of her art?

SUGGESTED READINGS

Bloom, Harold, ed. *Toni Morrison: Modern Critical Views.* New York: Chelsea, 1990.

Gates, Henry Louis, Jr. and K. A. Appiah. *Toni Morrison: Critical Perspectives Past and Pre-sent*. New York: Amistad, 1993.

Morrison, Toni. *The Bluest Eye*. New York: Holt, 1970.

_____. *Sula*. New York: Knopf, 1974.

_____. *Song of Solomon,* 1977. New York: Knopf, 1977.

_____. *Tar Baby*. New York: Knopf, 1981.

_____. *Beloved*. New York: Knopf, 1987.

_____. *Jazz*. New York: Knopf, 1992.

_____. *Playing in the Dark: Whiteness and the Literary Imagination*. New York: 1992.

_____, ed. *Race-ing Justice, En-gendering Power: Essays on Anita Hill, Clarence Thomas and the Construction of Social Reality*. New York: Pantheon, 1992.

Samuels, Wilfred D. and Clenora Hudson-Weems. *Toni Morrison*. Boston: Twayne, 1990.

Taylor-Guthrie, Danille, ed. *Conversations with Toni Morrison*. Jackson: UP of Mississippi, 1994.

Index